S
GUIDE TO
THE JUMPS
1999-2000

Editor: Mark Maydon

©1999 Invincible Press

ISBN 0-00-218901-1

Published in the United Kingdom by Invincible Press,
an imprint of HarperCollins*Publishers*,
in association with The Sun newspaper.

Invincible Press, 77-85 Fulham Palace Road,
London W6 8JB. Telephone: 0181 741 7070.

Printed and bound in Great Britain by Caledonian
International Book Manufacturing, Glasgow.

Photographs by Gerry Cranham

Distributed by Magazine Marketing Company Ltd.,
Woking, Surrey

Cover picture: Istabraq jumps the last on his way
to a second Champion Hurdle (Gerry Cranham)

Templegate's ten to follow

BRITAIN'S top tipster Templegate (Phil Logan) reckons these 10 will keep you warm over the winter

1 BARTON
Age: 6   Form: 1111111-   Trainer: Tim Easterby

HEARING Tim Easterby wax lyrical about one of his horses is about as rare as the summer's total eclipse.

So it was time to sit up and take notice when Easterby said Barton "could be a Champion Hurdle horse next season" following his bloodless win in the two-mile, five-furlong Royal & SunAlliance Hurdle.

Remember, that comment came a day after the highly-talented Yorkshire trainer had watched Istabraq bag a second Champion Hurdle.

Barton's nine-length defeat of Artadoin Lad (a smashing chasing prospect this term) at the Festival never looked in doubt when he led on the bridle after the second from home.

It was Barton's sixth straight win over hurdles and, while he was not so impressive when stretching his unbeaten run to seven at Aintree, he was probably feeling the effects of a long season.

Barton's change of pace at the end of the race and his fluent jumping have been the trademarks of his victories and I have no doubt he will be just as effective dropped to two miles. He won easily on the soft at Wetherby, but raced mainly on good or yielding thereafter.

Easterby is apparently considering a tilt at novice chases but I hope he keeps Barton over timber.

Istabraq has ruled the roost against ordinary opposition for the past couple of seasons, but in Barton he will face the acid test.

Jockey Lorcan Wyer says riding this horse "is better than sex. I'm on Viagra!"

Well, all I can say is that Barton is definitely on the up and up!

LORCAN WYER

3

CAROLINE BAILEY, who brought Teeton Mill through the ranks before the grey went to Venetia Williams, has another potential champion on her hands in Castle Mane.

The flashy chestnut was unbeaten in six races between the flags before graduating to be a top-class hunter chaser.

After strolling home in the mud at Warwick, he started a generous 9-2 for the Cheltenham Foxhunters run on good ground.

There he sustained a relentless gallop from the off before drawing clear to beat high-class Elegant Lord impressively by 13 lengths.

The runner-up gave the form a healthy boost when winning easily at Aintree, while the third, smart Last Option, also won a decent event next time.

Castle Mane did not jump quite so well at Punchestown in April, but won cosily by five lengths and a distance from market rival Sheltering and Dunaree (both winners since).

Although he is only small, I believe Castle Mane is the best hunter seen for years and the long-term plan is this season's Gold Cup.

However, the handicapper is often lenient with ex-pointers and hunters and I suspect connections may be tempted to run him in top staying handicaps in the meantime.

Like Teeton Mill last season, he is made for the Hennessy at Newbury in late November and two visits to the bank would be in order if he gets the green light (once to withdraw enough stake money and then back to deposit the winnings).

Castle Mane is a fluent jumper and relentless galloper who is proven on good and heavy ground.

MANE MAN . . . Ben Pollock guides Castle Mane to victory at Cheltenham

3 FLAGSHIP UBERALLES
Age: 5   Form: 22121111-   Trainer: Paul Nicholls

THERE is little doubt that Flagship Uberalles will find life difficult this time around.

He will not receive the now-reduced weight-for-age allowance and also picks up penalties in forthcoming events for winning the top two-mile novices' chases at Cheltenham and Aintree.

However, this half-brother to dual Champion Chase hero Viking Flagship has the physical scope, jumping technique and the right mental attitude to see him challenging strongly for top two-mile honours.

Flagship Uberalles, who joined talented Paul Nicholls from Irish trainer Paul Flynn after winning two bumpers, showed useful form on his first two starts over hurdles.

His attentions were soon switched to fences, however, and he made a bright start at Exeter in November. After meeting defeat over two-and-a-half miles at Chepstow behind Potentate, he remained unbeaten in four starts back at two miles.

The Flagship really came to the fore in the Arkle Chase at Cheltenham where he was settled just off the pace before taking command two out.

In close at the last, he ran on very gamely up the hill to extend his earlier Warwick supremacy over Tresor De Mai to two-and-a-half lengths.

Although he did not repeat that performance in terms of form, he won easily at Aintree by nine lengths from Grimes, again jumping superbly and racing with great enthusiasm.

The Flagship's best performances have come on good to good to soft, but he is also effective in the mud.

4 FROSTY CANYON
Age: 6   Form: 1217-   Trainer: Paul Webber

TRAINER Paul Webber thinks the world of this Arctic Lord gelding and Frosty Canyon has certainly done nothing wrong in four bumpers to date.

Despite drifting from 6s out to 12s, he made a winning debut at Chepstow back in November beating Star Of Dungannon (who went on to score twice subsequently).

Frosty lost little caste in defeat behind six-length winner Prominent Profiles back at the Welsh track next time, a race which produced no fewer than five next-time-out winners.

A well-earned place in the Champion Bumper at Cheltenham was then on the cards after he made all to beat highly-regarded Dorans Gold under a penalty at Sandown.

Starting an unconsidered 25-1 shot at the Festival, Frosty Canyon ran arguably his best race to finish around nine lengths seventh to Monsignor.

He deserves extra credit, too, as he probably burnt himself out by chasing the heavily-backed eventual runner-up Golden Alpha from the top of the hill.

Two miles over hurdles will probably be on the sharp side for Frosty Canyon, but I can see him developing into one of the best staying novices this season. He acts very well on soft ground but a faster surface clearly did not hinder him at Cheltenham.

5 GENEROSA
Age: 6   Form: 25013-   Trainer: John Hassett (Ireland)

A USEFUL stayer on the Flat, Generosa was having only her tenth start over hurdles when winning the Stakis Casino Handicap Hurdle at the Cheltenham Festival.

Given a brilliant hold-up ride by Norman Williamson, she stormed clear after the last to beat reliable yardstick Melody Maid by five lengths.

Remarkably, she was turned out the following day in the Coral Cup under a 7lb penalty.

Ridden on this occasion by Tom Treacy, she was again produced with every chance at the final flight.

However, this time she could not quite deliver the decisive turn of foot over the five-furlong shorter trip although only beaten a head and neck by Khayrawani and Miltonfield. Connections reported

she broke a blood vessel but that was probably the result of a second hard race in the space of 24 hours and it is to be hoped that it was just a one-off.

Only a six-year-old, I suspect this mare will once again be plotted up for the Cheltenham Festival in March where her acceleration will prove a potent weapon in staying races.

Generosa has proved her effectiveness in the mud, but good ground —, or slightly on the easy side — suits her ideally.

6 HORS LA LOI III
Age: 4   Form: 11111-   Trainer: François Doumen (France)

OWNER Paul Green's decision to remove his horses from Martin Pipe was a blow for the champion trainer.

Top French handler François Doumen has been the one to benefit as the high-class Hors La Loi III is back in his care for the forthcoming season.

Doumen sent out this full brother to Cyborgo — who won the 1996 stayers' hurdle for Pipe — to win his first three starts. After an easy success at Auteuil, he stamped himself as Festival material with a 16-length win from useful yardstick Wave Rock in the Grade 2

Summit Hurdle at Lingfield in December.

He returned seven weeks later to brush aside smart Behrajan at Cheltenham, despite pulling hard and the trainer's son Thierry taking him wide for most of the race.

Green then purchased the gelding for a sum not far short of £200,000.

Those who had backed Hors La Loi ante-post for the Triumph Hurdle (myself included) saw their money disappear down the drain.

The gelding was switched to the Supreme Novices at the eleventh hour by Green, who reportedly received sev-

HORS WELL . . . Four-year-old Hors La Loi III is destined for more top honours

eral "nasty letters" after making the decision (myself not included this time!).

Hors La Loi's display in the Supreme Novices was awesome.

Tony McCoy kicked, stretched the field from the top of the hill and stormed away to win by 17 lengths from the ill-fated Joe Mac, ridden by Conor O'Dwyer.

Before the race O'Dwyer had warned McCoy that Joe Mac had been catching pigeons at home. McCoy replied that his mount had not only been catching them, but also cooking and eating them!

The fastish ground at Cheltenham clearly proved no problem for Hors La Loi and, although unimpressive when winning on similar going at Aintree subsequently, it is fair to assume that his exertions at the Festival, rather than the underfoot conditions, had begun to take their toll.

Hors La Loi translates as 'outside the law' and there is little doubt that this brilliant jumper will take some catching wherever he goes.

 KHAYRAWANI

Age: 7   Form: 6112-   Trainer: Christy Roche (Ireland)

LEGENDARY gambler J P McManus must be rubbing his hands at the prospect of his reliable seven-year-old lining up for one of the top handicaps again.

Incredibly, Khayrawani has won three of his four starts at Cheltenham and Aintree in the past two seasons and finished runner-up in the other.

In 1998 he was second to well-handicapped Top Cees in the Coral Cup, before beating Cadougold a neck at the Grand National meeting 16 days later.

A year later he managed to go one better in the Coral Cup — beating Miltonfield and Generosa — despite drifting from 12s to 16s on the day. He then followed up his Aintree win but in unfortunate circumstances as the same owner's promising Budalus was fatally injured after crashing out at the final flight.

Khayrawani did his handicap mark no good when chasing home Anzum in a Grade 1 at Punchestown in April, but that effort proved he stays three miles.

He will no doubt be prepared with the big ones at Cheltenham and Aintree in mind and, given his tremendous record, he will not be one to oppose lightly.

His very best performances have come on good ground at around two and a half miles, though he has won in the heavy.

 LIMESTONE LAD

Age: 7   Form: 1112121113-   Trainer: James Bowe (Ireland)

THIS ultra-tough gelding must go down as the most-improved hurdler in Britain and Ireland last season, winning seven of his 10 starts and being placed in the others.

Limestone Lad scored off a rating of 99 at Naas in November and ended up in March winning off a whopping 43lb higher mark at Leopardstown.

He did it the hard way, too, winning most of his races from the front at two to two-and-a-half miles on ground ranging from good to heavy. He should stay three miles this season.

Tony McCoy took the reins on Limestone Lad on his final start at Punchestown in April and the pair finished eight-and-a-half lengths third to the mighty Istabraq, who was giving just 5lb.

McCoy was impressed despite reporting the going a shade fast, but also remarked that Limestone Lad will make a good chaser.

Limestone Lad will now have his chance to prove himself in that sphere.

Trainer James Bowe, who has handled the seven-year-old skilfully, said modestly: "This horse amazes me and gets better by the hour.

"I hope it continues when he goes chasing. Good ground suits him best."

He has the right physique to develop into a leading novice over fences.

However, given the Lad's record around Leopardstown (four wins from four starts last season) and his proven ability to carry big weights, connections may also be tempted to revert to hurdles for a tilt at the Ladbroke in January.

9 TREMALLT
Age: 8   Form: U12FF1F11-   Trainer: Tom George

FATE has not been kind to Tom Jenks in his riding career. He lost out on the ride on Earth Summit in the 1998 Grand National, but he has high hopes for Tremallt, a horse he hopes could be something special.

Indeed the Tom George-trained gelding looks just the sort to defy the handicapper for a while yet.

A bargain buy at the 3,000 guineas connections forked out for him at Doncaster Sales, Tremallt won all four completed starts last season over fences on soft or heavy — saving the best for last at Uttoxeter in April where he beat Yankie Lord impressively by 13 lengths.

A glance at his form figures also reveals some over-exuberant jumping cost Tremallt dear as he hit the deck four times.

That said, his technique was much better at Uttoxeter and the Murphy's Gold Cup at Cheltenham in mid-November was nominated immediately after that final success.

The eight-year-old is likely to have one run before the season's first major handicap chase.

He will probably need to win that prep to guarantee a place in the Murphy's, but Tremallt is definitely a couple of steps ahead of the handicapper — providing his jumping stays sound.

Cut in the ground is crucial to Tremallt — he has not been risked on fast going in the past two seasons.

10 YOUNG KENNY

Age: 8   Form: 22412U111-   Trainer: Peter Beaumont

THIS brilliant young staying chaser will be aimed at the Grand National after a 21lb hike up the ratings last term.

He was not seen out again in the 1997-98 season after winning at Kelso in December, undergoing an operation to sort out a chipped bone in his knee.

But Young Kenny has certainly made up for lost time and looked top class when asked to tackle three-and-a-half miles plus, winning at Market Rasen, Uttoxeter, Haydock and Ayr — all on ground softer than good.

He just got better and better, and the run of success culminated with a thoroughly convincing nine-length defeat of Hollybank Buck (received 10lb) in the Scottish National in April where he humped round top weight.

Trainer Peter Beaumont, who had no regrets about not entering the eight-year-old at Aintree, finds it difficult to compare Young Kenny with his star chaser Jodami, who won the Gold Cup in 1993.

Beaumont only says: "Jodami was a class three-miler, while Young Kenny is a class stayer."

Jockey Brendan Powell, who steered Rhyme 'N Reason to Aintree glory in 1988, reckons Young Kenny idles in front which suggests we have yet to see the best from the eight-year-old.

Bearing in mind that the Gold Cup is regularly won by a horse who simply outstays his rivals over Cheltenham's gruelling three miles, two-and-a-half furlongs, I will be having a small interest at Coral's 33-1.

Ladbrokes go a miserly 16-1 for Cheltenham and offer the same price for the National which is about right.

One note of caution is that our Ken is unlikely to be risked on fast ground, so supporters will need a bit of luck with the weather.

That is a chance worth taking given his current odds for National Hunt's premier prizes.

MARK MAYDON'S
Editor's Choice

SunRacing Editor Mark Maydon chooses 10 dark horses

LAST year's 10 included 16-1 Gold Cup hero See More Business, 6-1 Gerry Feilden Hurdle scorer Wahiba Sands, 3-1 Murphy's Gold Cup winner Cyfor Malta, and 5-2 Pertemps Christmas Hurdle success French Holly. This time around, the focus is on unexposed sorts.

1 BALINCLAY KING (Ferdy Murphy) is an exciting novice hurdle prospect who bolted up on his bumper debut at Ayr before finishing a gallant fourth in the big Punchestown bumper in April.

He will be kept to the smaller northern tracks to start with but is just the sort to run up a sequence.

2 BINDAREE (Nigel Twiston-Davies) has some smart Irish point-to-point form to his name. He has acclimatised well since his move to Gloucestershire and should not be missed in novice hurdles.

3 BRIGHT NOVEMBER (David Gandolfo) has had just five starts in the last two years. He was fairly useful over timber, winning twice in the 1997-98 season, but he promises to be even better over fences.

He had just the one chase start last season, at Kempton, and he would probably have won had he not tipped up three fences out.

Given time to recover from that unfortunate spill, this nine-year-old should do well in novice chases this time around.

4 CAPTAINE LEAU (Nicky Henderson) had some pretty smart form over hurdles in France but is yet to be seen this side of the Channel.

He will probably start off in conditions hurdles but may then switch to novice chases.

5 CARDIFF ARMS (M Johnston) is a four-year-old gelding who just came off worst in a three-way photo-finish in last year's New Zealand St Leger.

Regarded as "potentially the best jumper to come out of New Zealand since Lord Gyllene" by one shrewd judge, we should be hearing a lot more of Cardiff Arms in the near future.

6 CROCADEE (Venetia Williams) looked something special when winning a Bangor bumper last March in a common canter.

He may not have beaten much that day but should go on to better things over hurdles.

7 DOCTOR GODDARD (Philip Hobbs) was a lightly-raced maiden on the Flat in Ireland but might have beaten Martin Pipe's highly-regarded Hit And Run if he hadn't done the splits coming down the Cheltenham hill when running away with Richard Dunwoody last October.

That was his sole start last season so the Doctor remains a maiden over timber — but surely not for long.

8 KAISER STOLTZ (Ian Williams) is a five-year-old who won three times during his Flat career in Germany.

He appreciates cut in the ground and should put a smile on his up-and-coming trainer's face over the coming months.

9 MR LAMB (Martin Pipe) was snapped up for 125,000gns at the Doncaster Sales after running away with a Musselburgh bumper for Sally Hall last January.

He hasn't been sighted since but the word from Nicholashayne is that this four-year-old grey can really motor.

10 TARAWAN (Ian Balding) finally lost his maiden tag on the Flat at Newcastle on 31 August.

Previously placed no fewer than seven times, this son of Nashwan is just the sort to make his mark in novice hurdles and owner Robert Hitchins is no stranger to the winter game.

9

WHEN your workplace is the beautiful Dorset countryside and the tools of your trade are splendid National Hunt thoroughbreds, you have every reason to greet life with a smile.

So it is with Robert Alner as he prepares for the new campaign with boundless enthusiasm.

He has every reason to be bullish after ending the previous season with a career-best tally of 42 winners.

Not enough, perhaps, to make him the Alex Ferguson of racing, but sufficient to consolidate his position in the sport's Premiership list of trainers.

Gold Cup winner Cool Dawn may have been retired, but the prospect of handling some exciting new recruits as well as his dependable string of quality performers has Alner in good form.

"I'm not setting any targets, but simply looking forward to a lot more winners. I have never been the sort of trainer to look at a horse and say 'there's a Kim Muir winner' or 'that one's a Triumph Hurdler'.

"My way of training is to bring horses along in their own time, watch carefully how they are developing and then decide how much I can reasonably ask of them.

"It will be Christmas before the thought of a potential Cheltenham Festival winner even enters my head."

Here Alner gives Sun Guide readers an exclusive insight to his best prospects for the coming season.

COOLTEEN HERO, a fair handicap

ROBERT ALNER

Best Tracks

Towcester	.35%	6-17
Kempton	.34%	16-47
Southwell	.33%	3-9

Worst Tracks

Nottingham	.0%	0-6
Market Rasen	.0%	0-4
Windsor	.5%	2-39
Stratford	.6%	1-17
Newton Abbot	.6%	2-35
Bangor	.6%	1-16

Best months

None over 20%

Worst months

March	.10%	19-185
January	.12%	14-120
June	.13%	2-16

First time out

Chases

1994-95	.36%	5-14
1995-96	.26%	5-19
1996-97	.7%	2-27
1997-98	.19%	8-42
1998-99	.26%	9-34
Total	.21%	29-136

Hurdles

1994-95	.5%	1-19
1995-96	.8%	2-26
1996-97	.4%	1-26
1997-98	.11%	2-18
1998-99	.14%	3-22
Total	.8%	9-111

Jockey Watch

Mr R Nuttall	.32%	6-19
R Dunwoody	.32%	6-19
N Williamson	.31%	4-13

ALL THE STATS COVER THE LAST FIVE SEASONS

11

chaser at best, may be one of the yard's less progressive types but is a favourite of Alner's. A sound jumper who can always be relied upon to give his best, he won just one of his nine starts last season, on his second outing. His form tailed off before the end of the season and, uncharacteristically, he even failed to complete on his last two outings. But the lay-off has rekindled his enthusiasm and Alner insists Coolteen will pick up at least a couple of races this season.

EL MONTY is a stable star in the making. He ran twice in bumpers last season, the pick being a good second to the well-regarded King Of The Castle at Folkestone. "I am really excited about this one. He has just finished his road work and looks an absolute picture. He will start off in a bumper again, but he's already a lovely jumper. He skips over his hurdles and is such a natural he would jump a fence if you pointed him at one. I expect him to shape really nicely when we send him hurdling. Will he win many races? The man from El Monty, he say yes!"

HONEY MOUNT rounded off last season in good heart with hurdle wins at Fontwell, in April, and Towcester the following month. The winning distances were only half-a-length and a length-and-a-half, but the suspicion is that Honey Mount is a shade clever and won't do much more work than he has to. Alner said: "The handicapper has got a bit of a grip on him but the horse is really well and I'm looking forward to sending him chasing. He would be shouldering big weights in handicap hurdles and, because he shows an aptitude for the bigger obstacles, I'm ready to pitch him in some decent novice chases. He is another who should have a good season."

KATES CHARM, a soft-going specialist, was another Alner horse to try the handicapper's patience by rattling up a hat-trick, before disappointing late at the Cheltenham Festival. She has progressed over the summer and Alner expects more success this season. "Hurdling is her game and provided she has her ground she's pretty damn good at it. But be warned — she hates to hear her hooves rattle and must have give underfoot."

She's not alone, many of the Alner

horses prefer some give in the ground and for that reason he has few early-season successes. You can normally expect to see the winners start flowing in late October.

But two early starters, who like good going or firmer, are capable of getting the yard off to a flier. They are **MALWOOD CASTLE** and **MILLCROFT RIVIERA**.

The latter was off the mark at Huntingdon in September last year and is ready to strike again. He is not bred to stay extreme distances but is expected to pick up a two-and-a-half-mile handicap chase early in the season.

Malwood Castle had a light campaign last season, running only four times but winning a decent little race at Wincanton. He will also be sent handicap chasing with a view to early returns.

MENESONIC is a horse Alner has always had a soft spot for. He developed nicely last term following a successful novice chasing season in 1997-98. He won one of his six starts but also boasted four seconds and a third. No doubt the handicapper will give him cold respite for such consistency. "He's not the biggest horse in the world but he's as game as they come and we should be able to place him to win some more races this year."

MR CONDUCTOR is a versatile performer in handicap chase company, equally happy at two miles or three. He only won one from eight starts last season, at Towcester in November, but he slammed John Drumm by 17 lengths on that occasion. "He relishes three miles these days and we will see the best of him at that trip. Remember that he goes especially well when fresh so don't be afraid to back him the first couple of times he runs."

OSCAR WILDE is a highly-regarded chaser who will be having a crack at three miles despite flopping when tried at the distance at Kempton last November. He improved on that showing over shorter at Wincanton on his next three starts but Alner is convinced that staying is his game. "When we tried him at Kempton he blew up. He is older and stronger now, so I expect him to make his mark in three-mile chases this term."

One horse Alner rates particularly

highly is **OVER THE WATER**. He wasn't any great shakes over hurdles but won both his starts over fences last season at two-and-a-half miles. The handicapper has taken note but the trainer believes Over The Water will be even better this season, especially when stepping up in trip for the first time. "He was very impressive in winning at Kempton in November but did not show the same sparkle, despite winning again, at Wincanton next time. That didn't surprise me because the going was firmer than they officially called it at Wincanton and he loves the soft. He is rising in the ratings but will be even better at three miles with some give in the ground this season."

ROLLCALL won twice from five starts last season and Alner expects a speedy return to the winners' enclosure. Look out for this one in a three-mile handicap chase, either just before or just after the New Year because he usually seems to come to hand at that time. "He's looking well having just competed his road work. We will bring him along steadily and continue to pick up some nice handicap chases with him."

SPRING GROVE is another decent young prospect to quicken the pulse. The four-year-old won his only outing in a Chepstow bumper last season when the one-and-a-half lengths he had to spare over Antique Gold barely did him justice. "He has come on a treat and, while his first outing will again be in a bumper, he will soon go hurdling. At home, he has really taken to hurdles and it's obvious to me that he's a natural jumper. He is definitely one to follow next season. I expect big things of him."

SUPER TACTICS is the undoubted stable star. He kept company with the likes of Teeton Mill, Edredon Bleu and Lake Kariba last term and will be mixing

it with the best of them again. He won three times — at Wincanton, Sandown and Kempton and is clearly at his best on right-handed tracks. Alner is full of praise for his brilliant chaser: "He's a lovely horse, I've never seen one as genuine. He will never have an easy race because he would not allow himself one — he tries and battles every inch of the way." Most unusually, Alner has a specific target in mind for Super Tactics and the hint should not go unheeded. "He was brilliant in winning the Desert Orchid Chase at Wincanton at the end of October last year, beating Bertone by 12 lengths. The same race will be his first outing of the season but that is not a problem for him because he goes so well fresh."

One horse which may alter the Alner philosophy of never thinking ahead to the glittering prizes this season is newcomer **TORBOY**. He has just been switched to the trainer by owner Paul Green following his bust-up with Martin Pipe. Torboy was second to French Holly in the 1998 Royal & Sun-Alliance Novice Hurdle. Alner is hoping that Torboy now makes the grade over fences and the horse is already schooling brilliantly at home. "Any horse who can get within striking distance of French Holly is going to do well. He is ready to give his best over fences and I'm looking forward to a really good season with him."

Alner has another winner in mind for the Millennium — conditional jockey Robert Wolford from Malton, in Yorkshire.

Andrew Thornton will again take the majority of rides for the yard but Alner said: "Robert wrote to me asking for a start on the ladder and he is a good lad. He has yet to have a ride for me in public but he will get his opportunities. He could well turn out to be a useful prospect."

TIM EASTERBY embarks on his fifth jumps season with a licence in buoyant mood.

He has a grand mix of young and old at Habton Grange and, in Barton, he has a stable star who could be a leading Champion Hurdle contender, or challenging for top novice chase honours next March.

Here is Easterby's exclusive run-down on the mainstays of his string for the months ahead.

BAKKAR is a useful staying handicap hurdler who won on his reappearance at Wetherby last October but subsequently underwent an operation for a breathing problem. He sometimes wears a tongue strap and has been racing in Ireland during the summer. "He's only small but he's game and a great little jumper. He needs fast ground."

BARNBURGH BOY took well to chasing last term, winning four novice events at Catterick (twice), Musselburgh and Newcastle and finishing second on his other five starts over fences. He has been kept to two miles to date and is another who has been in action in Ireland during the summer. "He is a much better horse on fast ground. He's handicapped high enough but he should win more races."

BARTON, a non-thoroughbred, took the novice hurdling world by storm last term. He produced a scintillating display in the Royal & SunAlliance Novices' Hurdle when trouncing Artadoin Lad by nine lengths and ended the season unbeaten when taking care of Auetaler by two lengths at Aintree in April. He wasn't so impressive there and had to be shown the whip but may have been feeling the effects of a busy campaign which had included previous stylish wins at Wetherby (twice), Uttoxeter, Sandown and Doncaster. Although he has winning form at nearly three miles on soft ground, he has bags of speed. The sky is the limit for him this season — probably over hurdles but possibly in novice chases. "We haven't made our minds up what exact route we will take with him yet. We'll probably start him off in the Fighting Fifth Hurdle and then decide. He has the speed for two miles but will stay three miles plus if he needs to."

BOOGY WOOGY, whose grand-dam

was a very useful hurdler, has been running on the Flat this summer and is set to go juvenile hurdling. Watch out for him on soft ground.

CHOPWELL CURTAINS is going to be absent until around the turn of the year. He has only managed one appearance in the past two seasons but if he can stand the rigours of training and racing he might possibly be a dark horse for the Grand National according to Easterby.

CUMBRIAN CHALLENGE is a Wetherby specialist who sprung a 16-1 surprise in the Castleford Chase at his favourite venue last December when equipped with a tongue strap for the first time. He has now won an incredible **NINE** times at Wetherby but elsewhere has become rather inconsistent. He's a solid jumper but not the easiest of rides and operates between two and two-and-a-half miles. "Because he's rated so high there aren't a lot of options for him but I expect he'll go for the Castleford Chase again. I think two miles is his best trip."

CUMBRIAN MAESTRO has shown useful form in handicap hurdles, although he does race lazily and was blinkered for his last four starts last season. He won with first-time headgear at Catterick in December and wasn't seen out after finishing lame at Wetherby two months later. "We're sending him novice chasing, although he wouldn't want the ground too firm. He should get further than two miles."

EMPIRE PARK won on the Flat and over hurdles during the summer. His jumping success came at Market Rasen in early July and he will be seen to even better effect on softer ground.

EVASIVE STEP was pulled up early on over hurdles at Bangor in mid-August but she is rated much better than that initial venture in juvenile company and is sure to do better in time.

JACKSON PARK was restricted to just the one outing over hurdles last term due to a tendon problem but he has schooled well over fences and could make an exciting novice chaser.

JUSTICE PREVAILS has always shown plenty of promise at home but disappointed in his bumpers last season. "He's a very good jumper and he's going novice hurdling."

JUST TOM is now with Easterby having run in bumpers for Micky Hammond last term. He has schooled well and is set to go hurdling for his new trainer in the months ahead.

MIXSTERTHETRIXSTER was a reasonable two-year-old on the Flat in 1998 but has gone off the boil on the level this year. He could make a useful juvenile hurdler.

A Grade 2 Wetherby event was among **MONARCH'S PURSUIT**'s two hurdle wins as a juvenile in 1997-98 before he injured his back on his final start. He only appeared once last term — when fifth and not knocked about in a Wetherby handicap in October. He is best at two miles on good to firm ground and is just the type to show improved form this season. "He's going novice chasing and he could be all right. He's a big horse so we've given him plenty of time to develop. He could be a good prospect."

NICODEMUS is a half-brother to high-class stable companion Simply Dashing who still needs to fill out his frame. His dam was a winning hurdler but he was well outpaced on his hurdling debut after two runs in bumper company. He should improve this term.

PANAMA HOUSE was useful on the Flat and is a half-brother to winning hurdler/chaser stablemate Shining Edge. He made a winning debut over hurdles when favourite at Wetherby last November and had a tongue strap on and raced too freely when fourth on his only other start. This is a horse that should go the right way in two-mile handicaps if he learns to settle.

RUM POINTER has enjoyed a decent campaign on the Flat in 1999 and there is a chance this useful middle-distance handicapper might be sent over hurdles if he schools well enough.

SCOTTIE YORK was home-bred by the Easterbys and has been in action on the Flat. The plan is for him to go over timber at some stage this winter.

SCOTTON GREEN was a useful hurdler two seasons ago before taking well to fences last term, landing consecutive events at Haydock and Catterick. He jumps well and is suited by a test of stamina and plenty of give in the ground. "He stays three miles no problem and is tough. We're hoping he might make up into a Scottish National horse."

SHARE OPTIONS is a useful handicap chaser but not the easiest of rides and needs plenty of rousting along. He won consecutive three-mile-plus chases at Market Rasen and Uttoxeter last season and goes on most kinds of ground. "He's a grand type of horse and, you never know, he might even be our Grand National horse next Spring. He certainly jumps and the Aintree fences would be no problem for him."

SHINING EDGE reverted to hurdles after his first start last season but without success. He likes to come from off the pace and can idle if in front too soon. He has raced so far at around two miles and although probably better over hurdles than fences "we might go back

15

handicap chasing with him as he lost his way jumping-wise a little bit last season."

SHOP WINDOW was only plating class on the Flat over the summer but she had previously shaped quite well over hurdles and is expected to build on her timber debut when runner-up in juvenile company at Bangor in August.

SILLY MONEY won both his starts over hurdles in 1997-98 and shaped reasonably well in novice chasing company on his first three runs last term. Tenderly handled on a final run back over hurdles in a Catterick handicap, he usually races around two miles under both codes. "He was unlucky not to have won at Wetherby last season and he's going back chasing. We think he pulled some muscles in his back and we couldn't get him right after that."

SIMPLE TONIC did his job well in a couple of bumpers last term and is set to tackle timber this time. "He'll start off in novice hurdles over two miles although he should get further later on."

SIMPLY DASHING is a top-notch chaser who has had a couple of soft palate operations and normally wears a tongue strap. Although he didn't actually win a race last term, he was an excellent runner-up three times — in the Murphy's Gold Cup, Tripleprint Gold Cup and Peter Marsh Chase. He didn't jump well when pulled up in the King George VI Chase and reportedly choked when a well-beaten sixth in the Cheltenham Gold Cup. "We won't be trying him over three miles again this year as he doesn't appear to stay. So he'll stick to all the top two-and-a-half-mile handicaps. He's a much better horse on fast ground."

SIMPLY GIFTED was a progressive, smart, juvenile hurdler last season and his three wins included an excellent 12-length success under top-weight in the Victor Ludorum at Haydock in February. He travelled well for a long way before finishing seventh in the Triumph Hurdle and wasn't 100 per cent when fourth to Hors La Loi III at Aintree. Two miles is likely to be his optimum trip. "He got a little bit jarred up at Aintree and won't be back in until around Christmas. We've still to decide but he might go over fences this season."

SKILLWISE is back in the fold after missing a large part of last season having suffered a nasty leg cut. He only ran once last term but could develop into an exciting staying novice over fences. Keep an eye on him in three-mile events. "He injured his hock on his only start in a novice chase last October but should make a nice prospect."

DASHING TO SUCCESS . . . Simply Dashing jumps his way to the front

THERE should be exciting times around the corner for Micky Hammond, who embarks on the last jumps campaign of the century from a new base in Middleham.

Hammond endured a thoroughly miserable 1998-99 campaign, one he wants quickly to forget.

And at Oakwood, formerly Ferdy Murphy's yard, Hammond is hoping to make a fresh start. To that end, he has cut back slightly on numbers to concentrate more on quality.

"I had a wretched season last year — as a total of just 33 winners suggests — when we had the virus which basically wiped us out for much of the time.

"I have never been one to over-praise my horses — I'd rather let them do the talking.

"But I've got some good ammunition for the coming months and I am thrilled with my new stables."

CELTIC DUKE is still a maiden hurdler but took well to fences last term when winning a Perth novice chase on his debut and a Kelso handicap in April. Both those wins were gained at around three miles but he should be effective at shorter. He loved the fast ground and is an improving type that should do well again.

COMMANDER GLEN does his bit for the yard and, though often equipped with blinkers and a tongue strap, seems genuine enough. He doesn't appreciate extremes of going but has already been in the winners' enclosure this season. The Commander is a modest handicap chaser who is effective at two to three miles.

DEEP WATER was the leading juvenile hurdler of 1997-98 when he won three of his four starts including the Grade 2 Glenlivet Hurdle at Aintree's Grand National meeting. He suffered more than most by being badly out of sorts last term and only appeared once — when last of five in a minor event at Sandown in February — although he did travel strongly for a long way until lack of a race took its toll. He relishes heavy ground, should eventually stay further than 2m and is almost certainly still on the upgrade.

MICKY HAMMOND

Best Tracks

Stratford	33%	4-12
Worcester	30%	3-10
Uttoxeter	29%	4-14
Perth	21%	27-131
Newbury	20%	1-5
Kelso	20%	25-125

Worst Tracks

Huntingdon	0%	0-15
Warwick	0%	0-11
Sandown	0%	0-9
Leicester	0%	0-8
Kempton	0%	0-7
Ludlow	0%	0-5
Cheltenham	0%	0-5
Towcester	0%	0-4
Chepstow	0%	0-4
Ascot	0%	0-4
Doncaster	5%	2-44
Aintree	7%	3-41
Sedgefield	7%	5-70

Best months

July	35%	8-23
September	20%	12-59

Worst months

January	7%	13-186
November	9%	19-212
February	10%	18-188
December	12%	27-222
March	13%	28-216
May	14%	19-138
April	14%	26-183

First time out
Chases

1994-95	19%	3-16
1995-96	0%	0-20
1996-97	9%	2-22
1997-98	9%	2-23
1998-99	21%	6-29
Total	12%	13-110

Hurdles

1994-95	12%	5-41
1995-96	3%	2-58
1996-97	13%	8-63
1997-98	13%	9-71
1998-99	11%	6-53
Total	10%	30-286

Jockey Watch

A P McCoy	40%	2-5
C F Swan	25%	1-4
M Foster	25%	1-4
Mr D Parker	25%	1-4
R Dunwoody	25%	4-16
A Maguire	24%	5-21

"His first big target is the Christmas Hurdle at Kempton, It may be a blessing in disguise that he had just the one run last season as it has given him plenty of time to mature."

EASTERN PROJECT was an admirably consistent novice hurdler, who won twice (at Perth and Ayr) and was placed on each of his eight other starts last term. He races exclusively at two miles and is already making his mark in novice chases.

FISHKI'S LAD made all to land a Hexham bumper last term and appears as the type that will stay well. His mother, Fishki, was a grand money-spinner on the Flat and over jumps for the stable. Fishki's Lad will be tackling novice hurdles this time around.

FORREST TRIBE is a winning ex-Irish pointer but remains a maiden over hurdles. Last term he was successful on his chasing debut by a wide margin in a two-and-a-half-mile Ayr novice event. He didn't appear to get home over three miles, one furlong next time, but should be capable of holding his own in handicap company at the right trip.

GLENBOWER was a consistent staying novice hurdler in 1997-98 and was placed on his first three starts in novice chases last term. He races mainly at two-and-a-half miles but should stay further. He is hard to assess on bare form but is certainly capable of better over fences.

GRANDIOSO was fancied on his hurdling debut when runner-up at Perth this August. A shade novicey, he still showed enough to suggest losses will be recouped in the months ahead.

GREY EXPECTATIONS, a new arrival in the yard, is described by Hammond as "my Dessie — a strapping grey and a real chasing type." Plans are fluid for this one but he is obviously well-regarded.

GUN'N ROSES is a rangy French import with winning form on the Flat and over hurdles in his native country, as well as two placed efforts over fences. Last term he was a good second on his reappearance at Uttoxeter in a handicap hurdle but disappointed in his next two races. A grand chasing sort who should have no problem staying two-and-a-half miles. "He is owned by Stan Clarke and I shall be running

him in some of the better two-and-a-half-mile events over fences."

INVEST WISELY was a smart staying hurdler in 1997-98 who gradually got the hang of the chasing game last term. He won a 3m 5f novice handicap at Wetherby in April, demonstrating with that effort that he enjoys a good test of stamina providing the ground is not too soft. He is likely to continue on the upgrade, but don't back him when the mud is flying.

KEEN TO THE LAST was only a modest hurdler but returned in good heart in novice chasing company last term. He was an easy winner at Newcastle in March (when only two finished) and was runner-up in his other three starts over fences. He seems best at around two-and-a-half miles and is another who doesn't like heavy ground.

LUZCADOU, is now six and was only a maiden on the Flat but "is my most exciting prospect. He came from France and landed a nice little gamble when winning his only race for me, a novice hurdle at Carlisle back in December 1997. He was not entirely right last season which is why he did not run. But he is definitely one to look out for in handicap hurdles." He was twice successful over fences as a four-year-old in France so a switch to chasing is also on the cards.

MONYMAN is a sturdy sort of chaser who defied a three-month absence when bouncing back to his best at Newcastle in March. He was subsequently well beaten in the John Hughes Chase over the Grand National fences (when he blundered badly at Becher's). He only just gets two-and-a-half miles when conditions are not too testing but is clearly not done with winning yet.

ORSUNO was a useful winner on the Flat in Germany and took well to hurdling in this country last term. He impressed when winning a Uttoxeter maiden by 14 lengths and was placed in his other two starts. He raced only at two miles but is sure to improve and is one to keep on the right side in the coming months.

OUTSET is only small but is all heart and a decent handicap hurdler. Only seen out twice last term, he ran up to his best when chasing home Khayrawani in a valuable event at

Aintree in April. He's game and consistent and enjoys forcing the pace. He should stay three miles which would open new avenues.

PATRAS is another useful ex-French Flat performer, who was sold out of John Hammond's yard for 30,000gns at last year's Newmarket Autumn Sales. "He took well to hurdles and would have been unbeaten in all four starts last term had he not fallen at the last at Carlisle over Easter with the race in the bag. He will get two-and-a-half miles and perhaps a shade further. He is decent and should continue to progress this season — in fact I like this horse a lot and he is definitely one to follow this winter."

PORNIC is an ex-French maiden hurdler who is much better over fences and won two chases last term at Auteuil. Following a four-month break, he did well on his British debut at Newcastle to finish sixth in a novice hurdle and progressed to grab the runner-up spot in a novice chase at the same venue next time out. He gets two-and-a-half miles and should improve a fair bit yet over fences. One to keep an eye on.

PROFLUENT is a useful hurdler/chaser at his best. He quickened up nicely to win a slowly-run handicap chase at Wetherby on his reappearance but then failed to complete in three subsequent starts before obliging in a first-time visor at Market Rasen on his final run of the season. He's best at trips between two-and-a-half and three miles and raced exclusively over fences last term.

POLO VENTURE is a small, close-coupled gelding who ended a sequence of five placed efforts over hurdles with victory at Kelso in April. Attempting to follow up, he was second once more, this time to a Martin Pipe hot-pot at Cartmel. That was his final outing of the campaign in which he raced only at two miles but he is worth a crack over a little further. He should continue to pay his way around the small northern tracks.

RIVER MURRAY is a highly-regarded new arrival in the yard. "David Johnson has sent me this ex-French horse. I am very happy to have David as a new owner. River Murray has some useful jumping form in France and I am looking forward to seeing David's famous colours around some of the northern tracks."

RYALUX showed improved form last season to win his last two starts at Newcastle (two-and-a-half miles) and Hexham (two miles), having been runner-up on his first two outings. He has only raced on soft or heavy ground to date but still has plenty of scope and is a chasing type whose long-term future lies over fences.

STEEN is a French import who is a half-brother to the very useful hurdler Abzac. He won on his British debut for new connections in a novice chase at Kelso in October and was heavily eased (could have at least doubled the winning distance) when landing a moderate handicap over course and distance by 12 lengths in May. Has worn blinkers and a visor, acts on any ground and stays three miles plus.

TOHUNGA is a half-brother to useful Flat performers Hal's Pal and Minstrel's Gift. He made a winning debut on his only start last term when landing a Market Rasen bumper in April. Likely to improve further and should develop into a top-class novice hurdler if his trainer's predictions are fulfilled. "A really exciting prospect, he's my Istabraq! I bought him at the Newmarket Sales out of John Gosden's yard — just as Istabraq was."

> **Patras took well to hurdles and would have been unbeaten in all four starts last term had he not fallen at the last at Carlisle. He is definitely one to follow this winter**

19

IT'S onward and upwards for Nicky Henderson as he celebrates 21 years' training, the last five at Seven Barrows on the outskirts of Lambourn.

Winning totals have progressed to a personal best of 73 in 1998-99 and the 100 is a target this time around with Henderson emphatic that: "This is by far the nicest bunch we've ever had."

Here Henderson gives Sun Guide readers an exclusive A-Z rundown on his main prospects for the new campaign.

ADMIRAL ROSE comes from a talented, if temperamental family. "Stamina will be his strong point. He was a naughty schoolboy who finally started to behave and won his bumper. I'm pleased with him and he'll go straight over hurdles."

AMOROSO "is Sharpical's sister and because he improved so much from four to five I'd like to think she'd do the same. She won two novice hurdles but was very busy on the Flat before that and is looking good after a decent summer break."

ARTEMIS hasn't reached any dizzy heights yet but "he'll stay and will go novice chasing."

BACCHANAL is a horse Henderson hopes is destined for the top. "He was very nearly my banker for Punchestown but was beaten there although, to be fair, he was lame afterwards. He won at Sandown and was very impressive in the mud at Chepstow beating Davoski 23 lengths. The natural thing would be to send him straight over fences but I might just see how he goes in some early conditions hurdles although the handicapper is making it very hard. I'll start him over shorter distances but he'll stay all right."

BASSEY "is one I've always thought the world of. He won his bumper then missed last season but is back in action and looks fantastic. It'll be straight into novice hurdles for him."

BEAUFORT ZERO is from the same family as The Tsarevitch and Golden Spinner. "He has had a couple of bumpers and was immature but is learning quickly."

BE BRAVE has had just two runs in two years. "I thought she was going to be a very good mare last season but we kept getting problems, including a cyst on an eye. She's got a lot of potential."

BIG MATT is heading for retirement. "He's my hack at present and is not going to be easy to place because there are few races for him."

BLUE ROYAL "could be anything. He

NICKY HENDERSON

Best Tracks

Wetherby	75%	3-4
Ludlow	39%	13-33
Plumpton	38%	9-24
Folkestone	34%	11-32
Hereford	33%	9-27
Taunton	33%	9-27
Doncaster	32%	12-37
Leicester	31%	11-35
Fakenham	30%	3-10
Newton Abbot	29%	4-14
Ayr	27%	3-11

Worst Tracks

Aintree	4%	2-46
Nottingham	7%	1-15
Haydock	10%	2-20
Chepstow	11%	5-46
Cheltenham	13%	15-117
Ascot	13%	13-100

Best months

August	50%	4-8
December	28%	60-211
November	24%	43-180
May	24%	31-131
September	22%	2-9

Worst months

April	13%	23-175
January	14%	23-170
March	17%	36-213

First time out

Chases

1994-95	33%	7-21
1995-96	19%	4-21
1996-97	14%	4-28
1997-98	27%	6-22
1998-99	20%	6-30
Total	22%	27-122

Hurdles

1994-95	8%	3-39
1995-96	16%	8-51
1996-97	15%	10-65
1997-98	19%	13-68
1998-99	29%	18-62
Total	18%	52-285

Jockey Watch

T Hagger	33%	4-12
R Dunwoody	31%	8-26
Major O Ellwood	25%	1-4
M A Fitzgerald	22%	203-921
N Williamson	21%	3-14
Mr M Foley	20%	1-5
J R Kavanagh	16%	40-253
R Johnson	14%	1-7
M Lane	13%	2-16
Mr C Vigors	12%	5-43

amazed me last year. We bought him after one run in France and he got beaten a short head on his debut at Sandown which was a blessing because the race he won so impressively at Punchestown was for horses that had won just once. He's a quality chasing type and, if they hadn't taken the allowances to bits, I'd have sent him over fences as a four-year-old this season. I think he's certain to get two-and-a-half miles over hurdles. I hope he's a bit special."

BRANDY SNAP is owned by the Queen Mother and won a Bangor bumper. "She's a big strong mare who will go straight over hurdles."

BORO SOVEREIGN "had a funny sort of season. He won his bumper and should have won his hurdle at Wincanton but then came back lame after running second at Newbury. He'll improve."

CAPTAINE LEAU is a new French acquisition. "He's got some pretty smart French hurdle form being one of the better juveniles there. As he's won it's condition hurdle races although I may send him novice chasing."

CEANANNAS MOR is a full brother to Stormyfairweather. "I saw him win his point-to-point in Ireland and he was a joy to watch — seriously impressive. He will start in novice hurdles."

CLUB SANDWICH "will go over hurdles. She wasn't quite ready for her two bumper runs and took time to get over them."

DUSK DUEL won his Sandown bumper well. "He ran no sort of race at Aintree — with hindsight he's too big to be suited by the course. I wouldn't be worried by that because I think he's very talented."

EASTER ROSS will go novice chasing this season. "He's been weak and has needed time, He must have top of the ground. I couldn't believe it when he fell at the Cheltenham Festival because everything was right — two miles five furlongs and decent ground. He's the best jumper I've had in the yard for years."

ESPRIT DE COTTE joined Henderson late last season from France, having won there over fences. "He then won a novice hurdle at Stratford. I'm going to have to see what the handicapper does with him over fences — he's a wonderful jumper who needs cut in the ground."

FAR HORIZON won his only bumper start very easily. "Another who's going straight over hurdles."

FATHER MANSFIELD won two Irish point-to-points. "He's a proper chasing type so he won't be long over hurdles."

FIDDLING THE FACTS had an amazing year considering she failed to win. She collected £65,000 in place money, thanks to being narrowly beaten in the Welsh National as well as finishing runner-up in two National trials. "She never travelled better in a race than the Grand National until she fell at Becher's second time. She never had an easy race right from the Hennessy in November. The way the programme is it will be the Hennessy again, as long as it's wet enough, then the Welsh and English Nationals with possibly one of the Haydock trials in between."

GAROLSA is a French import that took time to get right. "He won a bad Chepstow hurdle well and is a natural born chaser."

GET REAL picked up a stress fracture after the Victor Chandler in which he was narrowly beaten by Call Equiname who went on to win the Champion Chase. "That won't do his handicap mark any good! The problem is he can only go right-handed so we are limited but his first objective should be the Haldon Gold Cup at Exeter, then the Tingle Creek at Sandown. He can't go to Cheltenham or Aintree, so long term it's Punchestown."

GRECIAN DART will go novice chasing. "He kept improving all year and he will start at two miles."

HIDEBOUND "had a problem with his knees after he was second to Behrajan at Sandown. We will be careful with him in staying novice chases."

IBORGA is a three-year-old full sister to Hors Le Loi. "She's gorgeous. I bought her three hours before the Supreme Novices Hurdle at Cheltenham. She's never run but I'd think about sending her straight over hurdles."

KATARINO had hard races at Cheltenham and at Punchestown but never flinched to make it five unbeaten for Henderson. "There's a big four-year-old hurdle in France in late autumn. Two miles is OK on soft but on faster ground it's not an option. Although he's not very big I wouldn't be frightened of sending him over fences — but races like the Cleeve Hurdle over two miles five furlongs are definitely on the agenda."

KINGS BOY "is a horse I like a lot. He won two novice hurdles nicely considering he is a complete playboy who never concentrated once the whole of last season. We may go chasing now."

LONG LUNCH won his only bumper start at Huntingdon in October but "then had a slight problem. He'll go over hurdles to start with."

LORD NATIVE "is a bumper winner who has only recently joined me but will go straight over hurdles."

LORD O'ALL SEASONS is a winning Irish point-to-pointer. "He will go into novice chases."

MAGIC CIRCLE "is huge. He was going the right way but then got a knee chip at Sandown. But he's fine now and is ready to tackle fences."

MAKOUNJI "will be best at two-and-a-half-miles although I think she will end up over three later on. She was very good winning at Leicester, Newbury and Kempton and was in season when pulling up at Cheltenham. We made sure she wasn't going to be in the same condition at Aintree when she went over three miles but she didn't appear to stay. She's not going to be easy to place because of her handicap mark."

MARLBOROUGH has joined Henderson from Henry Daly. "He is a very exciting horse. He's fallen at Haydock and Ascot when holding a winning chance in good races. As a second-season novice chaser it's going to be very interesting to see how he is handicapped."

MASAMADAS has summered well. "I'll look at the Free Handicap Hurdle at Chepstow for him."

OBELISK was bought at Doncaster in the spring. "He needs to grow up a bit."

PERFECT VENUE "got thrown in a bit deep towards the end of the season, having won twice at Taunton. He was still there two out in Hors La Loi's race at Cheltenham and was over the top by Punchestown. He could go chasing after starting in handicap hurdles."

PREMIER GENERATION had a good year, winning three hurdles. "The handicapper might have caught up with him so he'll go over fences."

ROMANTIC DREAM and **BELLA MACRAE** are four-year-old home-breds of the Queen Mother's. "I've had them in since the spring and they'll be ready to go shortly. They'll have a run in a bumper but they both jump well."

SALMON BREEZE "won two and should have won three — he went one way and Mick (Fitzgerald) the other at Fakenham. We think he had muscle problems behind when his jumping went to bits. I think he'll come back and he'll stay well on decent ground."

SERENUS is tiny but Henderson's ambition is to win a novice chase with him at Kempton. "That would mean he's won on the Flat, over hurdles and over fences at the track in the space of one year."

SHARPICAL came back with a problem after he won the Tote Gold Trophy in 1998. "We rather rushed him for this year and it backfired and he was wrong behind

after that. He'll go novice chasing as he's a fantastic jumper."

SILVER WEDGE is being aimed at staying hurdles, "possibly with a run in the Cesarewitch beforehand."

STEEL BLADE has joined Henderson from Kim Bailey. "He is a half-brother to One Man and won his only bumper. He hasn't been here long and is very laid back. He will go straight over hurdles."

STORMYFAIRWEATHER "had a couple of blips in the middle of the season — I wasn't sure if he wanted two or three miles. We made the right option in the end with the Cathcart at Cheltenham over two miles, five furlongs which is his trip on good ground. He was very brave in defeat at Punchestown."

STORMY ROW won a point-to-point in Northern Ireland. "He looks the part and will go straight over hurdles."

TAX EXEMPT won a Kempton novice hurdle "which in hindsight I wish he hadn't because he came back with a pelvic injury. We're not left with many options this season. I hope the handicapper gives him half a chance because I don't want to send him over fences yet."

TEMPESTUOUS LADY is quite well named — winning three novice hurdles last term but also throwing in two horrors. "She'd previously won three point-to-points and she'll go novice chasing. She stays and jumps on any ground."

TEQUILA won his maiden hurdle nicely before taking on the big boys at Aintree which proved too much. "He's been gelded and is much easier to train. He'll jump fences but he might have a decent handicap hurdle in him."

TIUTCHEV has joined the yard from David Nicholson. "The plan is to go over fences — he's already been schooled."

VIA DE LA VALLE "is a good-looking horse who won his only point-to-point in Ireland and will start over hurdles."

YOKKI MOPPIE "came from France and bolted up at Taunton only to return with a problem, so you won't see her until after Christmas."

There are a nice bunch of Henderson horses that didn't get to run last season, in particular: **KINGS RAPID, REGAL GALE, BUCKINGHAM, FAST FIDDLER** and **FIRST TOUCH** will all be ready to run quite soon, while two by Supreme Leader, **RULING THE ROAST** and **THE FULL NELSON**, are worth keeping an eye out for.

Henderson also has some nice French youngsters, among them **IRIS ROYAL, S'ASSAGIR, IRIS D'ESTRUVAL** and **HOPALONG**.

PHILIP HOBBS is one of the few who take on Martin Pipe on his home territory in the West Country and hold his own.

Not that Hobbs stays local — he's just as likely to send a box-full up to Perth in the early part of the season.

His impressive winning statistics of 84 winners with a 19 per cent strike rate put him fifth in the trainers' championship last season.

It also assured his Minehead stable was again at full capacity with 83, although as Hobb says: "We'll always make room for a good one."

The target is still 100 winners in a season and he came closest to that three years ago with 86.

Last season finished two short of that but was topped off by the Racing Post Chase victory of Dr Leunt.

"That was the best season we've had prize money-wise and now we've got a good base of quality horses to go to war with."

Here Hobbs gives Sun Guide readers an exclusive rundown on the pick of his yard's talent.

ATAVISTIC won two novice chases last season and is rated 110 "which might be high enough — he wants a long trip and soft ground."

ANTIQUE GOLD is a half-brother to Country Beau "who ran well in his bumpers. He is a big, strong horse who wants soft ground and will go straight over hurdles."

ARLEQUIN DE SOU's form doesn't look great over here "but he's won five chases in France, two of them claimers. I had to run him over hurdles because I couldn't run him in a handicap chase. The handicapper was very hard on him when he did give him a chase mark, 135, which is impossible. The officials are going to look at it. We claimed Arlequin for £18,000 which isn't bad when you consider a five-year-old handicap chaser with a rating of 135 should be worth nearer £100,000!"

ASHWELL BOY "got colic before he was due to run in the Galway Plate and then came back with a virus. But he's been a grand servant — we've had him since he was three and he's now eight. Two-and-a-half miles and fast ground are his ideal conditions."

BOUCHASSON "is an amazing

PHILIP HOBBS

Best Tracks

Perth	47%	15-32
Folkestone	44%	4-9
Huntingdon	35%	8-23
Newton Abbot	30%	57-191
Bangor	28%	10-36
Chepstow	27%	30-112
Taunton	24%	29-121
Sandown	23%	13-57

Worst Tracks

Leicester	0%	0-13
Haydock	3%	1-29
Ayr	8%	1-12
Cheltenham	9%	12-134
Ascot	9%	6-69
Plumpton	10%	2-21
Aintree	10%	5-49
Wincanton	12%	14-120
Newbury	12%	10-85

Best months

August	38%	44-117
July	30%	10-33
September	28%	31-109
June	25%	8-32
October	23%	49-209

Worst months

December	19%	48-248
May	17%	29-172
November	16%	45-273
April	16%	33-201
March	15%	36-235
February	14%	25-176
January	12%	24-193

First time out

Chases

1994-95	13%	3-24
1995-96	39%	9-23
1996-97	25%	7-28
1997-98	28%	7-25
1998-99	24%	6-25
Total	26%	32-125

Hurdles

1994-95	21%	13-62
1995-96	16%	10-64
1996-97	13%	9-67
1997-98	10%	7-71
1998-99	16%	14-89
Total	15%	53-353

Jockey Watch

A Thornton	42%	5-12
Mr J Creighton	33%	2-6
P Carberry	29%	2-7
C Maude	27%	20-75
A Maguire	27%	10-37
Mr P Flynn	25%	4-16

horse. I offered £20,000 for him last year and it was refused. Then he came up for sale at Saint-Cloud six months later after his owner died and we got him for 20,000 francs — about £2,000! He had three runs — third at Wincanton over too short a trip, before going to Ayr and winning the £25,000 Future Champion Novices Chase. He subsequently won a decent handicap by 20 lengths. I wouldn't want to say how good he is but he's won over two-and-a-half miles and he's crying out for three. We'll aim for the First National Bank Chase at Ascot for first and second-season novice chasers at the end of November and then take it from there."

BROTHER JOE won four races in New Zealand and was second in their St Leger. "He'll start in novice hurdles, possibly at two miles but maybe a bit further."

CALHOUN ran well in two bumpers last season and will go straight over hurdles. "He's a nice horse."

CELTIC NATIVE had one run in an Irish point-to-point last year. "He's by Be My Native out of a good mare."

CLIFTON BEAT's "jumping is coming right at last. He's won three chases and prefers faster ground. I'd like to think he could win a decent two-miler this season but he's rated 130, although, to be fair, I think he's capable of winning off that mark."

DOCTOR GODDARD had just one run last season — in a juvenile hurdle — but it was a good one. "He did the splits coming down the hill at Cheltenham and it would be no exaggeration to say he lost 200 yards but was beaten under two lengths by a decent horse of Martin Pipe's called Hit And Run. He injured a hock and couldn't run again but it's a blessing as he's a novice for this season. He could be very good but will start in a small novice hurdle before tackling the bigger boys."

DR LEUNT is rated 151 so is not going to be easy to place. "He's probably not up to the King George but he'll have plenty of weight in handicaps. That said, he's got better each year and he might get better again. He might also stay a bit further."

ENRIQUE won in Germany on the Flat. "He's a four-year-old who has been gelded since coming to England and is one to watch in novice hurdles."

FLYAWAY GUNNER has run in two point-to-points in Ireland, well clear when

he fell two out in the second of them. "He could do very well."

GAI MURMURE only had one run last season because he pulled back muscles. "He was fourth in a novice hurdle at Auteuil before he came to me and he's a big, strong horse who could have done with the time off anyway."

GLADIATEUR won at Lingfield although he had a slight breathing problem at the time. He's since had a soft palate operation which appears to have worked. "He'll have one run over hurdles before novice chasing. He wants two-and-a-half miles."

GOOD LORD MURPHY "had a terrible season considering I thought he was possibly my best horse. He pulled a muscle in his hind-quarters on his chase debut at Exeter. When he came back in February, we didn't want to lose his novice status over fences so he went back over hurdles only to disappoint me badly. Hopefully he'll do much better this year, although he must have it soft."

HANDYMAN had one outing in a bumper, a good second at Ludlow. "He needed time so we roughed him off after that."

IN THE BLOOD "is another one who wants it soft. He's won five of his last six chases and could still be improving."

KING WIZARD ran well in his bumpers, including when fifth at Aintree. "He's a great big, strong horse who has wanted time. He'll need two-and-a-half miles over hurdles."

LEABURN is still a maiden over hurdles but "is a lovely horse. I don't know why he disappointed at Sandown when we really fancied him on his third start. He'll definitely win over fences but he must surely win a hurdle first."

MAJOR ADVENTURE "has won a point-to-point in Ireland and was in training with us last season but had a minor problem — nothing serious. He'll have a run or two in novice hurdles but he's a chaser long term."

MONT ACA was bought from France as a three-year-old. "He's four now and finished second to Sagamix at Longchamp which sounds rather good but it was a maiden! He didn't cost a fortune but was placed in other maidens so showed signs of ability. He'll be ready in October and he might just run on the Flat first up. He'll want a trip."

NATIVE ARROW "is a really nice horse who won his bumper first time but wants fastish ground so will be out earlier than most in novice hurdles."

NATIVE FLING had a very good season, winning over hurdles and fences, but is rated 115 so he'll have to run at the better grade tracks. "I think he's up to it."

NORLANDIC took well to fences last season and "could still be improving because he was very backward and needed loads of time. He wants soft ground and three miles plus."

NUVELLINO showed fairly useful form in juvenile hurdles but "is still a novice which is a good job. After his first run in January he was quite highly tried but this season he'll start in an easier grade and move up."

ORSWELL LAD has been placed at the last two Cheltenham Festivals in amateur events. "He wants three miles and soft ground. He should win a decent chase given those conditions."

PAPO KHARISMA won four hurdles last season and now goes novice chasing. "He's completed over fences in Ireland for Arthur Moore so we know he can jump!"

PHARANEAR has joined Hobbs from David Nicholson. "He is rated 155 so it's going to be very difficult. He'll be aimed at the Stayers' Hurdle although I don't know if he's quite good enough."

PHARDANTE FLYER "ran brilliantly on his only start in a Cheltenham bumper but then developed a minor back problem so we gave him a year off. He'll win any ordinary bumper then go hurdling."

POT BLACK UK won a novice hurdle at Exeter last term. "He will go straight over fences this season."

QUALITY didn't run last season. He got an infected hock and Hobbs struggled to get him right. "He belongs to Des O'Connor and won two novice hurdles the season before last. I hope he is capable of winning a decent handicap hurdle and he might jump fences as well in time."

ROSS MINSTER "ran amazingly well in his novice hurdle at Exeter, coming from miles off the pace to finish second over 19 furlongs. That was great considering he's going to want three-and-a-half miles and soft ground over fences. But he's only five and he might stay in long-distance hurdles this season."

RUSCOMBE "is a half-brother to Edgemore Prince. He has done a fair bit of work and should do well in his bumpers."

SADDLERS REALM only won one hurdle last season but he was third in the Tote Gold Trophy, fourth at Cheltenham and third at Aintree. "He'll go straight over fences and he looks a high class novice chaser in the making."

SAMLEE broke a blood vessel in the National when still going well. "He'll be aimed at Aintree again and his first run will be in the Becher Chase there in November which he's won and been placed in before. He's better fresh and does seem to like the National fences."

SAXON DUKE "is a good, honest handicap chaser who will win a decent race over a long trip."

SOLVANG had only won chases in Ireland before he came over, so Hobbs shrewdly placed him to win a novice hurdle at Wincanton. "I then gave him the winter off because he wants fast ground. He'll be over fences in October at the better tracks because he's rated 125."

STORMY PASSAGE, a very decent handicap chaser on his day, "is capable of winning a good race somewhere but he is another who has burst blood vessels in the past. He runs better fresh and the Murphy's at Cheltenham might be his race."

STREET FIGHTER "ran very well at Taunton first time but was then outclassed at Cheltenham. He's a winner on the Flat in France and has benefited from a summer at grass. It'll be straight into novice hurdles for him."

TANTIVY BAY won his only race at Towcester, a bumper, but was very green. "He is sure to improve and will start in two-and-a-half-mile novice hurdles."

TEMPER LAD won three hurdles last year and will "pop up in a decent handicap hurdle somewhere".

THELONIUS was a winner on the Flat for Julian Smyth-Osborne but Hobbs is yet to really test him. "After we bought him we had him gelded and gave him a year off."

UPHAM LORD "is still a maiden but he's been placed in good bumpers and will win soon."

VILLAGE KING won five chases last season and is now rated 127 so won't be so easy to place. "He prefers faster ground and will be ready in October. He's got speed for two-and-a-half miles but also stays three."

WAVE ROCK was bought from Henrietta Knight. "He's ready to go over fences — he jumps really well considering he's only young."

LAST season saw a downturn in Henrietta Knight's fortunes — at least in terms of her total number of winners.

But as far as the Wantage trainer is concerned it was a case of down but definitely not out, and she is hopeful that the introduction over the summer of some attractive French-breds — as well as one or two from Ireland — will be enough for her fortunes to take a turn for the better.

Here she gives Sun Guide readers an exclusive insight into the best horses in her care this season.

ALPENSTOCK is a promising French three-year-old, purchased at the sales. "He ran fifth in his bumper in the Provinces and looks the part. He should be out in novice hurdles quite soon."

BE MY MANAGER is a winning point-to-pointer from Ireland. "He is a very big horse and I won't ask too much of him this season. I will play it very low-key until he tackles regulation fences. He will be out when there is some soft ground and will start off over two-and-a-half miles."

BEST MATE is another winner between the flags in Ireland who won't be rushed in his first season. "A year on and you could be looking at a fine chasing prospect."

BLOWING ROCK was twice placed in novices' chases at Sandown last winter, as well as making the frame at Towcester and Exeter in May. "He is a small horse with a big heart. He stays and jumps well, is best on good ground and is not badly handicapped at present."

BROWN LAD was fairly useful on the Flat in France before joining Henrietta Knight for his first season over hurdles. He kept on well for his win at Doncaster last December and later finished in the rear in the Citroen Supreme Novices' Hurdle at the Cheltenham Festival. "He is badly handicapped on his mark of 130 but is more likely to stick to hurdles than go novice chasing."

BRUTHUIMME ran well in point-to-points in Ireland and should develop into a good prospect in novice company. "He won't be rushed and will be better still with another season behind him."

HENRIETTA KNIGHT

Best Tracks

Plumpton	33%	10-30
Market Rasen	32%	13-41
Exeter	25%	36-144
Doncaster	24%	7-29
Taunton	23%	9-40
Folkestone	22%	4-18

Worst Tracks

Chepstow	0%	0-22
Lingfield	0%	0-14
Nottingham	0%	0-11
Ayr	0%	0-7
Wetherby	0%	0-4
Newbury	5%	3-55
Warwick	9%	6-66
Huntingdon	10%	4-42
Cheltenham	11%	8-76
Ascot	11%	4-35
Kempton	12%	6-52

Best months

September	22%	6-27
December	22%	40-185
May	20%	32-160

Worst months

June	11%	1-9
November	12%	25-210
October	13%	15-120
February	14%	25-175
January	15%	23-154
March	15%	33-215
April	15%	22-143

First time out

Chases

1994-95	29%	4-14
1995-96	8%	2-25
1996-97	12%	2-17
1997-98	21%	5-24
1998-99	12%	3-25
Total	15%	16-105

Hurdles

1994-95	14%	6-42
1995-96	16%	9-57
1996-97	9%	6-68
1997-98	7%	3-45
1998-99	7%	3-41
Total	11%	27-253

Jockey Watch

L Cummins	45%	5-11
A P McCoy	33%	6-18
Mr J M Pritchard	33%	3-9
Mr A Dempsey	25%	2-8
J F Titley	21%	64-308
T J Murphy	20%	3-15

CATFISH KEITH made a winning debut over hurdles at Windsor last November but was later beaten in handicaps. "He has done well over the summer and schooled nicely over fences. He will go novice chasing and will start off over two to two-and-ahalf miles. He goes on any ground."

CELTIC SEASON's campaign fell apart after he won as he pleased from weak opposition at Leicester in January. That 18-length victory caused the handicapper to put him up 12lb and he never looked the same horse again, finishing tailed off on all his three remaining starts. "He will carry on in handicap chases, and we may try him over three miles. He is accident prone but has come back looking very well."

CHARMERS PLACE has joined the yard after winning a point-to-point in Ireland. "He wants soft ground and will start off over two-and-a-half miles."

COLONEL BLAZER has won seven races for the yard, his two contributions last season coming in handicap chases at Exeter and Towcester in May. Sadly, the consequence is that he starts the new campaign on a mark he could not win off last winter. "He is still only seven, so I hope he will be that little bit better this time around. He doesn't mind fast ground and should pay his way if we keep him to the minor tracks and don't ask too much of him."

COXWELL COSSACK is a half-brother by Gildoran to three winners, but is still waiting for his first success. His best effort in five starts last season was a second to Doublet at Ludlow. "That was quite good form and he was entitled to run a lot better than he did when down the field at Stratford and Hereford in May. I am hopeful this will be his year."

DICTUM closed last season with a novices success (over fences), just as he had the '96/'97 campaign (over hurdles). "As that win came in May, he is still eligible to run in novice company this term. He beat seven previous winners at Stratford (hence his 20-1 SP) and that win should have done his confidence the world of good. He is best going left-handed and races over two-and-half miles."

DORAN'S GOLD took the eye in the paddock before his debut in a Sandown bumper last February, and ran a highly promising second of 11 to Frosty Canyon, who went on to run well at the Cheltenham Festival. "He put 10 lengths between himself and the third with the minimum of fuss. He was then put away for the season and has done well for the break. He is a chaser in the making but should pay to follow in novice hurdles confined to horses that have not raced on the Flat."

EDREDON BLEU got thrashed out of sight on his comeback in the William Hill Haldon Gold Cup Chase at Exeter in November. But he was back to his brilliant best at Huntingdon the same month, winning the Grade 2 Peterborough Chase. His later win off a mark of 155 at Sandown was sandwiched between seconds in the Mitsubishi Shogun Tingle Creek Chase and the Queen Mother Champion Chase, the two most important two-mile chases. "He will carry the flag in the same races and could be better still with another summer's break behind him. He has done really well and either Tony McCoy or our stable jockey Jim Cullotty will be in the saddle."

> **Edredon Bleu could be better still with another summer's break behind him. Either Tony McCoy or our stable jockey Jim Cullotty will be in the saddle**

FOLY PLEASANT won four chases and two hurdles in France, where he has been used to figure-of-eight tracks. "We will have to get him handicapped as he is not eligible to run in novice events. He wants soft ground."

HARDLY showed a good attitude on his debut in a Sandown bumper last November, so his success on his hurdles debut at Wincanton in January did not come as a total surprise, even though Boro Sovereign and Running

Water were preferred in the market. His subsequent placed efforts at Newbury and Exeter confirmed him a useful prospect. "He has schooled well at home and will go novice chasing. He would not want it too soft and will race over the minimum trip."

HELLO DE VAUXBUIN won a French bumper in the Provinces. "He is a nice prospect — ready to go on with and could be out soon."

HURRICANE DAWN is a Strong Gale mare who is closely related to Dawn Run. "She had just the one run — finishing third in a Worcester bumper last back-end. She needs to settle down a bit and is one to look out for in mares-only novices' hurdles, after an initial run in a bumper."

JEREMY FISHER won a hunter chase over two-and-a-half miles at Warwick in April. "He was an eventer and a showjumper before he came into training. A fine big horse, he likes it very soft and should pick up a novice chase or two."

LORD NOELIE kicked off with a win at Stratford last October, picked up a £10,000-to-the-winner hurdle at Wincanton in February and rounded off his season with a fourth to King's Road in the Grade 1 Sefton Novices' Hurdle at Aintree. He was tried over fences at Cheltenham on New Year's Day but came a cropper at the last. The plan for this season is undecided as he is still young enough to have a further season over hurdles, but at some point he is likely to run in another novices' chase. "He has come on very well and is an exciting prospect. He won't be risked on fast ground, but doesn't mind soft, and he stays three miles."

LORD OF THE FLIES had a good first season over hurdles, placed twice at Plumpton and once at Hereford before winning two novice events at Exeter in the spring. "We gave him a two-month break after some below-par efforts — including one in blinkers — and he returned to the track a changed horse. He is effective at up to two-and-a-half miles and won off a mark of 103 in May. He has only gone up 3lb, so I am hopeful there are more handicap hurdles to be won with him before he goes chasing in the New Year."

ONE NATION was strongly fancied to win his bumper at Ascot at the end of March, but came off third best to race-fit market-rival Barney Knows. "He had worked well beforehand but, in the race itself, pulled too hard for his own good and ran green. He will come on for the experience and is one for the future. We won't be hurrying him."

PERSROLLA is a half-sister to two winning hurdlers. She goes into the new season with two bumper runs and an outing over hurdles behind her and will be carefully placed to maintain her family's good record. "I can see her winning over two-and-a-half to three miles — if she calms down."

ROMAN LORD ran promisingly in all his three bumpers earlier this year. The fact that he lined up at Aintree in the spring suggests he is quite highly regarded. "He is a grand type who should do well over jumps in due course. He has not been knocked about and should soon repay some of the 29,000gns he cost in Ireland as a four-year-old — a very straightforward sort of horse."

SKIPCARL joined her trainer last summer after winning three of her five starts in Irish point-to-points earlier that year. She was unlucky not to make a winning debut at Warwick but quickly made amends with victories at Exeter and Fontwell. On her final start she ran third to Flagship Therese and Alta at the April Cheltenham fixture. "She may be tried over three miles and is a really nice sort. She always gives 100 per cent and is another who won't be risked on fast ground. Her target will be the Tattersalls mares-only series over fences."

SOUNDS LIKE FUN was bought as a fun horse and has done all that has been asked of him, winning eight times since coming into training in the 1995-'96 season. "He ran well on all his four visits to Sandown and his sixth (to the well-handicapped Majadou) at the Festival was the first time he had finished out of the frame in two and a half years. He acts on any going and has improved with each season. If the handicapper has not got the better of him, he should win more races."

WADE ROAD "is eight years old and has yet to run a poor race for me. If he can stay free of injuries there are handicaps to be won with him. He must go right-handed."

LEN LUNGO had plenty to cheer about in the 1998-99 National Hunt season, recording by far and away his best ever total of 56 winners and netting a highly-respectable £287,341 of prize money in the process.

But far from resting on his laurels, Lungo is thirsting for an even better millennium campaign with all 66 boxes fully occupied at his fabulous Hotland Hill Farm Stables.

The experienced Robbie Supple, plus two cracking young 5lb claimers — Bruce Gibson and Willie Dowling — will once again share the bulk of the rides for the yard.

On our exclusive visit to his Carrutherstown base in the south of Scotland, Lungo gave the inside track on the pick of his team.

BIRKDALE "is a lovely son of Roselier who stays forever and has been a great stable servant, winning eight races for us. Following three wins in very good company over hurdles last season he's now rated 150. There's hardly a single long-distance handicap hurdle left for him to run in and I don't think he's quite good enough for the conditions races. He also won a novice chase last season, and although Birkdale is not anything like as good over fences, he is now too high in the weights over hurdles, so we'll look for some good to soft ground and go back chasing with him."

CELTIC GIANT gave Lungo his biggest day to date by winning the Kim Muir at Cheltenham in March. "He has been treated for an irregular heartbeat. Although it's been put right now, there's no guarantee it won't come back. The plan this time round is to bring him in late, take him hunting, and then go for the Kim Muir again - which may well be his first race of the season because he seems to run best fresh. If all goes OK at Cheltenham then we might well pick out one of the races at Aintree, maybe the John Hughes or the Grand National."

CHUMMY'S SAGA "is a fun horse who won three chases for us last season. He went up the handicap, but he can win again and we'll be going round the little tracks like Hexham and

LENNY LUNGO

Best Tracks

Uttoxeter	42%	5-12
Perth	23%	12-52
Hexham	22%	23-105
Cheltenham	20%	1-5
Sedgefield	20%	10-50

Worst Tracks

Cartmel	0%	0-6
Market Rasen	5%	1-19
Haydock	8%	4-50
Kelso	13%	11-85
Aintree	13%	1-8
Ayr	14%	27-190
Bangor	14%	3-21

Best months

September	36%	4-11
June	25%	2-8
May	22%	16-74
October	21%	10-47

Worst months

April	11%	14-124
January	12%	14-116
February	14%	21-149
November	16%	26-158
March	18%	26-145
December	19%	26-140

First time out

Chases

1994-95	0%	0-4
1995-96	20%	1-5
1996-97	33%	3-9
1997-98	33%	3-9
1998-99	25%	3-12
Total	26%	10-39

Hurdles

1994-95	5%	2-44
1995-96	8%	3-36
1996-97	0%	0-32
1997-98	8%	3-36
1998-99	9%	4-45
Total	6%	12-193

Jockey Watch

A Dobbin	40%	2-5
L O'Hara	33%	2-6
R Garritty	25%	3-12
A P McCoy	25%	1-4
W Dowling	21%	29-136
R Supple	20%	64-321
Mr B Gibson	18%	11-61
T Reed	16%	27-174
M Foster	11%	4-38
F Perratt	11%	12-110
J Supple	8%	1-12
I Jardine	6%	2-36

Sedgefield trying to find a small race for him."

CORSTON JOKER "is a big strong horse with plenty of bone by Idiot's Delight. He has great talent with his own style of jumping — he tends to hurdle his fences but still gets to the other side. Two seasons ago he won five races for us, progressing up the weights all the time. Unfortunately he is a horse with a kink, and he has decided to give himself a few easy days by planting himself at the start and not jumping off with the field! However he's still a nice horse and if we can catch him in the right mood he can definitely win again."

CRAZY HORSE won three races over hurdles last season including the £20,000 Hennessy Final at Kelso. He wasn't beaten far when third in the Scottish Champion Hurdle. "He's quite a highly-strung horse with lots of nervous energy. He tends to pull too hard when fresh and perhaps he's a horse who might just need a race or two to settle down. Currently rated over 140, nevertheless we've still got high hopes for him because it looks like he will stay two and a half miles this season."

DANTE'S GLEN "is a nice young horse by Phardante, very tall and scopey. He ran over hurdles last season showing a bit of promise before disappointing on soft ground at Carlisle. He's only five and is still growing and improving, I see him as more of a chaser than a hurdler. He probably needs decent ground to show his best."

EVENING ALL "is from the family of General Crack. He has been very weak to date and needs fences, so should be going novice chasing this season. Maybe we'll give him one or two races over hurdles to get his eye in again beforehand. We're hopeful he will win a long-distance event or two."

FLIGHTY LEADER, by Supreme Leader, was placed a couple of times last season. "He ran into some very soft going on a couple of occasions and didn't really handle it — consequently we'll be scouting around for some good ground. He won a point-to-point in Ireland before he came to us and there should be a couple of long-distance hurdles in him this term. Straightforward to ride and train, it's just a question of finding the right race for him."

GLACIAL DANCER is related to I'm A Driver who was placed in the National. "He's a rangy sort who possesses plenty of power from behind. He was placed

a couple of times before winning a novice handicap hurdle at Hexham beating a large field. He wasn't that great over hurdles but we believe he will make a lovely two-and-a-half mile chaser, and get three miles in time. One of our novice chase team this season and should go very well. He handles any ground."

HEART OF AVONDALE was bought at the Doncaster Sales and only arrived with Lungo late on last season. "She'd been running in Ireland over two miles from the front without success. So we tried something completely different, holding her up over two-and-three-quarter miles — and it worked because she won twice using those tactics at Kelso. I like this mare — our only problem is she's gone shooting up the handicap. It's not going to be so easy to place her, although we've still got the option of schooling her over fences. But for the moment we'll see what we can do in middle-distance handicap hurdles."

LORD OF THE LOCH "is by Lord Americo. He's been a very frustrating horse who was second, beaten a neck in a bumper a few seasons ago. We thought he was a penalty kick for a novice hurdle but he had a slight tendon strain, had time off, then went lame again the day before he was due to run and had to have another break. He won in a photo at Perth in the spring after a two-year lay-off, in heavy ground. He'll be back over hurdles this season and looks a nice soft ground stayer in the making. A horse with plenty of ability."

LORD OF THE SKY was bought by Lungo after he had won his first and only start in a point-to-point at Wetherby. "He beat nothing that day but won very easily and has since had two runs in bumpers for us and won both. I'm quite hopeful he could be useful because he won his second bumper carrying a penalty with a great deal of ease — so he is an exciting horse for this season over hurdles."

MIKE STAN progressed well over fences, winning three novice chases this year. "He may not be the best in the yard, but he tries hard. Likes good ground, jumps well, and stays well. Although he's not very big he's a real battler, and I hope we can find some other opportunities for him over fences this term."

NATIVE AFFAIR bagged two bumpers last season, at Catterick and Musselburgh. "He'll go novice hurdling and

I'll be astonished if he doesn't win more races this season."

NOW YOUNG MAN "is a nice horse by Callernish who is 10 now. He won impressively fourth time out last season, at Carlisle in September when, unfortunately, he picked up a minor injury on the firm ground which explains why he hasn't run since. He's back in training and can win again."

PADDY MAGUIRE "is a horse I bought at Doncaster Sales having seen him win our local point-to-point at Lockerbie. He ran a couple of fair races last year, however he was still growing and could have been on the weak side. We'll start him off in novice handicap hurdles this season, then he'll join the novice chasing team. Stays forever and likes good ground."

PALACE OF GOLD is one of the stalwarts of the yard. "He's won a lot of races over the years, starting off with a couple of sellers, and then kept sticking his head out in front. We tried him over fences but he didn't like it. He's back over hurdles now and I think he can win again provided the handicapper gives him a chance."

PHAR ECHO won two handicap hurdles last season. "He's a gelding we like to switch between hurdles and fences. Has won on soft ground although I feel he's better on good. Still a maiden over fences and there are plenty of races for him to run in."

PLUMBOB "won a hurdle race at Hexham and was second in a decent three-mile chase at Ayr. He should win again over hurdles or fences."

RED HOT INDIAN "was one of our few disappointments last season. He won his bumper two campaigns ago and we thought he was very good. He then went hurdling and we found him a couple of winning opportunities, but he didn't take them. More worryingly, he appeared to be going well and then his head looked to come up a bit. However on his very last run he jumped a lot better than he had done before, and we just think the penny might have dropped. If we can find a small race that he can win easily, he might just get his confidence back and go on to win two or three more."

SANTA CONCERTO is one of the stable's leading lights, winning three staying handicap chases last season. "He is a lovely big sort by Orchestra. He ran well in defeat at both Cheltenham and Aintree. He's now in need of some sympathy from the handicapper, but we may have a crack at the Grand National with him."

SHE'S ALL HEART "is a small filly by Broken Hearted who won a seller and then a novice hurdle, both at Perth. She used to pull too hard, but seems to be relaxing much better now. She's probably best with cut in the ground and we'll try and find another small race for her."

SPOOF "is a small horse by Good Thyne we bought at Doncaster very cheaply. The plan with him is to go novice hurdling. An athletic type, I really feel we can find a race or two for him - he's very competitive."

SUPERTOP is getting a bit long in the tooth and this one-time useful hurdler is on the downgrade. "He's won lots of races and given plenty of experience to the claiming riders while they've been learning. Good ground over two-and-a-half miles are his ideal conditions."

SWANBISTER "is a lovely horse by Roselier. He won under top weight at Kelso last season and will be long-distance handicap chasing again this term. He's summered well and looks a picture."

THE GREY DYER "is a nice young horse who ran twice last season. He's only five years old, jumps well and shows promise. Chasing will be his game long-term, but he will hopefully pick up a novice hurdle or two first."

THE NEXT WALTZ won the Channel 4 Trophy for the most races won last season — nine in all. "As a result he was hiked up the handicap over two stones under both codes. But you couldn't ask for a more genuine and honest racehorse over both fences and hurdles. He's tough, but may well suffer for the time being for all of his successes last season."

TIME AFTER THYNE "ran a nice race in a bumper two seasons ago. We tried him twice over hurdles last term, although really he's too big and awkward for the smaller obstacles. I think he's a horse with a big engine and will eventually stay three miles. We might give him a couple more runs over timber before going novice chasing."

TO DAY TO DAY won two novice handicaps over timber last season. "We'll try to win a little handicap hurdle before he joins the novice chasing team. He likes a cut in the ground."

VALIGAN "is another earmarked to go novice chasing having won a couple of long-distance hurdles last season."

FERDY MURPHY has set himself a target of at least 50 winners this season.

And judging by the strength of his best ever team, the talented handler should not be far off the mark.

Leading the line from the front will be stable star, French Holly, back in strong work and looking every inch a future champion over fences.

He will as usual be partnered by Andrew Thornton, but it is Adrian Maguire who is poised to get the pick of the stable's rides.

On our exclusive visit to Murphy's West Witton yard, nestling snugly below Middleham's High Moor in North Yorkshire, the trainer hand-picked a selection of his horses for Sun Guide readers to follow.

ACKZO, a six-year-old Ardross gelding, won twice for the yard over hurdles last year. "He needs soft ground which we will wait for, then go novice chasing. I would say he has the potential to go right to the top. He's a very tough sort who will have no problem jumping a fence. He'll start off in the north, but is definitely a Cheltenham type and is being aimed at the Sun Alliance, all being well."

ADDINGTON BOY, a gallant fourth carrying the famous red and white Sun colours in last season's Grand National, heads for the Becher Chase over the spruce fences at Liverpool in November. "The outcome of that race will decide where his season goes from there. He's done exceptionally well over the summer."

ALBRIGHTON wasn't any great shakes on the Flat for Chris Thornton but improved when sent hurdling by Murphy. "He was very exciting last year, winning twice over timber for us. He is sure to win a couple more provided the handicapper gives him a chance." He's best at the minimum trip.

ANDY'S LAD goes novice chasing this season. "He's won one hurdle for the stable, but was unlucky not to win three or even four last season. As he is a little bit hard to settle, it took us a while to get to know about him. However I think the combination of Adrian Maguire and fences will suit him and he can win a few this time round."

ARDRINA, a useful staying handi-

FERDY MURPHY

Best Tracks

Perth	42%	5-12
Hereford	38%	6-16
Ludlow	33%	2-6
Musselburgh	31%	11-36
Kelso	30%	6-20
Taunton	29%	4-14
Cartmel	25%	3-12
Kempton	25%	1-4

Worst Tracks

Aintree	0%	0-12
Exeter	0%	0-11
Wincanton	0%	0-9
Leicester	0%	0-5
Stratford	0%	0-4
Worcester	5%	1-22
Warwick	9%	1-11
Haydock	9%	1-11
Bangor	9%	1-11
Sandown	9%	1-11
Newton Abbot	9%	1-11

Best months

May	27%	14-51
February	23%	18-80
April	20%	13-64
March	20%	22-109

Worst months

June	11%	1-9
November	11%	10-91
October	10%	3-31
September	0%	0-14

First time out

Chases

1994-95	0%	0-4
1995-96	0%	0-10
1996-97	8%	1-13
1997-98	0%	0-9
1998-99	6%	1-17
Total	4%	2-53

Hurdles

1994-95	14%	3-21
1995-96	15%	4-27
1996-97	0%	0-28
1997-98	10%	2-21
1998-99	22%	8-36
Total	13%	17-133

Jockey Watch

O McPhail	50%	6-12
M A Fitzgerald	50%	2-4
M Dwyer	36%	4-11
Mr K Whelan	29%	2-7
Mr J P McNamara	28%	15-53
A Thornton	27%	6-22
A Maguire	23%	18-78
R Dunwoody	22%	2-9

cap hurdler last term, will start off in handicap chases. "I would say the time to catch her is definitely first time out. You couldn't meet a more honest mare, although it doesn't take a lot to put her off. She can get a bit disillusioned so we plan to space her runs out a bit this season." She stays three miles and seems to act on most surfaces.

BALLINCLAY KING came to Murphy from the Irish point-to-point sphere where he had finished runner-up on his only start in 1998. "He won well on his bumper debut at Ayr and was then fourth in the Grade 1 Power Champion Bumper at Punchestown. This fellow wouldn't be far behind French Holly, he's got a real engine. He will go to Ayr or Newcastle for his novice hurdles, then possibly the Tolworth Hurdle at Sandown to see how good he is."

BALLYMANA BOY, a six-year-old son of Commanche Run, goes novice chasing straight away. "He's a tough and consistent stayer who ideally wants good ground. He jumped hurdles exceptionally well last season, winning three races on the bounce in May. I can't see any problem with him jumping fences. We'll keep him up north, certainly to start with, and I can really envisage him running up a sequence around the likes of Hexham and Cartmel."

/ Ballinclay King wouldn't be far behind French Holly — he's got a real engine /

/ Ballymana Boy could run up a sequence around the likes of Hexham and Cartmel /

BECCA'S ROSE cost 25,000 guineas at the Doncaster Sales but immediately began repaying part of that with a win on her bumper debut. She then ran three times in novice hurdles. "She wants three miles and good ground and will definitely win more races over hurdles."

BREA HILL has had three runs in bumpers. "He is a nice sort who will go novice chasing. He was a bit disappointing on his last two runs, but came home a bit sick from Huntingdon. We should be able to find a race for him.

He could improve when stepped up in trip."

BROOKSBY WHORLTON finished like a train when fourth at Carlisle in a bumper. "He will go novice hurdling and needs a trip to show his best. Again, he will stay up north but shouldn't have any problem winning a novice hurdle or two."

CLAIR VALLEY was third on her only run in a bumper at Bangor. "She is by Ardross and is tough as nails. Her dam was a fair stayer over timber, and Clair Valley jumps well and is certainly capable of winning her fair share of novice hurdles."

COOLAW won his only two starts over hurdles last season. "Adrian (Maguire) thinks he's really good. He'll go novice chasing and rates an exciting prospect." He is just the sort to improve considerably this season.

COUNT KARMUSKI won twice over fences last season but "it has been hard to establish what his best trip is. His owner is probably right when he says two-and-half-miles is his optimum." He certainly failed to stay three miles when tried on his last start.

FRENCH HOLLY goes novice chasing after finishing a valiant third to Istabraq in last season's Champion Hurdle. "I schooled him myself in France and he jumps fences superbly. He has done exceptionally well over the summer break and we may start him off at Wetherby, then go twice to Cheltenham for a bit of practice prior to taking his chance once again at the Festival. He's a very big horse with an outstanding engine, he's already won once at the Festival and there's no reason why he can't do it again."

FRENCH WILLOW "is out of a full-sister to French Holly and might just have been unlucky not to have won a bumper. Last time at Hexham she came up against one of Jonjo O'Neill's hot-pots. As a half-sister to Deano's Beeno, she'll definitely want three miles and a bit of cut in the ground over hurdles."

GENERAL LOUIS, who should stay further than two miles in time, "was placed in a couple of bumpers prior to finishing sixth at Punchestown. He's got a real good future over hurdles."

GRANIT D'ESTRUVAL is an impeccably-bred French horse who just had the one run when a not-knocked-about fifth in a Haydock bumper. "He will stay up north over two-and-a-half miles, maybe three, and should win a couple of staying novice hurdles. This is a very nice horse whose future will be over fences, so we'll have to be patient with him."

HEAVENS ABOVE failed to get his head in front last season in novice chases, but showed decent enough form, finishing runner-up three times. "I can't believe we didn't win with this fellow. He was very unlucky, particularly at Newbury when he tied up after the last having looked all over the winner. He's another who has done very well over the summer, and if he doesn't win three or four times over fences it will be a major shock."

MELDRUM PARK "is a well-bred filly who was extremely consistent over hurdles last season. She will be kept in the north, novice chasing this time round." She is just the sort to improve on her two modest runs so far over fences when sent over two-and-a-half miles or further.

NATIVE LEGEND, cost 16,000 guineas as a three-year-old and is yet to see the racecourse. "This Be My Native gelding is owned by Jimmy Gordon who has put an awful lot into the game and deserves a decent horse. Native Legend will go novice hurdling this season and is a gelding with a really promising future."

OSCAIL AN DORAS, a grand handicap chaser, did brilliantly for the stable last term, winning four races . "He goes on any ground, loves Huntingdon where he won three times last season, and will probably go back pot-hunting there." He is effective between two and two-and-a-half miles.

PADDY'S RETURN "has proved himself to be a high-class hurdler having won and been placed at the Cheltenham Festival. He'll be out early, novice chasing in the north, although he will go down south for the bigger prizes once his confidence is up. Adrian says he is ready to win first time up but we wouldn't risk him on fast ground." His two outings over fences to date were an error-strewn round at Ascot and a fall at Wetherby, so the seven-year-old needs to brush up his jumping.

PARIS PIKE was formerly with Paddy Mullins where he showed some decent form over hurdles. He has just had the one run for Murphy when winning at Perth. "I've ridden him in quite a bit of work myself and he gave me the feel of a really good horse. He'll be kept to the small tracks for the time being, and certainly won't be overtaxed for the present."

TONI'S TIP, a seven-year-old Phardante gelding, won a couple of times at Newcastle last season, showing stamina was his strong suit. "He's a horse who will develop into a Grand National type in time. Meanwhile the Eider or Kim Muir is on the agenda. A real old-fashioned staying chaser." He is effective with and without blinkers.

WOODBRIDGE "is a fun horse belonging to a syndicate. He always pays his way in two-and-a-half-mile handicap chases."

WYNBURY FLYER was only selling class over hurdles but managed to win a juvenile event over two miles at Catterick. "He jumps for fun and will go novice chasing."

> ◢ **Heavens Above failed to score last season. But he has done very well over the summer, and if he doesn't win three or four novice chases it will be a major shock** ◣

SATURDAY, November 7 last year was a day to remember for Paul Nicholls.

He sent out 10 runners and had seven winners. The accumulator came to 1,288-1. That night he said: "Everything went right and without a shadow of doubt it was my best day as a trainer."

Come March and Nicholls had another huge pay-day — when See More Business won the Cheltenham Gold Cup, a race in which he was so unlucky the previous year when carried out.

Sun Guide readers were told in this space 12 months ago that 'nothing less than winning chasing's Blue Riband will satisfy ambitious Nicholls.'

This time around it is a case of beating Martin Pipe to the trainers' championship. With a little help from the horses listed below, he might well do it.

Here Nicholls gives Sun Guide readers the low-down on the cream of his powerful team.

ARLAS won a valuable novices chase at Auteuil on his last start in France. He jumps exceptionally well and is a top prospect for similar events in this country. "As he is only four, there are no chases for him pre-Christmas, so he is still out at grass. He is one to follow in the New Year and will stay two-and-a-half miles."

BENGERS MOOR injured a knee at Wincanton last October. After some minor surgery, he was brought back for a spring campaign and won a handicap chase at Stratford. "He is fit, fresh and well and should win plenty more races at up to three miles. He wants fast ground."

BETTER OFFER "was a good horse on the Flat with Amanda Perrett. He had very good form over hurdles as a novice but was disappointing last year. I bought him at the sales in the hope the change of scenery and the challenge of chasing will rekindle his enthusiasm, as it did with Green Green Desert. I have done plenty of work with him and he could start off at Chepstow on October 2nd over two and a half miles."

BIGBANDSAREBACK, a winning point-to-pointer, is one to follow early in the season. "I am very pleased with his progress, and he could make a nice novice chaser if he regains his form. He has been off the course for 15 months."

BLUAGALE is a progressive chaser who "has won all five starts for us including

PAUL NICHOLLS

Best Tracks

Southwell	54%	7-13
Leicester	50%	2-4
Fontwell	43%	27-63
Ayr	40%	8-20
Sandown	32%	16-50
Kempton	31%	11-36
Folkestone	30%	3-10
Wincanton	30%	47-159

Worst Tracks

Doncaster	0%	0-5
Haydock	4%	1-23
Towcester	7%	1-15

Best months

September	37%	17-46
October	33%	46-140
August	29%	8-28
April	25%	40-161

Worst months

June	0%	0-6
February	17%	27-158
March	19%	38-197

First time out

Chases

1994-95	17%	4-23
1995-96	21%	6-28
1996-97	43%	17-40
1997-98	26%	11-43
1998-99	33%	14-42
Total	30%	52-176

Hurdles

1994-95	21%	4-19
1995-96	22%	5-23
1996-97	17%	4-24
1997-98	19%	4-21
1998-99	17%	6-36
Total	19%	23-123

Jockey Watch

Miss P Curling	46%	6-13
T J Murphy	34%	61-181
G Bradley	33%	2-6
N Williamson	30%	3-10
A P McCoy	29%	74-251

his only two runs last autumn. He suffered a minor leg injury but will be back to run after Christmas. He holds the course record at Chepstow over two and a half miles and remains an exciting prospect."

BOLD BUCCANEER "is the highest rated (by the Irish formbook) of all the former Irish point-to-pointers in the yard, on the strength of winning his sole start! He is a big strong gelding and will go novice chasing this season."

BUCKSKIN CAMEO "won a bumper and a novice hurdle last season and is a fun mare who should win more races."

BUCK'S PALACE "is a ready-made chaser who won twice over hurdles last campaign. He acts on soft and will race at trips up to three miles."

CALL EQUINAME is the apple of jockey Mick Fitzgerald's eye. Fitzgerald has told Nicholls that riding the horse "is a bit like driving a Ferrari. He has outstanding acceleration." This year's big target will again be the Queen Mother Champion Chase "but I might run him first in the Peterborough Chase at Huntingdon over two-and-a-half miles and then possibly in the King George on Boxing Day. Even though he is nine he is prone to sore shins, so is lightly raced with few miles on the clock."

CALLING WILD "started off last season winning a three-mile novice hurdle at Chepstow and a small handicap chase at Wincanton before picking up the Paddy Power Handicap Chase at Leopardstown last Christmas, worth £66,370. He was travelling well in the William Hill Handicap Chase at the Festival when falling. He will start off in the Badger Beer at Wincanton and, if he looks well handicapped, will then run in the Hennessy. There are plenty more races to be won hith him."

CHARLIE STRONG "is a lovely strong horse who has spent two seasons hunting and point-to-pointing with Richard Barber, winning several races. He will start his novice chasing career in mid-October, as his preference is soft going, and should pay his way."

DERRYMORE MIST "was plagued with sore shins last season but still managed to win two novice chases and ran very well in the four-miler at Cheltenham. As he matures he will improve and win more races, especially over marathon trips."

DINES improved out of all recognition when put over fences last season, winning four times and running second in the Grand Annual Handicap Chase at the Festival. "He loves to front run and is marginally better on a right-handed track. He has strengthened up over the summer and should get two-and-a-half miles."

DOUBLE THRILLER "aggravated an old leg injury when he got loose after falling at the first in the Grand National and is not back in training yet. I would love to run him in the King George but a more realistic target might be the Pillar Property Chase at Cheltenham at the end of January."

EARTHMOVER "suffered a near-fatal fall first time out at Newton Abbot and in hindsight I think it would have been better if we had not run him again last season. However he is in very good order after a lovely long rest and he will make his seasonal debut at Chepstow on October 2. He is well handicapped if he recaptures his best form."

ESCARTEFIGUE has moved to Nicholls from David Nicholson. "It will take 12 weeks to get him fit, so don't expect to see him before mid-November. He was runner-up in the King George last December and that is his immediate target — maybe the Gold Cup too, if everything goes okay."

EXECUTIVE DECISION won at Chepstow and ran well in the County Hurdle at Cheltenham. "He has had a wind operation, which will hopefully improve him, and goes novice chasing a lot heavier and stronger than before. He wants two miles on soft ground."

EXTRA STOUT won hunter chases at Sandown and Aintree in the spring when trained by Tony Martin. "He will be ready to run in mid-November. He could be a candidate for the National Hunt Chase at Cheltenham in March, and in the meantime should pay his way in staying chases."

FADALKO "is our top prospect. He ran well at Cheltenham and Aintree before winning the Scottish Champion Hurdle at Ayr. He is one of my favourites and will contest all the top novice chases after an easy introduction to boost his confidence. He jumps ever so well when schooling."

FALSE TAIL "missed last season with a leg injury but the rest has done him no harm. He is still only seven and should not be long in adding to his successes in point-to-points and hunter chases. He stays forever and prefers soft ground."

FATHER KRISMAS was placed in all his starts over hurdles last term. He might run in the Timeform Free Handicap Hurdle at Chepstow before going over fences. "Has done very well since last season."

FLAGSHIP THERESE won two bumpers and four hurdles last season. "She has shot up the handicap so fast that, given her physique, we will have to go chasing with her as she cannot carry big weights. She is in good order though."

FLAGSHIP UBERALLES, the Arkle winner, gave Nicholls his first Cheltenham Festival success. "He is a very exciting prospect for this season after winning five novice chases, including the Arkle and the Sandeman Maghull at Aintree. The only time he got beaten over fences was my fault because two-and-a-half miles on heavy ground was too far for him. When he started last season he would have been 20 lengths off Call Equiname at home, but by the end of the season he was finishing upsides! The Haldon Gold Cup early in November is an obvious starting point, then possibly the Tingle Creek and the Queen Mother Champion Chase if he keeps on improving. He goes on soft but is most effective on good ground."

FORTVILLE won a maiden point-to-point for Richard Barber. "His younger full brother has already won Listed chases in France so we have high hopes for him. He is quite speedy."

GALAPIAT DU MESNIL "won a novice hurdle for Nicky Henderson on soft. I would not be at all surprised if he won first time out over fences, at somewhere like Plumpton or Fontwell."

GEDEON is a promising five-year-old with a novice chase win at Auteuil under his belt. "He is eligible to run in similar races over here and should have a good season."

GIGI BEACH improved beyond all recognition last spring, winning marathons at Exeter and Cheltenham, and was only just touched off in a four-mile chase at Kelso. "He should continue to pay his way as he is still ahead of the handicapper.'

GREEN GREEN DESERT "is 100 percent genuine whatever you may hear to the contrary. He went from a mark of 120 up to 156 last season, hardly the sign of a horse that does not put it all in. He has thrived this summer and is capable of winning more races."

GROSVENOR "needs to get his confidence back after missing 18 months through injury. He loves soft ground, stays well and will be out by November."

HIGH GALE "is an exciting front runner. A half-brother to Morley Street and Granville Again, he will win plenty more races if we can get his jumping together."

IRBEE "was a model of consistency last year. He has done well during the summer and should win more races from two-and-a-half to three miles. He goes on any ground."

JUYUSH was a top-class staying hurdler with Jim Old, and "will hopefully be an equally classy chaser for me. I am very pleased with him, but won't be aiming too high initially, starting at the smaller tracks until his jumping says he is ready to go on."

KNIGHT TEMPLAR "stays forever and ought to win several long-distance chases this winter. He acts on any going."

LIZZYS FIRST won three over hurdles for Rod Millman in his first season under National Hunt Rules. "He should pay to follow in ordinary novice chases."

LORD JIM won all his three starts in his first season with Jim Old but disappointed last campaign. "He will go novice chasing."

LYPHARITA'S RISK "was purchased in France this summer after winning over 10 furlongs at Longchamp. He won several other races at up to a mile and a half and I am hopeful he will win plenty of races. A seriously nice prospect."

MICHEL DE MOEURS won five on the Flat in France where he ran in very good company. "He is a nice stamp of a horse with a good turn of foot and should win novice hurdles this winter."

NORSKI LAD "is one I got from Sir Mark Prescott. He won four of his starts over hurdles and was particularly impressive at Ayr last time. The Cheltenham Stayers' Hurdle will be his target and he will be hard to beat on soft."

ONE OF THE NATIVES "is a long term prospect. He had a couple of runs in bumpers for David Nicholson and might pinch a novice hurdle or two before he comes into his own over fences."

RAID "won on the Flat in Ireland over 12 furlongs and had three educationals over timber for us. He has done very well. He will go chasing from January but is worth following in novice hurdles before then."

RELKANDER should have little trouble adding to the two novice chase successes he had when with Jenny Pitman. "He is a nice big sort who loves fast ground."

SEE MORE BUSINESS "had been a bit of a lazy jumper but what a difference a pair of blinkers make! This year the plan is to start him off at Down Royal in November, then go for the Rehearsal Chase at Chepstow, which he has won for the last two years. Then it is the Irish Gold Cup at Leopardstown or the King George before going to Cheltenham to defend his Gold Cup crown."

SOLDAT "joined me from David Nicholson. Injury has restricted him to one run in the last two seasons but I am very pleased with him. He is a chaser with a future."

THE HOBBIT has been winning point-to-points for the last two seasons. "He should win his fair share of staying novice chases."

TORN SILK won a novice chase for Paul Webber. "I got him at the Doncaster sales and he should be a good fun two-mile chaser to follow in the West Country. He certainly wouldn't want further."

YOUNG DEVEREAUX may be last but is certainly not least. "He is my favourite young horse in the yard. He sustained a very minor leg injury after winning his maiden hurdle and has done really well during his break. He will go novice chasing this winter and he has so much ability I am hopeful he will go right to the top."

MONTHS of speculation were finally ended in late August when David Nicholson confirmed that the 1999-00 season would be his last.

The Duke, who has finished in the top three in the trainers' table for the past nine seasons, is retiring at the peak of his profession.

And while numbers may be slightly down on recent years, Jackdaws Castle is still jam-packed with top-class talent.

Nicholsons's powerful string just missed out on several of the top prizes last term, including the King George VI Chase, the Cheltenham Gold Cup and Leopardstown's Hennessy Gold Cup.

But hopes are high that the new exciting clutch of novice chasers can help the more established stars take Nicholson well past the 1,500 winner mark before he bows out.

Here Nicholson gives Sun Guide readers an exclusive insight into the pick of his string.

AIR SHOT missed last season due to a tendon strain but prior to that was a very useful staying chaser. "Providing the wheels stay on, he should win plenty more races, but he will not run until we get soft ground."

ANZUM "was our number-one star last season and is arguably the leading staying hurdler around after his victories at the Cheltenham and Punchestown Festivals. He is extra tough and is effective on any type of going."

BARONET, the 1998 Scottish National hero, is an out-and-out staying chaser and won over four miles at Cheltenham over the New Year. "He is best on fast ground so the going was against him for the most part last term. We fancied him to go well in the National, but unfortunately he overjumped at the fourth and paid the penalty."

BLUEDONIX "came to us from France last season and has won twice over hurdles. Unfortunately, he slipped a tendon off his hock at Aintree, but he has made a fine recovery and hopefully he will retain his ability. He is now owned by a syndicate which includes myself and we should have a bit of fun with him. He handles all types of going and will go handicap hurdling this season."

CALL IT A DAY struggled with big

DAVID NICHOLSON

Best Tracks

Fakenham	38%	3-8
Lingfield	37%	7-19
Ludlow	37%	26-70
Towcester	35%	31-88
Stratford	32%	20-62
Worcester	32%	30-94
Market Rasen	31%	11-36
Kempton	30%	23-77
Hereford	28%	10-36
Newton Abbot	28%	7-25

Worst Tracks

Fontwell	0%	0-5
Kelso	0%	0-5
Folkestone	0%	0-5
Newcastle	10%	1-10
Ayr	10%	3-29
Cheltenham	14%	35-248

Best months

August	71%	5-7
July	40%	4-10
May	32%	40-125
September	31%	8-26
November	28%	100-358
June	27%	3-11
October	26%	27-104
January	23%	66-282
December	23%	76-330

Worst months

March	13%	37-295
April	16%	35-214
February	20%	60-301

First time out

Chases

1994-95	22%	7-32
1995-96	32%	8-25
1996-97	32%	13-41
1997-98	23%	7-31
1998-99	10%	3-29
Total	24%	38-158

Hurdles

1994-95	23%	13-57
1995-96	18%	11-62
1996-97	31%	18-59
1997-98	45%	28-62
1998-99	12%	8-65
Total	26%	78-305

Jockey Bookings

P Niven	43%	3-7
Mr F Hutsby	29%	5-17
A P McCoy	27%	3-11
N Williamson	26%	5-19
J R Kavanagh	25%	1-4
C F Swan	25%	1-4
A Maguire	25%	185-753

weights last season after winning the 1998 Whitbread and failed to get his head in front. However, he ran some great races in defeat, notably when a brave third in the Grand National. "He was given a great ride by Richard Dunwoody at Aintree and they gave an exhibition of jumping. That race is the big target again. It's the one thing I'd love to win before I retire."

CAPTAIN ROBIN was too immature to run last season, but is now beginning to look the part. "He is owned by Jenny Mould and will be running in bumpers when there is decent going."

CASTLE OWEN has taken a long time to learn to settle in his races, but came good last term, winning three times. "He has schooled well over fences and will be running in novice chases this term. He gets two-and-a-half miles well."

CASTLE SWEEP struggled with big weights last season after reaching the top of the handicap. "As a last resort we ran him over fences at the end of the season and he won both races. But because that was in May he is still eligible for novice chases this season. He acts on most ground conditions."

COLONEL HOOK is closely related to Gold Cup second Go Ballistic and "is sure to stay well. He had a couple of runs over hurdles last season and was placed once."

FOREST IVORY ran a great race to finish third in the Welsh National but then "developed a problem with his teeth that affected his digestive system. It also affected his form later in the season, but we have had a specialist dentist in to treat him and the problem seems to have been sorted out. He is back in good nick, loves soft ground and long distances."

FULL MINTY "is a full brother to Picket Piece and Land Afar, but is a size bigger. He has been broken and educated and should be ready to run in a bumper when the going is suitable."

GONE BALLISTIC is closely related to Go Ballistic and "should improve on his two placed efforts over timber last season."

GO BALLISTIC "only returned to the yard in the middle of last season and ran a tremendous race to finish second in both the Pillar Property Chase and the Cheltenham Gold Cup. On his day he is a very high-class, genuine horse and he deserves to win a top prize."

HAILSTORM won over hurdles the season before last, but missed the 1998-99 campaign with a leg injury. "He has a reasonable handicap rating and will continue over hurdles this season."

HURRICANE LAMP, an honest two-mile chaser, won at Sandown last season and was third to Space Trucker in the Grand Annual at the Festival. "I am sure there is a good race in this fellow."

KOVACH "was immature last season and, though he worked well enough at home, he was unable to put it together on the racecourse. He has developed well over the summer and will be running over hurdles again this season."

KING ON THE RUN "is a young horse with tremendous potential. He has won over hurdles and fences and will continue to improve for some time yet. He has only been lightly raced so far but that's simply due to immaturity."

LORD SCROOP showed promise on his only outing in a bumper last season. "He is a bit of a live wire and was unable to follow this up after sustaining an injury when he got loose on the gallops."

MIDNIGHT LEGEND "returned from a season at stud with great enthusiasm and performed well against the very best over hurdles last term. He has returned ready for the new campaign after covering 35 mares and will probably go over fences with an outing over hurdles beforehand."

MINI MOO MIN "has summered very well and should be able to build on her bumper form from last season when she is sent over hurdles this term."

MULLIGAN put the 1997-98 season of blunders behind him with some solid efforts in chases over two and two-and-a-half-miles last term. "We made a mistake in running him in the King George at Kempton as he is essentially a speed horse and he will probably start off this year in the Desert Orchid Chase at Wincanton."

NEW BIRD "had a tough time last term as he was gelded as soon as he arrived from Germany. He was running over hurdles by December and was very consistent, winning twice. He can only improve for his summer's break and has the size to make up into a high-class chaser."

NOISY MINER "had a good first season over fences and there should be more good opportunities for him if the handicapper is not too severe on him. He seems to like Ludlow."

ONLY SO FAR had just one bumper run last season and may take in another before embarking on a hurdles career. "Two-and-a-half miles could be the trip and we have yet to see the best of her."

PENNYBRIDGE "was bought with the 1998 Marlborough Cup timber race as the objective but he had to miss that event with tendon trouble. However he won the race this year and will now be aimed at the Virginia Gold Cup in America in May."

PERK ALERT "was bought to replace one of our stalwarts Storm Alert. He won one bumper and was second in one of his two other starts. He goes well and is big enough to jump a fence. However he will go hurdling this season and looks a good prospect."

RAYBROOK was bought in Ireland in the spring and has yet to see the racecourse. "He comes from the same family as Mighty Moss and has done everything asked of him so far. He is another with great potential."

PICKET PIECE had a long time off with injury but bounced back last season to win three times. "He will start off over timber this term, but may switch to fences later on. He is not that big but is strongly built and he jumps really well."

RELKEEL's career has promised so much only to be ruined by injury time and time again. "He is a once-a-year wonder! He has won the Bula Hurdle for the past two seasons, but on each occasion has been unable to run again after developing an injury. He is a hugely talented, if frustrating, giant, and the plan is to aim for the Bula again."

ROCABEE was placed in bumpers and over hurdles last season and "will continue over timber for the time being. Has plenty of ability and will improve as he matures."

RUFIUS showed plenty of promise in his work at home last season but was a bit disappointing on the racecourse. "Hopefully, this was due to immaturity and a summer's rest will prove the answer. He seems a much nicer horse this year and he could prove to be really well handicapped. Two-and-a-half miles should be his best trip."

RUSSELL ROAD showed bags of

potential in bumpers and hurdles and is now ready to make his mark over fences. "He has schooled very well over fences and this season could be the one we have been waiting for. The Fred Rimell Novice Chase at Worcester is a possible starting point."

SAMUEL WILDERSPIN needed time to recover last season after breaking a blood vessel on his first outing over fences. "He later reappeared to win three times and has plenty of ability so should add to his tally in handicaps this year."

SHEEPCOTE HILL "came back after a long injury lay-off last season and was still backward. He has shown ability at home and we are hoping fences will be the answer."

SHOTGUN WILLY had just two runs in bumpers last season. "This is a youngster with plenty of potential. He may have one more run in a bumper before going over hurdles."

SIMBER HILL won first time out in a bumper last season, but "was only lightly raced because his owners wanted to preserve his novice status over hurdles for this season."

SPENDID is one of the stable stars and developed into a high-class novice chaser last season. "He is a very tough individual and a little further improvement could see a big prize within his grasp — provided the handicapper is not too unkind."

TOTO TOSCATO was a top hurdler in France and showed he was a high-class and consistent performer this side of the Channel as well last season. "He will be running over fences this time around and he is a very exciting prospect for Stan and Hilda Clarke."

WINDROSS "is a very tall homebred half brother to Air Shot and Flying Gunner, who was second in his two bumpers and won his first two hurdle starts. He has schooled very well over fences and is another I am excited about for novice chases."

ZAFARABAD "was a top-class juvenile hurdler two seasons ago, but then had to take on the top older horses and, though he ran consistently well, he was always up against it. He schooled over fences before going on holiday and is yet another top candidate for novice chase honours this season. He's just the sort to do well."

MARTIN PIPE was given quite a fright by Somerset rival Paul Nicholls last season.

But he still stormed clear to be champion trainer for a record **NINTH** time with 187 winners and £1.2 million in prize money.

In terms of numbers of races won, the Wellington Wizard has been top dog every season since 1985-86.

Last season's title was clinched on the final Bank Holiday Monday of last season with a staggering 10,460-1 eight-timer.

Then, on August 30, Pipe galloped into the record books yet again by beating Arthur Stephenson's 20th century record of 2,644 winners.

So what is the big target now? Cheltenham's Gold Cup remains the one elusive prize, but Pipe revealed: "I don't think I'll ever do it. Anyway, it's not top of my list. My greatest ambition is to go through the card at Exeter - but I probably won't do that either!"

Pipe has lost Paul Green's horses — including aces Unsinkable Boxer and Hors La Loi III — but is greatly looking forward to the comeback of 1997 Champion Hurdler Make A Stand — who has finally recovered from injury.

It seems less likely we will see Cyfor Malta this season, although Pipe has not given up hope.

Nevertheless, Nicholashayne is chock-a-block with both quantity and quality and here Pipe gives an exclusive insight into the main hopes from his unrivalled winners' factory.

ABACUS was bought by owner David Johnson from Eddie O'Grady in Ireland. "He is a nice big strong sort who won a decent bumper at Punchestown. He'll start over hurdles with a view to a chasing career later."

AUETALER was snapped up by jockey-come-bloodstock agent Graham Bradley after winning five races on the Flat in Germany. Brad sold the gelding to footballing chums Robbie Fowler and Steve McManaman. "He won on his hurdling debut for us at Taunton and was far from disgraced when tenth behind Hors La Loi III in the Citroen Supreme Novices Hurdle at Cheltenham. Then he ran a fine second to Barton at Aintree. I see that he

MARTIN PIPE

Best Tracks

Perth	83%	5-6
Wolverhampton	63%	5-8
Sedgefield	60%	3-5
Cartmel	55%	11-20
Doncaster	50%	2-4
Plumpton	45%	35-78
Fakenham	33%	2-6
Hereford	33%	38-115
Worcester	33%	60-182
Lingfield	30%	17-56
Fontwell	27%	32-120
Newton Abbot	27%	99-369
Bangor	26%	29-111

Worst Tracks

Ayr	5%	1-22
Cheltenham	14%	49-348
Aintree	14%	17-118
Kempton	15%	9-59

Best months

August	39%	79-201
July	34%	44-129
June	29%	38-131
October	29%	80-276
September	27%	46-171
May	27%	123-461
November	26%	103-391
February	20%	81-408
April	20%	80-402

Worst months

March	16%	87-534
January	19%	72-376

First time out

Chases

1994-95	17%	5-29
1995-96	18%	7-40
1996-97	25%	9-36
1997-98	21%	7-33
1998-99	30%	13-44
Total	23%	41-182

Hurdles

1994-95	20%	21-104
1995-96	20%	23-117
1996-97	29%	35-122
1997-98	36%	41-113
1998-99	21%	33-156
Total	25%	153-612

Jockey Watch

Mr A Farrant	39%	16-41
S Durack	33%	3-9
J A McCarthy	33%	2-6
A P McCoy	33%	359-1082
Mr M Rimell	33%	2-6
R Johnson	32%	12-37
S Wynne	30%	6-20

is quoted an early-season 33-1 for the 2000 Champion Hurdle. I hope the bookies are right putting him in the list but he will start off in handicap company. He goes on any ground."

BAMAPOUR went into the record books when he gave the champion trainer his 2,645th winner. "He hates jumping fences so I'll just keep him going in claiming hurdles. He's done us proud over the years and I'll never forget that race at Newton Abbot."

BETTER THINK AGAIN is another new Irish purchase by David Johnson. "He is rising six and came to us from Paddy Mullins for whom he won a good bumper race at Punchestown. He is a good, well-made sort who will go hurdling."

BLOWING WIND had a tremendous season the year before last when pulling off the Imperial Cup, County Hurdle and Scottish Champion Hurdle hat-trick. Things didn't go as well last term when the gelding failed to progress as anticipated. "Richard Dunwoody was brought down on him at the fifth flight in the Champion Hurdle on his final start. He will go chasing now and I rate him a good prospect over the bigger obstacles."

CHALLENGER DU LUC has talent galore but has become a professional loser. He predictably failed to win last season but ran one of his better races when third to Teeton Mill at Ascot in February. "I just wish the handicapper would drop him a bit and give him a realistic chance. He's so high in the weights that it is going to be very hard to win races with him. He fell at the first in the Grand National so I don't think he will be going back to Aintree."

CYFOR MALTA is arguably the best of the legion of French imports at Nicholashayne. Best suited by left-handed tracks, he has won five out of his six races since joining Pipe and was still on the upgrade when he injured a leg, which forced him to miss the big prizes at Cheltenham and Aintree. But who can ever forget the way he surged round Aintree to win the John Hughes Chase over the Grand National fences as a five-year-old — or his Murphy's Gold Cup victory last November? "He is still turned out and we'll just have to see when — or if — he can make a comeback. He could return this season, or we could wait

and give him another year off. I am hopeful that it will be this season. Everybody knows what a fantastic horse he is and we certainly do not want to rush him. He has yet to be beaten in three races at Cheltenham and the Gold Cup is an obvious target, but he skipped round those Aintree fences as a five-year-old which means the Grand National is also a possibility."

DEANO'S BEENO was off the course for a year with a knee injury before running a blinder to be second to Princeful at Ascot in December. He subsequently beat Moorish by 22 lengths to win the Long Distance Hurdle at Haydock, before disappointing on unsuitably fast ground in the Stayers' Hurdle at the Cheltenham Festival. "He's a lovely horse and it was the fast ground that also caused him to run a bit tamely in the Martell Hurdle at Aintree behind Istabraq, when he finished fifth. He will probably go chasing, although I still haven't decided for sure."

FAR CRY, a very useful Flat campaigner who came from Sir Mark Prescott, was second in the Ascot Stakes at the Royal meeting and also won the Queen's Prize at Kempton on the level. "I bought him specially to go hurdling but he has done really well on the Flat and the highlight was winning the Northumberland Plate, when Kevin Darley rode him out of his skin. He's got top Flat race targets in the autumn like the Cesarewitch but hurdling will be his programme mainly from now on." Two-and-a-half miles will probably prove to be his trip over timber.

GALANT MOSS was a maiden on the Flat in France but is another exciting Gallic recruit. "He won the Grosvenor Casinos Long Distance Hurdle at Ascot in fine style and later took the Crowther Homes Long Distance Hurdle at Haydock. He will be aimed at all the top long-distance hurdles and obviously is a lovely three-mile hurdler to have about."

GOLDEN ALPHA was a bumper "talking horse" in Ireland when trained by Paddy Mullins. He made a winning debut in England at Newbury and was then second to Monsignor in the big bumper at the Cheltenham Festival when Tony McCoy went for home a good half-mile out. "He will now go hurdling and I am sure he has a bright future. He only just got caught at Cheltenham and it could have been that he just didn't quite get home on the day."

HANAKHAM won the SunAlliance Chase in 1997 (beating Pipe's ill-fated Eudipe) when trained by Ron Hodges. His first run for the champion trainer saw him finish third of four runners at Sandown in February. He was widely touted as a Cheltenham Gold Cup and Grand National prospect but was pulled out of both big races. "He wasn't injured, it was just decided not to run him again. He is fine and is back doing light roadwork. He has some top form to his name and I will start him off in handicap chases."

HIT AND RUN is an ex-French horse who won his first four races over hurdles. He missed the Triumph Hurdle through lameness but returned after a three-month lay-off to win on his handicap debut at Warwick. "He was just not right and we were quite right to miss the Triumph. He will go in handicap hurdles and is a really nice sort."

LADY CRICKET is yet another French-bred who won her English debut over hurdles under automatic top-weight at Newbury and then went on to score in a three-horse event at Fontwell. She later ran ninth in the Champion Hurdle. "She went up so dramatically in the weights that basically we had to run her in the Champion. The handicapper caught her out and that was that. She was entered for chases at the Cheltenham Festival but now is the time to try her over fences and I am sure that she will do well in that sphere."

LANKA is yet another newcomer who will be carrying the David Johnson colours. This youngster came from Ireland where he was trained by John Oxx. "He is a lovely

bumper horse but he's still just a four-year-old so it's early days yet."

MAKE A STAND won the 1997 Champion Hurdle but picked up an injury on his next start at Aintree and had the whole of the next two seasons off as a result. "When he won the Champion Hurdle he broke the course record so it's obvious he is a bit special. In fact, on his day he is as good as I've seen. He had a slight leg problem but he is now back in training and appears to be fine. It is going to be very difficult to place him but I'm sure we will find some races to ease him back into action. If all goes well he will be there attempting to regain his Champion Hurdle crown."

MAJADOU won his first four races after arriving from France, including when he justified hot 7-4 favouritism to win the Mildmay of Flete Handicap Chase at Cheltenham by a runaway 16 lengths. "He was my banker bet at the Festival and he never looked like letting me down. I think that Aintree came too quickly for him afterwards so that's why he failed to sparkle there. He is basically a two-and-a-half-mile chaser, so that could put the Gold Cup beyond his reach, while the Queen Mother Champion Chase over two miles may be too short. But he is very exciting. He'll probably be entered for the Murphy's Gold Cup at Cheltenham on November 13 although that might just come too soon."

MR LAMB was bought at the Doncaster Sales for 125,000gns after he had won a good bumper race at Musselburgh for his former trainer Sally Hall. "He is a full brother to the very useful Lord Lamb and has yet to race for us. He will go hurdling and is definitely one to follow through the winter months."

POTENTATE has won nine times at Chepstow and won the Welsh Cham-

> *Mr Lamb is a full brother to the very useful Lord Lamb and has yet to race for us. He will go hurdling and is definitely one to follow*

43

pion Hurdle there for the third time in April. "He has only ever been beaten twice at Chepstow. He was also second in the Scottish Champion Hurdle. But he also won novice chases at Plumpton and Chepstow and was fourth in Cheltenham's Cathcart Chase. He's a lovely horse to own as he can jump fences well but can always revert to hurdles. I'd like to see him win a fourth Welsh Champion Hurdle but he will also be going chasing to start with."

PRIDWELL was never keen over fences, although he won one of his three starts. Famous for his head defeat of Istabraq in the Martell Hurdle at Aintree in 1998, he failed to notch a win in three starts last season. That might suggest his best days have been and gone. "I am hoping that he can win again over hurdles. But nobody will ever forget Tony McCoy's display when he beat Istabraq at Aintree — he was fantastic that day."

RAINBOW FRONTIER won the Swinton Hurdle at Haydock in 1998 but was only fifth when trying for a repeat win last season. He also failed to score in four other outings. "He is a lovely horse and has been consistent on the Flat and over hurdles. The problem is that he is judged on his very best display and that means that he is always burdened with plenty of weight. It is so difficult to place him over hurdles, he will probably go chasing."

RASH REMARK joined Pipe from Ireland where he won three out of his four hurdle starts. "He is an exciting front-runner and it probably came too quickly after his previous runaway victories at Haydock and Newbury when he finished down the field in the SunAlliance Novices Hurdle at the Cheltenham Festival. However, he got back to winning ways at Chepstow. He will now be aimed at novice chases

and it will pay to follow him as he goes on any ground."

ROYAL PREDICA is a typical Pipe plundering job from France where he was claimed for £20,000. Only fair over hurdles, he has improved over fences. "He won a Plumpton chase in November and later won the Chivas Regal novices' event at Aintree by nine lengths. He will now go handicap chasing."

STAR OF DUNGANNON could be a real money-spinner for Pipe judging on his wins last season over hurdles at Kempton in February and Cheltenham in April. "When he scored at Cheltenham he beat several previous winners and he could not have been more impressive. He is a big strong gelding and I think he could be a really nice horse. He is certainly one to follow in handicap hurdles."

TRESOR DE MAI came from France and made a winning debut at Lingfield before three times coming up against Flagship Uberalles, notably when a good second in the Arkle Chase at Cheltenham. He was probably over the top when fifth behind the same horse at Aintree. "He is one I like a lot and he will go handicap chasing. He is an out-and-out two-miler."

WAHIBA SANDS won the Gerry Feilden Hurdle at Newbury last November from subsequent Tote Gold Trophy hero Decoupage. He also finished second to Master Beveled in the Champion Hurdle Trial at Haydock. "His future now lies over fences but we might run him in a couple of hurdles first."

YOU'RE AGOODUN has lived up to his name, being a progressive handicap hurdler who won at Haydock in December and Cheltenham in April. "He has worn blinkers on his last five starts but is as genuine as they come. He went up 15lb between his Haydock win and Cheltenham but still won very easily."

◢ Star Of Dungannon beat several previous winners at Cheltenham and could not have been more impressive. One to follow in handicap hurdles ◢

A CRACKING score of 104 winners last season represented a new personal best for the remarkable **Mary Reveley.**

She has again assembled a formidable string and, as usual, her Groundhill Farm yard looks well worth following in the months ahead.

The Reveley team is particularly powerful in the novice chasing department this term, as the Saltburn handler detailed in an exclusive interview for the Sun Guide.

ALLOTROPE was bought at Newmarket Sales for 42,000gns last back-end with a view to tackling two-and-a-half-mile novice hurdles. A useful-looking Nashwan gelding, he has schooled well at home.

ALPINE PANTHER won his first three races last season — a claimer at Plumpton and two handicaps at Newcastle and Bangor. He's a decent staying hurdler on his day and wasn't disgraced when second to impressive Lady Rebecca at Cheltenham in January. He is set to go novice chasing.

BROTHER OF IRIS made a tremendous start to his chasing career last term when winning three times. He was particularly impressive when trouncing Zaitoon by 11 lengths at Doncaster in January before injuring a pastern when falling at the 12th in the Royal & Sun-Alliance Chase when fourth and still going well. "He's coming back but obviously he was quite badly injured at Cheltenham so we're just hoping he'll recapture his best. He's reasonably well handicapped and, all being well, we'll be going for three-mile chases with him."

BUDDY MARVEL was a useful juvenile hurdler in 1997-98 and was trained until after his third start last season by Oliver Sherwood. He ran reasonably well in the County Hurdle and a valuable Aintree handicap for Mrs Reveley and races mainly at around two miles. The sort that may do better from his change of scene in novice chases this term, "he has schooled well over fences."

DRAGONS BAY is a decent handicap chaser and showed no signs of ageing last season when successful at Carlisle, Doncaster and twice at Market Rasen. He operates at up to two-and-a-half miles and should pick up more races..

FOUNDRY LANE is a good-looking,

MARY REVELEY

Best Tracks

Ludlow	40%	2-5
Towcester	38%	3-8
Southwell	38%	5-13
Cartmel	38%	5-13
Ascot	36%	4-11
Huntingdon	34%	16-47
Carlisle	31%	37-120
Perth	31%	25-81
Kelso	27%	38-140

Worst Tracks

Worcester	0%	0-7
Cheltenham	4%	2-52
Stratford	7%	1-14
Hexham	12%	7-59
Newbury	12%	2-17
Aintree	14%	5-37
Uttoxeter	14%	9-66
Musselburgh	15%	7-47
Haydock	17%	12-69

Best months

August	45%	14-31
September	30%	28-92
October	29%	49-169
November	25%	83-328
December	24%	56-233

Worst months

July	14%	3-22
June	15%	5-34
April	18%	37-208
January	18%	40-219

First time out

Chases

1994-95	18%	4-22
1995-96	19%	3-16
1996-97	24%	5-21
1997-98	22%	4-18
1998-99	13%	3-23
Total	19%	19-100

Hurdles

1994-95	24%	18-74
1995-96	20%	16-80
1996-97	21%	16-75
1997-98	26%	22-85
1998-99	16%	12-77
Total	21%	84-391

Jockey Watch

A Dobbin	50%	3-6
Mr S Swiers	50%	6-12
L Wyer	32%	9-28
Mr A Dempsey	29%	43-150
Mr M H Naughton	26%	7-27
P Niven	26%	287-1115
M A Fitzgerald	20%	1-5

useful hurdler but not quite so good over fences . . . yet. He still managed to win a novice chase at Wetherby in January and is effective at two to two-and-a-half miles on any ground. "He'll start off on the Flat in the autumn and then we could switch him in between chasing and hurdles through the winter. His jumping in chases seems to be getting better and he should win more races."

FULLOPEP is set to go straight over fences and should make the grade. "We're pleased with his schooling. He's from the same family as Simply Dashing so he should make a decent chaser at around two-and-a-half miles."

GRAY GRANITE carries the colours of the Mary Reveley Racing Club and should give members some fun in the coming months. He won a Huntingdon bumper on his only start last term and is expected to go over hurdles in the second half of this season.

HIGHBEATH is a reasonable handicap chaser and is best at a stiff two-and-a-half miles. He won at Market Rasen and in amateur company at Ludlow last season but tends to idle. Despite his high head carriage he should still pick up more races on top of the ground.

IL CAVALIERE has already secured a Market Rasen bumper in June. He is highly rated and may remain in bumper company this term.

JUNE'S RIVER won twice in the soft at Carlisle last season and he will be competing in two-mile handicap chases this time.

KATHRYN'S PET progressed quite well over hurdles last season winning her first three races at Huntingdon (twice) and Doncaster. She was well beaten on soft ground but acts on good to firm and good to soft and should get further than two miles. Look out for her in mares-only novice chases.

LINGDALE LAD is still unexposed as a bumper horse. Chasing will be his game eventually but "he'll be novice hurdling for the time being".

LORD LAMB took well to hurdling last season and was an easy winner of his first three races, at Newcastle (twice) and Wetherby (all over 2m). He didn't jump so well when well-beaten in a Grade 2 event at Aintree in April but has bags of toe and should get further than the minimum jumps trip. He carries his head high but seems genuine enough and also has winning form on the Flat. "He didn't quite fulfil his early promise and was probably over the top at

Aintree. He'll stick to decent hurdle events on good ground this time."

MARELLO is a high-class staying hurdler who had a light campaign last season. She won the Grade 2 West Yorkshire Hurdle at Wetherby on her reappearance but pulled very hard when a well-beaten fifth in a similar event at Newbury next time. She may have had enough for the season when tailed off and pulled up in a Grade 1 hurdle at Punchestown in April. "She could well be going novice chasing this season. We've schooled her and she jumps very well. Obviously we'd be disappointed if she didn't make a nice three-mile novice over fences."

MERRY MASQUERADE is a strapping big sort who should make a chaser. He won staying hurdles last term at Newcastle and Ayr and likes testing ground. He's fairly lightly-raced but has a good strike rate. "He's a very big horse who stays further than three miles and needs soft ground. He's built to be a chaser and he's okay now after he went wrong in the middle of last season."

MR BUSBY is another set to tackle fences this term. He also enjoys plenty of cut. Two-and-a-half miles is his trip.

NO MORE HASSLE is a big, scopey sort. Fairly useful over hurdles and fences, he won 2m 4f novice chases last term at Huntingdon and Market Rasen. He's possibly best when the ground is not extremely fast or soft and his last win was gained in a manner that suggests he can progress further, especially over fences.

OCTOBER MIST's only run last term was when finishing second in a Wetherby bumper and this grey is well regarded by Mrs Reveley. He is closely related to Lord Dorcet and will start off in bumpers before graduating to novice hurdles later on.

OLD HUSH WING was trained on his first two starts last season by Pat Haslam and recorded a third course win when landing a handicap hurdle at Sedgefield for Mrs Reveley. He was also successful on the Flat in 1999 and stays three miles over hurdles.

ONCE MORE FOR LUCK is not the easiest of rides but nevertheless won three times over hurdles last season at Leicester and Wetherby (twice). His winning form ranges from two to two-and-a-half miles and he goes on most ground. He is usually well placed by his shrewd trainer.

RANDOM HARVEST turned into a

smart handicap chaser last season, winning staying events at Market Rasen and Wetherby (twice). He wasn't disgraced when third to General Wolfe in the Peter Marsh Chase and stays three-and-a-quarter miles. He acts on most ground and is a grand big improving horse that should have another good campaign. "He's a nice chasing type and he's still open to a little bit of improvement yet. He's a fine big horse and will be entered in all the good staying handicap chases."

ROBBO won a couple of two-and-a-half mile handicap hurdles last season at Ayr and Newcastle but was well beaten in the Coral Cup where the ground was too lively. He should stay three miles and likes plenty of cut. Another set to go novice chasing.

SAD MAD BAD took well to chasing last season and won four of his eight starts over fences, although he disappointed in his last three runs. He was probably outclassed in a Grade 1 event at Punchestown on his final outing and requires a good test at two miles. He will get further than two-and-a-half miles in time and loves heavy ground — just the sort to make an interesting prospect in handicap chases this season.

SANDABAR completed an early season hat-trick over hurdles at Perth (twice) and Sedgefield before emerging from an eight-month break to make it four out of four with a Wetherby victory in late May. He's probably best in spring and autumn on faster ground and may be the type to progress further when conditions are in his favour.

SEVEN TOWERS won a five-runner affair at Ayr in November but was mainly disappointing last season. He's a high class staying chaser at his best but has had his share of problems and wasn't seen out at all in 1997-98. He was talked about as a Grand National prospect and claimed the scalp of 1997 Aintree hero Lord Gyllene in the Midlands National three seasons ago — which shows what he can do. He didn't appear after mid-January but "has had a good long rest and is set to return around Christmas."

There should be races to be won on fast ground with **THE GRANBY** over two-and-a-half miles while **TIME OF FLIGHT** might be a dark horse to follow this season. "Time Of Flight is a horse I particularly like. He won his first bumper and then we never got him quite right over hurdles. He'd be a horse that would go hurdling then novice chasing and he could be decent."

TURNPOLE won the Cesarewitch on the Flat in 1997 and is a useful hurdler. He was runner-up in a Grade 2 stayers' hurdle at Ascot before winning twice in minor novice chasing company. He's effective from two-and-a-half to three-and-a-half miles and is almost certainly capable of a lot better over fences which will be his game this time round. "I hope the handicapper rates him on his chasing form and not his form over hurdles. He'll be running in soft-ground three-mile chases."

WOODFIELD GALE was a progressive sort over hurdles last season, winning a maiden at Wetherby and two handicaps at Newcastle. He needs plenty of cut to be at his best and all his wins have been gained at two-and-a-half miles, a trip which suits him well. He's a nice type of horse who is going novice chasing. "He's getting better as he grows older and he jumped well when we schooled him at home."

WYNYARD KNIGHT has progressed from a successful bumper horse and hurdler to make the grade over fences. Last season he won novice chases at Ayr, Doncaster and Wetherby. Although he lost his jumping confidence in the Arkle Trophy and made mistakes again when last of four in a Grade 1 event at Punchestown in April, he may still be on the upgrade. "He's best at two miles and because of his mark he'll have to go for some decent handicap chases this season."

WYNYARD LADY, effective from two to two miles six furlongs, trotted up on her final start over hurdles last term and is set for a novice chasing campaign this time round.

OLIVER SHERWOOD has held a permanent presence among the leading jump trainers for longer than he cares to remember, but the Millennium season brings a set of new challenges for the Upper Lambourn handler.

First, he must do without the services of Jamie Osborne, his long time stable jockey, adviser and friend who has retired to, of all things, the Flat trainers' ranks.

Sherwood has appointed David Casey, one of the most exciting young talents from Ireland as replacement, but Osborne is a very tough act to follow and it will be interesting to see how that relationship "beds down" in the weeks ahead.

Then, on the equine front, both Lord Of The River and Kadou Nonantais, his two high-class novice chasers from last season, have spent the summer recuperating.

They will be brought along only gradually during the autumn in an attempt to nurse them back to their very best form, following the injuries sustained towards the end of the 1998-99 campaign.

Hopefully they will fulfil their great potential come the spring but in the meantime, Sherwood must look to an exciting clutch of mainly novice chasers and novice hurdlers to keep his name among the top players.

Here, in an exclusive interview for the Sun Guide, he discusses the prospects of both the familiar names and some of the less exposed types, starting with his chasers.

CALLISOE BAY "may not be the horse he once was, but he did make a noise in a couple of races last season and has had his wind operated on. However, he was third in the Peter Cazalet in January which was a good run. It has taken us a while to learn that he wants three miles and soft ground and, if things work out well, he could still win some good races, even though I would like to see him a few pounds lower in the handicap."

CHEROKEE CHIEF is a novice going handicapping this season. "He had to stop in February after chipping a couple of bones in his knee, but they have been

OLIVER SHERWOOD

Best Tracks

Fakenham	40%	4-10
Southwell	33%	5-15
Newbury	29%	17-59
Uttoxeter	29%	20-69
Exeter	27%	7-26

Worst Tracks

Market Rasen	0%	0-4
Ludlow	4%	2-45
Chepstow	8%	2-26
Leicester	10%	2-20
Aintree	10%	2-20
Folkestone	11%	4-36
Worcester	12%	4-33
Huntingdon	14%	9-65

Best months

October	34%	28-82
June	29%	2-7
November	23%	43-191
March	22%	33-149

Worst months

January	12%	17-142
May	12%	12-98
August	14%	1-7
April	16%	20-125
February	17%	24-144
December	18%	30-171
September	19%	5-27

First time out

Chases

1994-95	24%	4-17
1995-96	20%	4-20
1996-97	22%	4-18
1997-98	18%	3-17
1998-99	20%	4-20
Total	21%	19-92

Hurdles

1994-95	19%	7-36
1995-96	26%	11-43
1996-97	24%	10-42
1997-98	11%	4-38
1998-99	13%	4-31
Total	19%	36-190

Jockey Watch

P Niven	50%	2-4
R Dunwoody	26%	5-19
P Carberry	25%	3-12
G Bradley	23%	3-13
J McCarthy	21%	3-14
D Leahy	20%	1-5
Mr G Baines	20%	1-5
A Maguire	17%	1-6
J A McCarthy	16%	70-428

It would be nice to think Kadou Nonantais could make his mark against the very best one day, but that is a long way off and we shall think more about the staying handicaps for the time being

operated on. He won around Haydock last season, but he does take the odd liberty. A nice horse who should stay three miles eventually."

CENKOS is a French horse Sherwood has inherited from Kim Bailey following his decision to move back to his Northampton roots. "He was a very good horse across the Channel and showed promise on his only outing for Kim last year behind Zafarabad at Newbury. He is not an easy horse to place over hurdles and my gut feeling is to send him over fences sooner rather than later."

FOREVER NOBLE was very consistent over hurdles last season and will go novice chasing. "He likes good ground and will get three miles in time. He will probably be kept to the smaller courses."

GOOD VIBES was bought at the Doncaster August Sales. Formerly trained by Tim Easterby, he ran a blinder when second to Whip Hand on his only outing last season. "He has had a leg problem, but if he stays sound he could be a smart chaser."

HIM OF PRAISE, a classy out-and-out stayer on his day, won the valuable National Trial at Uttoxeter in February. "We all know he is a character and we all know he can do much better! He will be geared towards similar staying handicaps again and he will be given a Grand National entry this year, but I have to admit that Martin St Quinton, his owner, and myself have thought about a change of scenery for him. We will start him off here, but if he shows that he needs a change of routine, we may think about doing something different and perhaps send him over to Ireland to join Arthur Moore. The fact that he is so laid back makes him a frustrating horse to train sometimes, but he is so talented I would not mind a yard full of horses like him."

KINGSMARK is owned by Robert

Ogden and did Sherwood proud last season, winning four of his six races. "He loves it hock deep and goes novice chasing this year. He is not all that big and just how he handles the Newburys and Ascots when he gets there remains to be seen. But he should handle the smaller courses without much problem. A bonny little horse and one to keep on the right side."

KADOU NONANTAIS developed into a top-class novice last season, winning five of his eight starts, including an impressive success in the Towton Novices Chase at Wetherby. "We opted to go for the William Hill Handicap Chase at Cheltenham and he duly started favourite. He jumped really well but then made a right mess of the 12th and took a crashing fall. Unfortunately, he injured himself and had to have an operation in late April to have some chips removed from his shoulder. This means he will be late getting going this season but we could not perform the surgery any earlier because we thought he had problems with his back and he had to undergo a scan and other tests. He has spent a nice time out in the field, will be brought back gradually, and a lot of his preliminary work will be undertaken on the horse walker.

We have one thing going for us and that is the fact that he takes no time in getting him ready. Having said that, he wants soft ground so there is no point rushing him anyway. At the moment we have no major plans besides getting him back ready to run. I have to confess that at the start of last season I thought he might be a two-miler but he is a relentless galloper and stays really well. It would be nice to think he could make his mark against the very best one day, but that is a long way off and we shall think more about the staying handicaps for the time being."

LORD OF THE RIVER will not be

49

seen out too early either, and Sherwood has ruled out a crack at the Hennessy. "His campaign is being geared towards Cheltenham. He did have a little niggling problem just above a joint towards the end of last season so we abandoned the Punchestown Festival and opted for a low-key start this term. He achieved everything we hoped of him over fences last season and more. Not too many horses win the Feltham at Kempton and the Reynoldstown at Ascot in one season. We hoped he could do the hat-trick in the Sun Alliance at Cheltenham but things did not go his way during the race and he had to be content with a well beaten second. He came back with a badly twisted plate which had stuck into his foot and Tony McCoy, who rode him that day, said he started to hang badly in the second half of the race and stopped very quickly at the top of the hill. I'll take nothing away from the winner who is clearly a very good horse, but it was not Lord Of The River's true form. Number one priority again is to get him back on course, but if all goes well I would like to think he would develop into a Gold Cup horse at some stage. He has plenty of class."

MERRY PATH won a novice hurdle at Newbury last season, but did not run up to expectations on other occasions. "He is only five, has summered really well and looks a much stronger horse this season. He likes good ground so might well be in action earlier than most. Goes novice chasing and looks a nice prospect."

SAINT JOE won twice last season and is another going novice chasing. "He jumps for fun, handles any ground and should win his races."

WELCOME CALL "has not been on the racecourse for a couple of years and my main ambition this season is to get him back in action. He got to within a week of running last season but then he went and fractured his pelvis. He has been ticking over all summer and hope-

fully will be able to fulfil his potential this season."

First up alphabetically among the hurdlers is **DEALER'S CHOICE** who won his only race last season, a bumper at Fontwell. "He is quite laid back and is still a bit 'leggy'. Will go novice hurdling and should win, but is more of a chaser long term."

HULYSSE ROYAL has come from France "where he won his last three races before he was gelded. He could be anything."

LIGHTNING STRIKES ran three times in bumpers last season, "which is unusual for me. He took his racing really well and showed some very good form. He is a full brother to a good horse of Mark Pitman's called Santabless. I am almost tempted to go straight over fences with him because he is a big rangy, striking horse, but he will have a go over timber. Look out for him over two-and-a-half miles in the second half of the season."

MILLENNIUM WAY "is an Irish import who was placed in a point-to-point."

OSOCOOL "is closely related to Cruising Altitude and Bear Claw and did well to finish third to Stand Easy on her only outing in a Newton Abbot bumper."

STYX "is another chasing type by Over The River and showed promise on his only outing behind Dromdoran in a bumper at Folkestone.

THE BUSH KEEPER "was bought from Eddie Hales, Kim Bailey's former assistant, who has some really nice young horses in Ireland. He has finished placed in a bumper and point-to-point across the water. A lovely, big, strong horse."

UN JOUR A VASSY was favourite for the bumper Dealer's Choice won at Fontwell and finished a close fourth. "He is more of a hurdler than a chaser."

There are a few other unraced young horses that did not run last season for one reason or another and three Sherwood likes particularly are **DRUMLIN**, **INTERCITY** and **MOSSY BAY**.

> ◢ **Lord Of The River's campaign is being geared towards Cheltenham. He had a niggling problem at the end of last season so we're opting for a low-key start this term** ◢

NIGEL TWISTON-DAVIES has again maintained his lofty position in the trainers' premier division. Last season he finished seventh in the table with his 65 winners and £531,322 in prize money.

The fast ground at Aintree was against stable standard-bearer Earth Summit in his repeat attempt on the Martell Grand National. But the 1998 winner will be back again for a crack at the first Aintree thriller of the new Millennium.

Fun-loving Twiston-Davies, who works well in partnership with his more subdued assistant Peter Scudamore, is publicity shy and only has to see a camera, or a notebook, to scurry into hiding.

His Naunton base is a definite no-go area for reporters but, as usual, Twiston-Davies gives Sun Guide readers an exclusive preview of his main hopes for the new season, with much of the stable's strength coming in the novice chase department.

ALTA, who won a novice hurdle at Exeter last season, now goes novice chasing. "She did well in mares' only races. She likes soft ground — the bigger the test of stamina the better — and always races prominently."

ASHLEY MUCK "is from the amazing family that has done us so well over the years. He will be entered for handicap hurdles. Last season he did well when second to Hoh Invader in a pretty hot Grade 2 novice hurdle at Cheltenham. Previously he had won at Exeter. There have been questions over his temperament but he seems fine and has summered well."

BALLYNABRAGGET was knocking at the door last season in bumpers and novice hurdles. "He is sure to pay to follow this winter, especially when he switches to novice chasing."

BARNEYS BELL won a 15-runner novice hurdle race at Lingfield on his debut by six lengths. He was then off the track for two months but "he's back in strong work now and I think he is well handicapped over hurdles."

BEAU won over hurdles at Newton Abbot in December and subsequently ran behind the outstanding Barton,

NIGEL TWISTON-DAVIES

Best Tracks

Perth	39%	7-18
Carlisle	25%	3-12
Market Rasen	25%	7-28
Leicester	23%	8-35
Lingfield	23%	9-39
Doncaster	22%	5-23
Haydock	22%	19-85

Worst Tracks

Newcastle	0%	0-6
Wincanton	8%	4-49
Fontwell	9%	2-23
Cheltenham	9%	22-234
Towcester	10%	9-93
Ayr	10%	3-30
Taunton	11%	5-44
Sandown	11%	9-79
Worcester	12%	12-99
Stratford	12%	7-60
Huntingdon	12%	10-83

Best months

August	28%	5-18
July	27%	3-11
September	22%	17-76
May	22%	40-185
October	20%	33-168

Worst months

February	11%	35-323
June	12%	3-25
March	12%	38-313
April	14%	35-256
December	14%	36-253
November	15%	56-379
January	16%	39-248

First time out

Chases

1994-95	29%	9-31
1995-96	22%	7-32
1996-97	8%	2-25
1997-98	11%	3-28
1998-99	17%	3-18
Total	18%	24-134

Hurdles

1994-95	23%	17-74
1995-96	19%	15-79
1996-97	21%	14-66
1997-98	9%	6-67
1998-99	14%	12-84
Total	17%	64-370

Jockey Watch

Mr J Goldstein	29%	4-14
Mr S Joynes	25%	5-20
W Marston	22%	2-9
M Keighley	18%	6-34
C Llewellyn	18%	188-1054
G Bradley	17%	1-6

when fourth of six to Tim Easterby's hotpot at Doncaster. "He wants further than two miles and he will go novice chasing."

BINDAREE "is a very exciting newcomer for us who won point-to-points in Ireland. He will start in novice hurdles and is one that I would advise Sun punters not to miss. Definitely one for the notebook."

BORA BORA had a good 1998-99 season, winning mares-only hurdle events at Huntingdon, Towcester and Uttoxeter. "She was also very unlucky when hampered and 10 lengths third to Conchobor at Ayr. Like so many of my team she will now go novice chasing. She was bred by Peter Scudamore's father Michael, who still rides out for us daily."

BORAZON is another one earmarked for novice chasing. He won a handicap hurdle at Worcester in October and "will be really suited by tests of stamina over the bigger obstacles."

BOSUNS MATE "could not have done us better last season. He is closely related to Young Hustler and won good novice hurdle races at Cheltenham and Newbury. He's a tough sort and will now go novice chasing. The longer the distance, the better for him."

CAMELOT KNIGHT, a gutsy long-distance chaser, may be 13 but does not seem to have lost too much of his zest. "He failed to win in four starts last season but this time I expect to start him off in the Becher Chase at Aintree on November 21, which Earth Summit won last year. Whether he tries to win the Grand National as a 14-year-old must be open to question, though."

CAUGHT NAPPING "broke a blood vessel on his hurdling debut at Worcester and he also suffered a hairline fracture injury. But he is back in full work and will be aimed for novice hurdles."

CHOPINS REVOLUTION will run in novice hurdles and is rated better than her uninspiring form figures suggest.

DAMP COURSE showed some ability when placed in conditional jockeys' races at Newbury and Newton Abbot last term. "He will stick to novice hurdling for the time being."

EARTH SUMMIT won the 1998 Grand National at Aintree to complete the unique treble of the Welsh and Scottish Nationals. "He was an easy winner last season of the three-finisher Becher Chase at Aintree, when he started a bigger SP than when he won the Grand National! I had him spot on for his repeat bid last April but the fast ground was all against him and, more importantly, he was very badly hampered at Becher's Brook on the second circuit. That rather took the running out of him and he weakened over the last four fences before finishing eighth. Obviously his main target will be another crack at the National. He is just an out-and-out stayer, who much prefers a bit of cut in the ground. I was going to let him run in the Becher Chase at Aintree on November 21 but the programme book states that it is a 0 to 145 race and obviously he is too good for that. I hope that the rule can be changed to allow him to run. He seems to be in very good form and has been a marvellous servant to us over the years."

ESKLEYBROOK is on the upgrade and did well for the yard last season, winning four small-field handicap chases at Hereford, Warwick, Bangor and Startford. "He acts well on soft ground and is one of the most improved horses in the yard."

FLAPJACK LAD "ran eight times for us last season without troubling the judge. Hopefully we will be able to get him back into the winner's enclosure in a modest handicap chase somewhere."

FREDDIE MUCK "is another from the famous Muck family. He won a three-runner handicap chase at Newton Abbot in November but failed to get his head in front again in five races. He jumps for fun and I'm sure there are more races for him to win."

GENTLE RIVAGE showed useful form in bumpers before running a fine race to finish fourth at Ayr in a novice hurdle. "He will remain in novice hurdles. Extended trips will be no problem."

JAGUAR "will be my main Triumph Hurdle hope. He is a colt by Barathea and was trained on the Flat by Gay Kelleway. Although he failed to lose his maiden tag on the level, he is a horse I like a lot and hopefully he will be there with a fighting chance come Cheltenham next March."

KERAWI was a smart hurdler on his day, finishing fifth behind Istabraq in the 1998 Champion Hurdle. Last season he failed to get his head in front and made little impression when eighth at 50-1 in the Stayers' Hurdle at the Cheltenham Festival. "He is another one set for novice chases."

KING'S ROAD is one of the stable's leading lights. Two seasons ago he won the prestigious bumpers at Aintree and Punchestown, while last term he was never out of the first four over hurdles. The ground was probably too quick for him in the Royal & SunAlliance Novices Hurdle when he finished fourth behind Barton. But stamina is no problem and he was running on best of all up the hill. He had previously won at Chepstow and Newbury but his best display came when winning the big novice hurdle at the Grand National meeting where he beat Martin Pipe's Ballysicyos. That makes it two consecutive years he has won at the National meeting — perhaps one day he will complete the hat-trick at Aintree and win the Grand National itself! He schools well over fences and I am really looking forward to launching him on a novice chasing career."

LADY OF GORTMERRON won over hurdles at Cheltenham and Exeter and this mare is another being aimed at novice chases.

LADY PADIVOR, a cheap buy who landed a gamble in a slowly-run Warwick bumper last term, "will be kept to novice hurdles."

MADAM MUCK has shown only modest form over hurdles and fences so far. "She will go handicap chasing."

MAHLER, a top class novice over fences in 1997-98, failed to fulfil his potential last season. "He had back problems which explains why he never reproduced his previous form over fences. He will start out in the Becher Chase at Aintree on November 21 and his long range target is the Grand National."

MISTER MOROSE was having his first race for nearly two years when he landed a bit of a gamble in the Tote Silver Trophy Handicap Hurdle at Chepstow last season. He subsequently ran fourth in the Champion Hurdle behind Istabraq, belying his 100-1 starting price. "He has also won over fences so it's hard to decide which way to go forward with him."

MOORISH "had only three races last season but won by a head from Bold Gait at Newbury and was also second to Deano's Beeno at Haydock. I am persevering with him in handicap hurdles."

OCEAN HAWK was very smart over hurdles and looked to have a big future in front of him when winning on his chase debut at Exeter in October. Even though he subsequently won at Worcester, he failed to progress as anticipated. "He will continue over fences."

QUEEN OF SPADES was pulled up on her two starts last season and has had time off since to put her right. "She will make her comeback in handicap chases."

ROLLER BLADE showed much improved form to win a Ludlow bumper by 18 lengths. Despite subsequently flopping at Aintree he looks one to follow, especially when upped in trip. "He won at Uttoxeter in May and will stay novice hurdling."

SCARLET PIMPERNEL "came to us from Criquette Head and progressed to finish sixth in the Triumph Hurdle. I'm afraid it will be difficult to place him this season."

UPGRADE won the Triumph Hurdle two seasons ago but that hard-earned victory seemed to bottom him as last season he couldn't return to winning ways, eventually finishing down the field in the Champion Hurdle. He may well be worth trying over further than two miles. "He's yet another going novice chasing."

YOUNG THRUSTER, has the build of a chaser but won over timber at Newton Abbot, Huntingdon and Worcester last season. "He is an out-and-out stayer and is certainly one to follow in novice chases this time around."

◢ **Young Thruster, an out-and-out stayer, is one to follow in novice chases this time around** ◢

IN percentage terms the most successful trainer in the winter game stands head and shoulders above the rest.

Venetia Williams posted a fantastic strike rate of 28 per cent last season — a figure all her rivals must envy. Even champion Martin Pipe, once Venetia's boss, can't match her protege — as his 21 per cent winners-to-runners ratio demonstrates.

There are lies, damn lies and then there are statistics, but in this case the numbers paint the complete picture — Williams, the long, tall tomboy trainer based at her family's Aramstone acres outside Ross-on-Wye, has surged right to the top of the profession in double quick time. Only four seasons ago she posted just seven winners. That total rose to 33 at the end of the next campaign, had reached 45 a year later, and last season she sent out 74 winners worth a whopping £606,334.

A meteoric rise by anyone's standards.

Flying grey Teeton Mill was the star of the 1998-99 show with a fabulous Hennessy-King George VI double. His Cheltenham Gold Cup bid was wrecked by a cruel injury in the race itself but there is still hope he can make a full recovery.

Here, Stephen Winstanley of the Winning Line, the syndicate which is the stable's main backer, gives an exclusive preview of Venetia's main hopes for the new season.

ARTIC CAMPER was second in the 1998 Cheltenham Festival bumper and returned to Prestbury Park 12 months later to run sixth of 18 to Barton in the Royal & SunAlliance Novices Hurdle. He had previously scored at Cheltenham and Fontwell over hurdles and will be an exciting recruit to novice chasing.

BACK ON THE LASH is an improving novice hurdler, who was formerly with Ferdy Murphy. He made all to win at Towcester, and then scored at Market Rasen. On the back of those victories he was made 4-1 favourite for a decent novices' handicap hurdle at Sandown in March but could only finish eighth, spoiling his chance by pulling too hard. He will be winning again if he learns to settle.

BELLATOR joined Venetia from Toby Balding and his best run came when he was seventh to Istabraq in the Champion Hurdle at 50-1. He ran a blinder then, only half a length down at the second last flight. He subsequently ran fourth in a

VENETIA WILLIAMS

Best Tracks

Doncaster	57%	4-7
Folkestone	50%	5-10
Huntingdon	50%	5-10
Chepstow	44%	8-18
Fakenham	40%	2-5
Warwick	40%	4-10
Plumpton	39%	7-18
Fontwell	39%	11-28
Wetherby	36%	4-11
Stratford	35%	8-23
Newton Abbot	35%	6-17
Haydock	33%	4-12
Perth	33%	2-6
Ludlow	33%	8-24
Newbury	31%	4-13
Kempton	30%	3-10

Worst Tracks

Exeter	0%	0-7
Ayr	0%	0-5
Sandown	7%	1-14
Wincanton	7%	3-18
Aintree	11%	2-18
Worcester	16%	5-31
Uttoxeter	16%	5-32

Best months

September	67%	6-9
October	39%	14-36
December	36%	23-64
November	32%	21-65
January	32%	20-62
February	29%	20-70

Worst months

July	0%	0-9
April	13%	11-85
August	14%	1-7

First time out

Chases

1995-96	40%	2-5
1996-97	0%	0-13
1997-98	35%	7-20
1998-99	40%	10-25
Total	30%	19-63

Hurdles

1995-96	9%	1-11
1996-97	29%	5-17
1997-98	28%	8-29
1998-99	22%	11-50
Total	23%	25-107

Jockey Watch

Miss S Vickery	75%	3-4
T J Murphy	50%	3-6
A P McCoy	40%	8-20
A Maguire	40%	4-10
R Dunwoody	35%	7-20
R Farrant	33%	7-21

handicap at Aintree before disappointing at Ayr. He will probably be better suited by further than two miles and is one to watch in handicaps.

BOOTS MADDEN has had his confidence restored and has progressed from a decent hurdler to a winning handicap chaser. He scored last season at Warwick and Stratford and is sure to be placed to win again.

BOWL OF GOLD is a home-bred filly who, after a modest career in bumper races, was fourth of eight at Wincanton in a mares-only race on her hurdling debut. She was rather outpaced that day and will need a greater test of stamina.

BRAMBLEHILL DUKE came from David Nicholson but failed to sparkle at first before winning a conditional jockeys' hurdles race at Newbury by a neck. Not seen out again after November, he is the type to stay further than two-and-a-half miles in time.

CARDINAL RULE is rising 11 but he is still a useful handicap chaser on his day. A winner at Warwick and Wetherby last season, he wants two-and-a-half miles.

CAREYSVILLE is an improving chaser who should do well in handicaps this season. The highlights of his 1998-99 campaign were wins at Folkestone and Newbury. This front-runner is suited by a good test of stamina and is normally the safest of jumpers.

CROCADEE was purchased for 26,000gns at the 1998 Doncaster May Sales and could not have made a more impressive debut for his new stable when winning a 17-runner maiden at Bangor by 18 lengths. He cruised into the lead and won as he liked. A very exciting prospect who is certain to be a big name this season.

DAVOSKI was formerly with Barry Hills on the Flat. He is as tough as they come and was cleverly placed to win novice hurdles at Hereford, Uttoxeter and Kempton and handicaps at Newton Abbot and Uttoxeter. Very consistent and should continue to do well.

EDEWEIS DU MOULIN finished third on his belated reappearance for Venetia in the Cathcart Chase at the Cheltenham Festival, which was a fine display considering that he had been off the track for 334 days. He then won at Aintree over an extended three miles. More success awaits this Robert Ogden-owned chaser and the Murphy's Gold Cup is a possible first target.

EFFECTUAL won five races in 1997-98 and added to that tally in small fields at Doncaster and Fontwell last season. He

was not disgraced in better races such as the Tote Gold Trophy at Newbury and the Sunderlands Imperial Cup at Sandown. One to watch out for in heavy-ground handicap hurdles.

FOURTH IN LINE was greatly improved by his new trainer to win four races and caught the eye as well when fifth behind Royal Predica in a valuable novice chase at Aintree. This front-runner is sure to be placed to win more races.

GENERAL WOLFE is a top-class chaser owned by the Winning Line. Winstanley said: "He goes best after a good break and last season came out and won the Peter Marsh Chase at Haydock first time up, beating Simply Dashing by four lengths, after being off the course for a year. He subsequently was not firing on all cylinders in the Uttoxeter Grand National Trial — falling at the last when tired, It was a similar story in the Grand National itself, when he was 12th of the 18 finishers. He is pretty high in the handicap but absolutely loves Haydock and it would be fabulous if he could win the Peter Marsh for the third time in a row in January. Before that he might go for the Hennessy Gold Cup at Newbury in late November. With good to soft ground and after another decent holiday, he might just run a big race."

GOLDEN GOAL is a fabulous looking three-year-old who came from Germany and could well develop into a leading contender for the Triumph Hurdle at Cheltenham next March. He has form-lines that tie in with the top German middle-distance performers and will be a very interesting newcomer, having been gelded in the summer.

HAPPY CHANGE was being aimed at the Champion Hurdle last year but could never quite get his act together and failed to make a single appearance over timber. However, he won on the Flat for Mark Johnson in August and is now back with Venetia. "He has schooled well over hurdles and the plan is for him to make his hurdling debut at Wetherby or Uttoxeter early on. Obviously we are looking ahead to this season's Champion Hurdle if he lives up to all our hopes."

IN QUESTION, once trained on the Flat by Barry Hills, was purchased by The Winning Line for 60,000gns at the Doncaster November Sales out of Chris Thornton's Middleham yard, having won for Thornton on his hurdling debut at Kelso. "He scored first time out for us by 12 lengths at Ludlow but then disappointed in his next two races. He was made second favourite for the Imperial Cup at

Sandown on the back of his easy Ludlow win but lost his chance by running far too freely on his way to post and could only finish sixth, after trying to make all. Some good judges have said that one day he will win the Arkle Chase at Cheltenham and we hope he'll go places over fences."

ITSONLYME has good form in bumpers having been shrewdly placed to win at Aintree, Folkestone and Huntingdon. He should pay to follow when he switches to novice hurdles.

JOCKS CROSS was formerly with the late Gordon Richards. He won three hurdles on the trot at Fontwell, Stratford and Ayr and is sure to be in the money again as he stays really well.

KINGDOM OF SHADES took well to novice chases last season, scoring at Lingfield and Plumpton. Finished distressed when beaten on his final outing at Uttoxeter when his tendency to break blood vessels was the problem.

LADY REBECCA's progression was fairytale last season. This tiny but gutsy mare cost a mere 4,500gns for the Kinnersley Optimists syndicate but scooped a magnificent £75,951 with four wins from six starts. In all, she has won 11 of her 14 starts and bagged well over £100,000 — including no fewer than five successes at Cheltenham. She started 3-1 second favourite for the Stayers' Hurdle at the Festival but had suffered an interrupted preparation just prior to the big race and, in the circumstances, ran a blinder to finish third to 40-1 shock winner Anzum, beaten less than three lengths. If she is back to her best, she is the one they all have to beat in the Stayers' Hurdle next March.

LAKE KARIBA was trained by Paul Nicholls last season but joined the Winning Line team for 35,000gns. "He is still only eight and will be aimed at all the top two-mile chases, because the competition does not seem too hot in that division, even though I think he could stay as far as three miles. Last season Paul Nicholls started him off in the Haldon Gold Cup at Exeter — which he won by a distance — and that's where he is likely to make his debut on November 2 for us. I am sure that Paul Nicholls only let him go because he also has the top two-milers Call Equiname and Flagship Uberalles and he didn't want to have all three running against each other in the big races at Sandown, Cheltenham and Aintree."

MASTER PILGRIM won a hurdle at Fontwell in February last season by a runaway 19 lengths and then went on to score at the Sussex track again two weeks

later. The ground was clearly a bit too quick for him when he finished a very respectable tenth of 30 behind Khayrawani in the Coral Cup Handicap Hurdle at the Cheltenham Festival. He is one to note when he comes out in novice chases.

MEPHITIS, who was trained in France by Alain de Royer-Dupre, has been snapped up by the Winning Line and two of his owners are well known in cricket circles — England opener Mike Atherton and ex-coach David Lloyd. This five-year-old gelding has yet to make his debut but should make an early-season appearance. "We want him to run and win for Mike and David before they go off on the winter tour to South Africa."

NORDANCE PRINCE only had two starts last season — in small-field novice chases at Towcester and Cheltenham — but won both. Niggling problems kept him off the track after October but he remains one to follow in handicap company when he returns.

SAMAKAAN had already won three novice hurdles before his fine five-length second to Martin Pipe's highly-rated Star Of Dungannon in a competitive 17-runner hurdle at Cheltenham on his last start. He is one to follow in handicaps.

TEETON MILL's future still hangs is the balance. In late August Venetia was able to say: "He is back being ridden but we will not know what the situation is until he gets into full work. I really can't forecast for sure whether he will run again or not." But Winstanley is more optimistic. "I am more than hopeful that he will run again. He's out in a paddock and the vet is pleased with him. We have a bit of time before Cheltenham and Aintree and don't forget that he is a low-mileage horse and has had less than a dozen races in public. In fact he has won nine out of his 10 races and has never been beaten when he is right. We will never risk him again if there are any fears but hopefully he will come back as good as new." Officially rated the equal top chaser with See More Business, Teeton Mill would be a formidable opponent for all the other Gold Cup contenders if back to his best come next March.

THE OUTBACK WAY is yet another who carries the Winning Line colours. "He ran well for us in the Mildmay of Flete at Cheltenham when fourth., It was probably a mistake to try and match strides with Martin Pipe's Majadou. He will have an early start to the season and hopefully he'll creep into the Murphy's Gold Cup at Cheltenham in mid-November on the minimum 10-stone mark."

STABLE TOUR INDEX

58

Your insider's guide to the top talent lurking in the Emerald Isle

YOU didn't buy this book just to be told that Istabraq will join the all-time greats by winning a third Champion Hurdle next March.

Of course he will, but there's strength in depth in Irish jumps racing these days.

Istabraq's trainer Aidan O'Brien, fresh from another fantastic Flat season, is aiming a few others at Cheltenham as well.

Bumper horse **KILCASH CASTLE** tops the list. He was actually being prepared for the Festival last season but never ran due to a series of minor setbacks.

But he looked awesome when making a winning debut at Galway in July and is a name you should be hearing a lot more of in the build up to the first Festival of the new Millennium.

The Ballydoyle handler also has great hopes for **YEOMAN'S POINT**, a three-year-old who was placed in Group company on the Flat. The Triumph Hurdle is the obvious target.

French import **LE COUDRAY**, so unlucky at Cheltenham, may well go chasing but surely deserves another crack at the Stayers' Hurdle.

Istabraq's owner J P McManus topped the tables on both sides of the Irish Sea last season and, despite losing such stars as Joe Mac and Cardinal Hill, he still has an army of top jumpers to represent him in the coming months.

They include the Christy Roche-trained **YOULNEVERWALKALONE** who will be aimed at the top novice hurdles.

Stable companion **GRIMES** is still

SECONDS OUT . . . Istabraq on his way to Champion Hurdle number two

59

qualified for novice chases having registered a tremendous second on his only start over fences at Aintree last April.

Watch out for him when the money is down.

As every Irish form book anorak will tell you, Noel Meade has yet to train a winner at Cheltenham

But he made a breakthrough of sorts by becoming champion Irish trainer last season and his stable continues to grow in strength.

Four to follow from his yard alone are **NOMADIC** in two-mile novice chases, **NATIVE ESTATES** in handicap chases, novice hurdler **OA BALDIXE** and the exciting **SYDNEY TWOTHOUSAND**. The last-named could end up in either the Champion Chase or the Gold Cup come next March.

Willie Mullins went without a winner at Cheltenham for the first time in five years last season, so he will be anxious to put the record straight this time around.

He reported **FLORIDA PEARL** to be "good and strong" after his summer break and the Gold Cup third is being aimed at the Ulster Champion Chase at Down Royal on November 6th.

DERMOT WELD

That could be some race with **DORANS PRIDE**, See More Business, **IMPERIAL CALL**, **MOSCOW EXPRESS**, Strong Promise and **LOOKS LIKE TROUBLE** all intended runners. Whether all of them turn up is a different matter altogether.

However, Dorans Pride, due to run in the Irish Cesarewitch on October 2nd, should win this round but Florida Pearl remains the most likely of the pair to win a Gold Cup — if only because he has youth on his side.

But the suspicion remains with Florida Pearl that there isn't quite enough in the stamina locker to bag Gold.

ALEXANDER BANQUET was no match for Barton at Cheltenham last March and this former Festival Bumper

winner is likely to go over fences after an opening spin at Down Royal where there is a suitable race for second season novice hurdlers. He has the scope to do well over the bigger obstacles.

BALLA SOLA will be harder to place thanks to his gallant second in the Triumph Hurdle.

Connections resisted the temptation to run the four-year-old on the Flat this summer, a break which will have freshened him up.

However, they are toying with the idea of sending Balla Sola over fences with the Arkle Chase as the ultimate target.

Arthur Moore had a quiet season by his standards, although **NATIVE UPMANSHIP** did win a Grade 1 hurdle at Punchestown. This one should put a winning sequence together over fences when sent over a more stamina-sapping trip than he has tackled to date.

Moore loves nothing more than a successful raid across the Irish Sea for one of the big English handicap hurdles. With that in mind, **DOUBLE ACCOUNT** is probably the best-weighted horse in the yard.

A note should also be made of **FEATHERED LEADER**, especially when he has his favoured good ground. He was second in the Irish National but is still qualified to run in novice chases.

Dermot Weld only keeps a few jumpers on the go but looks to have a most exciting novice hurdler in **STAGE AFFAIR**.

Second to the mighty Daylami in a Group 2 race last year, Stage Affair was hugely impressive on his three outings over hurdles this summer and Cheltenham beckons.

Looking around the other major yards, Francis Flood's **TO YOUR HONOUR** appeals as a type to do well in novice chases.

Enda Bolger is aiming cross-country specialist **RISK OF THUNDER** at the Aintree Grand National while stablemate **SPOT THEDIFFERENCE** failed to see out the trip when third in the four-mile National Hunt Chase at Cheltenham.

He is still held in high regard and there is surely a valuable handicap chase with his name on it.

BOSS DOYLE and **HIS SONG** both went off the boil for Mouse Morris in the second part of last season and can't be followed with confidence just yet.

But stable companion **FOXCHAPEL KING** has done little wrong and is bound to pick up a big prize or two in staying handicap chases.

A new set of Anglo-Irish jump ratings are of some help in allowing us to gauge what is well-handicapped and what is not.

The one that jumps off the page on that former score is Ted Walsh's **RINCE RI**. He left a lasting impression when slamming some top performers in the Power Gold Cup Novices Chase at Fairyhouse last April and his shrewd trainer is sure to lay him out for a valuable prize.

Big wins this summer for ex-novices Moscow Express and **SIBERIAN GALE** also suggest that Rince Ri is well-treated on a mark of 136.

Walsh has revealed that the Orchestra gelding's first big target is the First National Gold Cup at Ascot on November 20th.

He said: "That race is over two-and-a-half miles and that will very much tell us which way to go distance-wise.

"I think Rince Ri could develop into as good a horse as Papillon and don't forget he's rated 145."

Walsh won a Triumph and a Ladbroke Hurdle with **COMMANCHE COURT** and he looks to have another good young timber-topper in **BUSHMAN'S RIVER**.

Rated a stone behind Ireland's best juveniles last term, he has been lightly-raced and can only improve in his sec-

ond season. The trainer's tip that this French import will be aimed at the big handicap hurdles should be taken.

The aforementioned Siberian Gale, so impressive at Tralee, is likely to be given a light campaign by Paddy Mullins this winter to keep him fresh for some big prizes next spring.

His stamina should stretch to three miles on good ground which should open up some opportunities.

The last three Gold Cup winners began their racing careers in point-to-points, so the Sun Guide has dug deep to uncover a selection of future stars which ran between the flags in Ireland last season.

BE MY MANAGER (Henrietta Knight), **GUIDING LIGHT** (Jonjo O'Neill), **MURT'S MAN** (Paul Nicholls), **LORD MOOSE** (Henry Daly), **DARING NATIVE** (Howard Johnson), **CEANANNAS MOR** (Nicky Henderson) and **INCH ROSE** (Noel Chance) were the best to leave the Emerald Isle with winning point-to-point form.

However, no amount of money could persuade Antrim trainer Billy Patton to part with **SOUTHSEA NATIVE**.

A winner of two races between the flags, Southsea Native also collected a valuable bumper at Fairyhouse last season.

He has summered "fantastically well" according to the trainer's son Robert and will start off in novice hurdles this season.

Robert added: "He has grown into a real chaser and Cheltenham is the long-term plan.

"But he won't be risked on fast ground because he is such a big-bodied horse."

He has also got bags of talent and, in the immortal words of Yazz, the only way is up, baby!

> **THREE TO FOLLOW**
>
> **NOMADIC**
> **STAGE AFFAIR**
> **KILCASH CASTLE**

▌ Rince Ri slammed some top performers at Fairyhouse last April. His shrewd trainer is sure to lay him out for a big prize ▐

LEADING TRAINERS WITH 6-YEAR RECORDS

98/99		97/98	96/97	95/96	94/95	93/94
187	M PIPE Wellington	208	212	177	137	127
110	P NICHOLLS Shepton Mallet	82	56	53	28	29
104	MRS M REVELEY Saltburn	89	86	86	100	103
84	P HOBBS Minehead	72	64	79	84	64
76	D NICHOLSON Temple Guiting	103	100	86	96	81
74	MISS V WILLIAMS Hereford	45	33	7	–	–
73	N HENDERSON Lambourn	54	58	48	44	48
65	N TWISTON-DAVIES Cheltenham	69	51	74	81	72
56	L LUNGO Carrutherstown	34	28	14	28	27
47	MRS J PITMAN Upper Lambourn	36	17	49	36	26
42	R ALNER Blandford	36	24	25	27	26
40	K BAILEY Northampton	48	77	69	71	89
39	F MURPHY Leyburn	28	9	19	12	9
38	J J O'NEILL Penrith	32	18	18	27	19
38	MRS S SMITH Bingley	52	42	25	22	22
37	C MANN Upper Lambourn	25	24	17	16	15
36	O SHERWOOD Upper Lambourn	37	49	47	47	41
35	H DALY Ludlow	–	–	–	–	–
34	G M MOORE Middleham	29	32	17	28	26
33	M HAMMOND Middleham	47	47	34	42	44
32	P R WEBBER Banbury	14	27	13	–	–
32	P BOWEN Haverfordwest	38	33	7	5	–
32	MISS H KNIGHT Wantage	42	47	59	44	25
31	I WILLIAMS Alvechurch	14	5	–	–	–
28	T EASTERBY Malton	31	32	14	–	–
26	J OLD Wroughton	31	30	17	10	22
26	N MASON Brancepeth	9	2	3	4	12
25	M PITMAN Upper Lambourn	6	–	–	–	–
25	S SHERWOOD Upper Lambourn	–	–	–	–	–
24	D GANDOLFO Wantage	20	30	24	29	16
22	S BROOKSHAW Shrewsbury	14	15	6	3	3
20	C EGERTON Chaddleworth	15	17	13	15	26
20	M TODHUNTER Ulverston	11	9	3	–	–
19	P BEAUMONT Brandsby	10	25	21	12	17
18	MRS M JONES Lambourn	13	14	9	7	2
18	T GEORGE Slade	11	7	4	2	4
18	J HOWARD JOHNSON Crook	27	23	35	32	32
17	C GRANT Billingham	9	5	–	–	–
17	J FITZGERALD Malton	23	29	22	37	23
17	J GIFFORD Findon	25	41	40	47	51
16	G L MOORE Brighton	21	13	8	6	2
16	D WILLIAMS Newbury	13	2	9	7	1
16	J KING Swindon	26	28	13	17	19
16	R HODGES Somerton	20	22	25	24	35
15	J GOLDIE Glasgow	11	13	2	8	3
15	N RICHARDS Greystoke	–	–	–	–	–
15	J JEFFERSON Malton	29	24	14	16	11
15	M W EASTERBY Sheriff Hutton	12	11	13	10	11
15	G McCOURT Wantage	16	22	9	–	–
15	R FROST Buckfastleigh	23	20	8	8	13
14	A STREETER Uttoxeter	7	8	14	–	–
14	R LEE Presteigne	14	14	3	9	17
14	G HUBBARD Woodbridge	24	11	9	9	1
14	P MONTEITH Rosewell	15	27	24	18	20
14	R DICKIN Stratford-on-Avon	16	8	10	12	12
14	G BALDING Andover	8	21	45	42	16
14	B LLEWELLYN Bargoed	15	11	7	5	8
13	K BURKE Newmarket	6	6	8	8	11
13	D WINTLE Cheltenham	7	2	–	1	2

TOP JOCKEYS

98/99		97/98	96/97	95/96	94/95	93/94
186	A P McCOY	253	190	175	74	7
133	R JOHNSON	120	102	53	6	3
121	M A FITZGERALD	102	82	68	68	68
117	N WILLIAMSON	77	85	24	130	105
108	R DUNWOODY	103	111	101	160	198
91	J TIZZARD	27	11	2	–	–
78	C LLEWELLYN	82	57	58	45	39
73	T J MURPHY	60	28	23	–	–
73	A MAGUIRE	93	81	60	130	194
62	A DOBBIN	53	73	67	57	45
57	W MARSTON	45	18	45	64	34
52	R SUPPLE	42	49	24	11	10
52	S DURACK	41	3	–	–	–
50	J A McCARTHY	40	14	31	10	–
48	L WYER	41	23	66	32	48
47	MR A DEMPSEY	–	–	–	–	–
47	A THORNTON	80	38	50	26	18
44	P NIVEN	73	84	84	106	89
40	R McGRATH	31	12	10	5	1
39	B HARDING	17	7	31	12	7
38	J OSBORNE	16	131	53	111	105
38	B POWELL	42	36	27	31	34
36	R THORNTON	72	30	3	–	–
35	R WAKELEY	27	11	1	1	–
34	J CULLOTY	31	32	40	3	–
34	MR R FORRISTAL	–	–	–	–	–
33	G BRADLEY	46	33	44	41	37
33	D GALLAGHER	27	19	27	41	25
33	B FENTON	26	35	29	–	–
33	C MAUDE	49	56	38	20	15
31	R GUEST	45	50	33	36	19
30	C McCORMACK	14	6	2	–	–
29	R WIDGER	–	–	–	–	–
28	B STOREY	32	48	36	27	34
27	MR J CROWLEY	1	–	–	–	–
26	R FARRANT	31	26	24	30	24
24	G LEE	21	16	11	20	6
23	L CUMMINS	15	12	–	–	–
23	S WYNNE	30	27	14	10	12
22	N HORROCKS	10	6	3	–	–
22	R GARRITTY	45	62	35	17	24
22	J GOLDSTEIN	9	–	–	–	–
22	G TORMEY	26	19	29	15	3
21	J CALLAGHAN	20	16	14	26	25
21	P HIDE	22	35	39	34	16
20	M BATCHELOR	9	5	–	–	–
19	J MAGEE	13	4	3	–	–
18	S KELLY	16	–	–	–	–
18	E HUSBAND	15	9	15	4	6
18	J R KAVANAGH	20	22	36	26	28
17	MR J P McNAMARA	–	–	–	–	–
16	D LEAHY	11	6	5	6	7
16	MICKEY BRENNAN	28	25	–	–	–
15	W DOWLING	11	5	–	–	–
15	J FROST	16	19	8	9	29
14	R GREENE	5	4	4	16	7
14	MR S STRONGE	2	–	–	–	–
14	P HOLLEY	13	13	9	16	29
14	S TAYLOR	15	10	2	2	2

November

Developed a serious allergy to the Flat form book? Bored to tears of unpronounceable Arab-named beasts winning everything under the sun?

I know the feeling. You need a break, a switch to proper racing. And, thankfully, November provides just that.

After over 5,000 races, it's time to wave goodbye to another turf Flat season as it finally winds down at Doncaster on November 6.

A week later the winter game gets into full swing, thanks to the three-day Murphy's Craic meeting at Cheltenham, National Hunt's glorious HQ.

If you have never made it to Cheltenham before, you owe yourself a trip. When it comes to atmosphere, there's nothing quite like the hallowed amphitheatre of Prestbury Park. So dust down your waterproofs, fill your hip flask with your favourite tipple and get on down.

Had you done just that last year you would have been able to see the magnificent physical improvement that Cyfor Malta had made over the summer. A pre-race visit to the parade ring would have resulted in you backing him on those grounds alone.

But even if you cannot make it to Cheltenham, the great thing is that pinpointing the winner of the 2m5f **Murphy's Gold Cup** (Sat 13), the first big handicap chase of the jumps calendar, is as easy as 1-2-3.

1 Chuck out any contender who has not won over at least 2m4f. Cheltenham's demanding 2m5f is probably the equivalent of 3m on a flat track, so avoid two-milers stepping up in trip — they don't win.

2 Past winning form at Cheltenham is a

huge plus. Seven of the last 11 Murphy's winners had already won over the course, while two of the four exceptions had made the frame at the previous season's Festival meeting. Horses often run well in this race year in, year out.

3 Restrict your selection to the younger brigade. The oldest Murphy's winner in the last 10 years has been nine, so you are safe ignoring the claims of the pensioners.

A couple of other points to bear in mind. Senor El Betrutti's 33-1 shock in 1997 aside, this is a race for fancied runners — 12-1 is the next longest winning SP in the 37 other runnings of this great race.

And a previous outing is not essential. Cyfor Malta, last year's heavily backed 3-1 jolly, was the third beast in the last four to win the race on his seasonal reappearance.

My short list of two here last year — which included Cyfor Malta — was drawn from the previous year's Murphy's and the Cathcart.

Following that successful formula, I suggest you carefully examine the credentials of Stormyfairweather and Cyfor Malta once again, although I also rate Edelweis Du Moulin (Cathcart third).

The feature race on the Sunday is the **Murphy's Draughtflow Hurdle**, the season's first big handicap hurdle.

Stamina is again the trump card as Grey Shot showed last year. You need a horse with form over further than the bare 2m minimum.

It's a bigger certainty than Tony McCoy being clobbered with yet another whip ban that whoever wins the Draughtflow will be talked of as a Champion Hurdle contender.

But beware. Even if Istabraq should suddenly fall in a hole, the record of the Draughtflow winners back at Cheltenham the following March is not one to get excited about.

Instead, pay close attention to the names of those who finish in

NOVEMBER 5-YR TRAINER FORM

Trainer	Wins	Runs	%
M Pipe	103	391	26
D Nicholson	100	358	28
Mrs M Reveley	83	328	25
K Bailey	60	281	21
N Twiston-Davies	56	379	15
P Nicholls	55	231	24
J Gifford	51	251	20
P Hobbs	45	273	16
N Henderson	43	180	24
O Sherwood	43	191	23

behind. Three years ago Barna Boy (third) and Make A Stand (fifth) went on to Festival glory in the County and Champion Hurdles respectively.

A season later the race threw up classy future winners in the shape of Kerawi and Star Rage.

And 12 months ago, Polar Prospect (subsequent William Hill Handicap Hurdle victor at Sandown) and Decoupage (went on to win Newbury's Tote Gold Trophy) ran down the field.

With Haydock's midweek meeting now consigned to the dustbin of history, we have to wait for the weekend of Sat 20/Sun 21 for more top-class action.

But what a weekend it is. Top of Saturday's menu is the appetising **First National Bank Gold Cup Chase** at Ascot.

This limited handicap has almost unique conditions in that it is only open to horses that have not won a chase before May 2, 1998 — in other words, first and second-season chasers.

As a general rule, novices don't win this.

What you want is a contender with progressive form as a novice from the previous season, and clearly continuing on the upgrade.

> **The Becher Chase is a graveyard for Grand National prospects — it is yet to throw up the winner of the great race**

Last year's renewal wasn't up to the race's usual standard with the top-weight rated just 135. And 5-1 joint-second favourite Red Marauder, running off 122, was the lowest-rated of the past 10 winners.

But he did fit the trends having had a previous outing (only two winners of this event have landed the spoils without the benefit of a pipe-opener), being aged nine or under and being one of the fancied runners.

The race tends to fall to horses lightly-raced over hurdles before the switch to fences and Red Marauder, having only his ninth ever outing, fitted the bill on that score.

Highlight of Huntingdon's TV card the same day is the **Peterborough Chase**, a Grade 2 2m4f event.

Henrietta Knight's Edredon Bleu ran out the most impressive winner of a below-par renewal last year, having previously had a warm-up spin round Exeter in the William Hill Haldon Gold Cup.

Historically that Exeter event, together with the Desert Orchid Chase at Wincanton in late October, are the sources of the Peterborough winner.

Aintree's resurrected November meeting has now been transferred to Sunday 21. With the drastically-modified National fences no longer the feared obstacles they once were, a decent turn-out for the **Tote Becher Chase** is almost guaranteed.

Until Earth Summit upset that stats apple-cart last year, no horse had won the Becher on its first start of the season. And weight had proved difficult to carry — in the six other runnings, only Young Hustler had successfully shouldered more than 10st 6lb.

So Earth Summit, carrying 12st and never previously a winner on his seasonal reappearance, was one of the first I crossed off my list in last year's race.

Of course that well-known Law of Sod dictated that he should run out the oh-so-easy 6-1 winner, although the result was due in no small part to the moodiness of favourite and runner-up Samlee, together with the wayward jumping of Ottowa and Cavalero.

Just three finished, which told you how uncompetitive the Becher was . . . and strongly suggested the form should be treated with a healthy dollop of caution.

And so it proved: Earth Summit failed to score in four further runs, nor did runner-up Samlee trouble the judge in his subsequent outings. In fact, of the eight that started the Becher Chase, only Shanagarry and the now-deceased Ottowa managed a win at all last season.

This isn't an ideal punting race with just one winning favourite to date. If you must have a bet, restrict yourself to an animal with proven stamina — all seven winners of the Becher Chase had previously collected a chase over at least 3m1f.

Another point to bear in mind is that no horse has won the race twice, which counted against Samlee last year.

One final note is to repeat the advice that the Becher is a graveyard for Grand National prospects — it is yet to throw up the winner of the great race.

If you are searching for National clues, wait until Saturday 27 and Newbury's piece de resistance, the extended 3m2f **Hennessy Cognac Gold Cup**. In recent years

National heroes Party Politics and Rough Quest have used the Hennessy as the spring-board to Aintree success.

What's more, the race often throws up genuine Gold Cup contenders and the Hennessy's 42-strong role of honour reads like a Who's Who with hooves.

That said, Burrough Hill Lad (1984) was the last horse to win both races, but we will never know if Teeton Mill, last year's Hennessy winner, would have followed in those hallowed footprints as serious injury robbed him of his Blue Riband chance.

The profile of a typical Hennessy winner is straightforward — you are looking for a progressive, relatively unexposed chaser, preferably at the bottom of the handicap and the top of the betting.

Suny Bay, the 1997 winner, was the exception that proves the rule, defying an official rating of 162 and a burden of 11st 8lb.

Six of the last 10 have carried 10st 5lb or less, while nine of the last 10 winners have been sent off 10-1 or shorter. No winner in the past decade has been aged more than nine.

So nine-year-old Teeton Mill, the 5-1 second favourite and lumbered with exactly 10st5lb, fitted the trends to a tee.

The Badger Beer Chase has often been a useful Hennessy pointer and Teeton Mill won it off a very similar mark to Coome Hill two years previously

The last three Hennessy heroes came into the race with a penalty for winning their warm-up race, so don't let that put you off.

In fact, this decade only Wellington wizard Martin Pipe (with Chatam in 1991) has won the race with a horse making its seasonal appearance.

Principal supporting race on the Newbury card is the Grade 2 **Long Distance Hurdle**.

Princeful broke the mould by being the first winner without the benefit of a previous run that season.

He was sent off 6-1 third favourite and landed the spoils thanks in no small part to odds-on hot-pot Marello's flop. But this is normally a good race for the market leaders — in the nine runnings to date, six jollies have obliged.

Newbury's **Gerry Feilden Hurdle** is now a limited handicap so I am wary that analysing the trends could be misleading.

Similar comments apply to Newcastle's **Fighting Fifth Hurdle** the same day which has now changed from a limited handicap to a conditions event.

December

The festive month kicks off with a mouth-watering double-header courtesy of Sandown and Chepstow (Sat 4).

Queen Mother Champion Chase aspirants will be out in force in Sandown's feature, the 2m **Mitsubishi Shogun Tingle Creek Chase**, which is always a cracking spectacle.

Five of the 13 who lined up for the Queen Mother also ran in the Tingle Creek, making the Sandown race the second most important two-miler in the calendar.

With the retirement of Viking Flagship and Martha's Son, the tragic loss of One Man and an injury to Ask Tom, last year's renewal lacked an established star.

But, in beating a classy field of new pretenders, Direct Route, fit from a run round Exeter in the Haldon Gold Cup, again demonstrated that jumping is the name of the game when it comes to top-class chases over the minimum trip.

Direct Route's prep was a big pointer — all but two of the previous 10 winners had already had an outing. And the Haldon Gold Cup is the most popular warm-up — four of the five English-trained winners contested the Exeter race.

The Tingle Creek may be the purists' highlight, but the big punters get stuck into the 2m **William Hill Handicap Hurdle**.

And last year they really got stuck in with a monster plunge on Martin Pipe's Blowing Wind. Punters had clearly taken note of Pipe's tip-top record in the race — he has landed it five times in the last decade.

But, for once, those who joined the Pipe bandwagon got a nasty Good chill as McCoy's mount struggled into fourth behind 16-1 shot Polar Prospect.

That was the second shock result in as many years, following hot on the heels of Major Jamie's 25-1 1997 upset.

A closer examination of the trends would have rung warning bells over Blowing Wind. The biggest concern was the 12st he had to shoulder — of the previous 10 winners, only Land Afar in 1993 had successfully carried more than 11st.

It was also Blowing Wind's seasonal debut and only one of the past 10 winners had managed a first-time-out success (the Pipe-trained Balasani in 1991).

Polar Prospect fell into the favoured five and six-year-old age bracket, and like seven of the previous 10 winners, was in his first season outside novice company.

Across the Severn Bridge Chepstow's

card revolves around the **Rehearsal Chase**, the recognised trial for the Welsh National later in the month. The race has been plagued by small fields in recent years but it normally pays to side with that man Pipe again. He could only manage second in 1998 with Dom Samourai — but that was hardly surprising given the subsequent Gold Cup exploits of winner See More Business.

We have an excellent Cheltenham/Haydock double-header on the middle Saturday (11) of the month.

Last year I warned that Cheltenham's **Bonusprint Bula Hurdle**'s record as a trial for hurdling's Blue Riband was nothing short of disastrous. 12 months down the line little has changed. Relkeel's Champion Hurdle odds were halved after the injury-prone gelding won the Bula for the second year on the trot. But the talented 10-year-old did not even make the big one in March.

A niggling injury robbed Cyfor Malta of the opportunity to follow up his Murphy's win with victory in the **Tripleprint Gold Cup**, the big handicap chase of the day.

Chances are that he would have emulated Senor El Betrutti 12 months earlier in bagging both races.

The two big handicaps are inexorably linked. Four of the last nine winners came from the Murphy's and for further proof just look at the 1998/99 form book — Simply Dashing and Dr Leunt, second and third in the Murphy's, finished second and fourth in the Tripleprint.

Even without Cyfor Malta, the all-conquering Pipe-McCoy team still won the Triple-print, courtesy of the diminutive Northern Starlight. He fitted the trends on the age front, being at the lower end of the seven-to-nine-year-old bracket.

He also came into the race on the back of a third in Ascot's First National Bank Chase — highlighted as a key trial here last year.

Up at Haydock the big one is the **Tommy Whittle Chase**, a three-mile conditions event bedevilled by small fields. Suny Bay followed up his Edward Hanmer win by beating Earth Summit at level weights, a reversal of the 1998 Grand National form.

If the race had been a handicap, Earth Summit would have received the best part of a stone in weight, which explains why Suny Bay was sent off the 4-11 favourite.

It is time the Tommy Whittle was changed to a limited handicap to encourage bigger fields and a more punter-friendly shape to the race. Newbury's Gerry

Feilden Hurdle has been transformed by such a switch.

Your final chance to stock up with some pre-Christmas lolly comes at Ascot on Sat 18 and the big race of the day, the **Betterware Cup**, is a must-bet affair.

In the last 20 years just four winners have not started first or second favourite, so keep following the money and you won't go wrong. More specifically still, the recent trend is for in-form, second-season chasers landing the spoils.

Ascot's three miles takes some getting, and only Raymylette of recent winners had not previously scored over the trip.

Tamarindo was an expensive Pipe flop behind Torduff Express in this event last year but stats anoraks would have swerved the favourite because the Betterware is one of the few big races Pipe has yet to win.

Half an hour earlier on the same card, the **Smurfit Long Walk Hurdle** is invariably a top-class event. Last year's running was no exception, attracting an outstanding field of the best staying hurdlers around.

Princeful was the first winning favourite since 1985, but would probably have lost out to Deano's Beeno in a thrilling finish had Tony McCoy, riding the latter, not been worried out of using his stick by the prospect of yet another whip ban.

Be quick about thanking your mad aunt for the tasteless matching nylon tie-and-socks combo because Boxing Day's fare offers some of the best action outside the Cheltenham Festival.

The main event is Kempton's **Pertemps King George VI Chase** (Mon 27), jumps racing's mid-winter mountain peak.

In recent years this particular summit has been as white as they come with Teeton Mill, last year's victor, following in the hoof-prints of those other dashing greys, Desert Orchid and One Man. Unfortunately, an injury sustained in the Gold Cup will prevent Teeton Mill from becoming yet another back-to-back King George winner.

So whose name will join the illustrious band of previous winners? History can give us a few pointers. Favourites have a solid record in this traditional Christmas cracker — six of the last 10 have obliged.

Winning chase form over a variety of distances is also a common thread linking King George heroes. It seems the race requires a fine balance between speed and stamina.

French trainer Francois Doumen did not have a runner in the

DECEMBER TRAINER FORM

Trainer	Wins	Runs	%
M Pipe	90	425	21
D Nicholson	76	330	23
N Henderson	60	211	28
Mrs M Reveley	56	233	24
P Hobbs	48	248	19
Miss H Knight	40	185	22
P Nicholls	36	178	20
N Twiston-Davies	36	253	14
K Bailey	31	202	15
O Sherwood	30	171	18

1998 King George but any cross-Channel raider of his demands respect as he has given us Brits a stuffing four times in the past decade.

Doumen has been sent the talented Unsinkable Boxer and if the gifted handler can keep the ex-Martin Pipe chaser from bursting blood vessels, the 10-year-old could develop into a leading contender.

Put the winner of the **Feltham Novices Chase**, earlier on Kempton's Boxing Day card, straight into your notebook. The beast is usually destined for the top.

Highlight of the second leg of Kempton's meeting is the **Pertemps Christmas Hurdle** (Tue 28), the mid-season timber championship. The race has suffered in recent years from small fields and 1998 was no exception, the topically-named winner French Holly beating just four rivals.

Ferdy Murphy's gelding was promoted to 6-1 for the Champion Hurdle after his Kempton romp. But, in common with all the recent winners, French Holly could not break the Christmas jinx in Cheltenham's big one, eventually finishing third. The last horse to complete the double was Kribensis and that was back in 1989/90.

On recent form, the same day's **Coral Welsh National** at Chepstow is only about even-money to beat the weather.

Kendal Cavalier was the second double-figure priced winner in the last two renewals . . . but six of the previous Welsh Nationals had fallen to the favourite.

Martin Pipe farms this race. Admittedly, he has often applied the machine gun technique with over 20 runners in the last decade, but he has won four of the eight runnings during that period, as well as sending out six placed horses.

Last year's **Finale Junior Hurdle** on the same card was a disappointing affair but this event is usually worth keeping an eye on for Triumph Hurdle clues.

Northern racegoers after a quality end to the Millennium's sport should head to Wetherby for the **Castleford Chase** (Tues 28), a limited handicap over the minimum trip. Cumbrian Challenge caused something of an upset in this event last year by beating Direct Route. The gelding's improved form was down to the use of a tongue strap.

It was that result, among others, that persuaded the Jockey Club to make the declaration of tongue straps mandatory.

About time too. Now let's have sectional timing on every course, weighing of racehorses before each race and some accurate going reports from clerks of the course.

As the 20th century draws to a close for the rest of us, the Jockey Club big wigs are dragging themselves out of the 19th.

Jumps racing ushers in the new Millennium with a hangover . . . and a day off.

Saturday 1st will be a blank day (unless you fancy a trip to Tramore in Ireland), leaving Uttoxeter, Plumpton and Exeter to pick up the baton on Sunday 2nd.

Cheltenham tries to raise the temperature with a televised Bank Holiday card on Monday 3rd, but it's the Sun-sponsored day at Sandown (Sat 8) that really gets things hotting up again.

Get there if you possibly can because it is a cracking card that almost always beats the weather.

The **Sun King Of The Punters Tolworth Hurdle** is invariably one of the best novice events over timber outside the festivals. Last year's one-two, Behrajan and Hidebound, may not subsequently have matched the heady heights reached by the likes of French Holly, Grey Shot and Upgrade from the previous year, but they remain two hurdlers to follow.

The Tolworth usually falls to a form horse, so I suggest you limit yourself to the first or second favourite.

The big race over fences is the **Anthony Mildmay Peter Cazalet Memorial Handicap Chase** which often produces a live National contender — the likes of Rhyme 'N Reason, Mr Frisk and Party Politics have recently used this event as a stepping stone to Aintree glory.

Like Him Of Praise 12 months earlier, Eudipe failed to add to that record, but was gaining deserved reward for a series of excellent placed-efforts in top class staying chases including the Hennessy (twice) and Scottish National.

Top-weight Eudipe broke the stranglehold that the 10st7lb-11st7lb weight range had had on the Sandown marathon.

Over in Ireland the same day, the massive pot that the sponsors put up for Leopardstown's **Ladbroke Handicap Hurdle** always ensures a massive field.

And, to no-one's surprise for a bookie-backed cavalry charge, the Ladbroke is fiendishly difficult.

To start with, there seem to be more plots in the race than Guy Fawkes could shake a stick at. Half the field — or more — will have been laid out for this.

And, after a rare victory for the favourite in 1998, last season's Ladbroke reverted to type — 25-1 winner Archive Footage ensuring the sponsors' satchels were once again

EU ONLY WIN ONCE . . . Eudipe finally succeeded in Sandown's Cazalet Chase

bulging. A great spectacle, but definitely **NOT** a race to have a bet in.

Cornerstone of Ascot's meeting the following weekend is the **Victor Chandler Chase** (Sat 15), which has quickly established itself as the best two-mile handicap chase in the calendar.

Last season Ascot was waterlogged so, for the third time since 1994, the race was moved. This time the lucky beneficiary was Kempton the following Saturday where Call Equiname made his belated seasonal debut to win a shade cosily from Get Real.

Call Equiname was only the third in the race's short history to carry more than 11st to victory — a big pointer to his chance in the Queen Mother Champion Chase at Cheltenham, which of course he won.

That again underlined the star-studded nature of the Victor Chandler — other winners since Desert Orchid took the inaugural running in 1989 include Viking Flagship, Martha's Son, Waterloo Boy and Sybillin.

Call Equiname was the first horse to win the VC on his seasonal debut, but, at nine, did fit the favoured seven-to-nine-year-old age bracket. When Kempton is not

lucky enough to inherit the Victor Chandler Chase, pride of place on the card is the **Tote Lanzarote Handicap Hurdle** (Sat 22), another bookie-sponsored event that is never easy to solve.

15-8 shot Tiutchev's victory last season was a rare victory for us punters because he was only the fourth winning favourite since 1980.

Other Lanzarote trends are a bit thin on the ground but the winner almost invariably gets a short-priced quote for the following month's big handicap hurdle, Newbury's Tote Gold Trophy.

Haydock's **Intercity Champion Hurdle Trial** (Sat 22) has been nothing of the sort since 1994, principally because it clashes with the **AIG Europe Champion Hurdle** at Leopardstown the following day (where you can expect to see Istabraq putting the final touches to the defence of his Cheltenham crown).

The **Peter Marsh Limited Handicap Chase** on the Haydock card is billed as a Gold Cup prep but that is also a bit of a misnomer with only Jodami (1993) successfully using it for that purpose in recent times.

Last year's hero Gen-

JANUARY TRAINER FORM

Trainer	Wins	Runs	%
M Pipe	72	376	19
D Nicholson	66	282	23
Mrs M Reveley	40	219	18
N Twiston-Davies	39	248	16
Mrs J Pitman	29	164	18
P Nicholls	26	126	21
P Hobbs	24	193	12
Miss H Knight	23	154	15
N Henderson	23	170	14
Miss V Williams	20	62	32

69

eral Wolfe, winning the Peter Marsh for the second consecutive year, didn't even go to Cheltenham.

Anyone who thought Deano's Beeno was a good bet for the Stayers' Hurdle after he won the **Tote Premier Long Dist-ance Hurdle** hadn't read last year's Sun Guide.

I pointed out then that Haydock's third big race of the day was yet another grave-yard for Cheltenham aspirants, and Deano's Festival flop proved the point in spades.

Nigel Twiston-Davies' Moorish chased home Deano's Beeno at Haydock and the Gloucestershire trainer's record in this race is second to none.

January closes with a last chance for Festival hopefuls to test their mettle on Cheltenham's unique undulations before the main event just six weeks later.

The **Pillar Property Chase** (Sat 29) has become a highly significant Gold Cup trial since it was opened up to all comers in 1991 and last year's renewal did nothing to undermine that view despite only attracting five runners.

The Gold Cup one-two, See More Business and Go Ballistic proved no match for Cyfor Malta in the Pillar, suggesting Martin Pipe's six-year-old would have played a leading part had injury not cruelly curtailed his season.

In the **Marchpole Cleeve Hurdle**, run over an extended 2m5f, make sure your selection will get the trip — which probably means siding with a stayer dropping back in trip rather than a two-miler stepping up.

Course-specialist Lady Rebecca proved that point when out-battling Silver Wedge and Commanche Court last season.

Over at Doncaster the big-betting race of the day is the **Stakis Westgate Casino Great Yorkshire Handicap Chase** in which Major Bell caused a 20-1 upset last term.

The 11-year-old's first victory since the 1996-97 season was a blow to a firm trend that suggested in-form top-weights win this race.

If we ignore Major Bell's success, history strongly suggests we are looking for a pro-gressive chaser aged between seven and nine who made the frame on his previous start.

Previous to Major Bell, you have to go all the way back to 1983 to find a winner of this race that had not won at least twice before during the same season.

That, of course, will point you towards those at the head of the betting which is as it should be — Bob Tisdall (1988) was the only other recent winner returned at bigger than 10-1.

Keep your fingers crossed for a mild month because February is often the worst hit by the vagaries of the British weather.

Sandown's **Agfa Diamond Handicap Chase** (Sat 5) has suffered over the years from small fields and last season was no exception — for the sixth time in seven years six or fewer runners went to post.

This is not the only staying chase in the calendar that consistently struggles to pro-duce decent fields — Haydock's Tommy Whittle and Edward Hanmer are other clas-sic examples — which suggests the whole chase programme needs an overhaul by the men in grey suits at the BHB.

The big-betting heat on Sandown's high-class card is the **Tote Handicap Hurdle** where you want to keep a close eye on hors-es at the foot of the weights.

Teaatral's convincing success last sea-son means eight of the 12 winners since the race was first run in 1986 have carried just 10st2lb or less.

Stan Clarke has turned round Uttoxeter in the last couple of years and the Midlands track now boasts some really decent days, the **Singer and Friedlander National Trial** card (Sat 5) being a case in point. Expect some big Aintree pointers there this season, especially now the course manage-ment have introduced a valuable bonus scheme which ensures a decent turnout.

The big draw at Newbury the following weekend is Britain's richest handicap hur-dle, the **Tote Gold Trophy** (Sat 12).

And unlike some of the season's other big handicaps over timber, this is no pin-sticker's paradise.

Rather, it is a race which can easily be reduced to just a handful of runners.

Recent renewals of this prestigious event have tended to fall to an up-and-coming hur-dler carrying between 10st10lb and 11st5lb.

Decoupage, a seven-year-old in his first season outside of novice company and off 11st dead, duly fitted the bill last season.

Winning form leading up to the race is a favourable, if not essential, attribute, but more important is your selection's position in the betting market.

You have to go back to Jamesmead, the 11-1 winner in 1988, to find some kind of shock result.

If the Tote Gold Trophy winner does hump more than 11st 5lb round, back him for the Champion Hurdle without a second's hesitation.

The only two horses who have successfully carried that kind of weight in the race's 28 runnings have been Make A Stand and Persian War, both subsequent champions.

Chief attraction on Newbury's supporting card is the **Mitsubishi Shogun Game Spirit Chase**, a 2m1f conditions event that has been on the wane when it comes to providing Queen Mother pointers.

But keep an eye on the closing bumper which is increasingly being used by the top trainers as a final trial for their youngsters before Cheltenham.

A week after Newbury it is Newcastle's turn to take the limelight, courtesy of the marathon **Tote Eider Chase** (Sat 19).

Hollybank Buck provided a rare Irish success in this event last season but should have been on anyone's shortlist, even though he was considerably helped by the departure of favourite Young Kenny at the first fence.

Hollybank Buck carried less than 11st which put him the right side of a barrier only Seven Towers (1997) has broken in recent years.

He also had scored earlier that same season — a stat common to all of the last 10 winners.

And his SP of 10-1 was in line with previous winning odds — Eider shocks are rare.

The same Saturday there should be plenty of Cheltenham clues at Ascot's former midweek fixture.

The feature is the **Mitsubishi Shogun Ascot Chase**, which last season heralded the successful return to action of Teeton Mill after a niggling muscle complaint saw him miss his intended Gold Cup prep run in the Pillar Chase three weeks previously.

Run over 2m3f110yds, an unfamiliar trip for most chasers, this event ought not be the greatest from a betting point of view, but is, in fact, invariably won by the favourite, usually the highest rated on official figures.

On the same card pay close attention to the **Reynoldstown Novice Chase**, a key prep race for the Royal & SunAlliance Chase, while at Warwick there is usually some Cheltenham-bound talent also on display.

Kempton's **Racing Post Chase** day (Sat 26), positioned just over two weeks before Cheltenham, is often cited as the most significant Festival pointer in the whole jumps calendar.

That was certainly the case in 1994 when no fewer than **EIGHT** Festival winners were fine-tuned at Kempton. 1995 saw three winners and two seconds warm up there, while in 1996 five subsequent Cheltenham seconds were on show.

1997 threw up just one winner while a firm-ground 1998 drew a blank.

But we were back on the winning streak last season courtesy of Katarino and Anzum, so pay particularly close attention to the Kempton form when you come to picking your Festival fancies.

The feature 3m Racing Post Chase suffers from the alternative attraction provided by Haydock's more valuable Greenalls Trial the same afternoon (yet another example of where the chase programme could do with some major surgery).

Ten of the last 11 Racing Post Chase heroes carried 10st7lb or more, while recent winning form is also crucial — all of this decade's winners had either won or been placed second previously in their successful season.

The betting market is also a reliable guide — only Mudahim (1997) and Zeta's Lad (1993) were sent off at double-figure prices.

David Nicholson has had four and Martin Pipe two of the past seven **Rendlesham Limited Handicap Hurdle** winners, a recognised Stayer's Hurdle trial.

Triumph Hurdle aspirants line up for the **Voice Newspaper Adonis Juvenile Hurdle** — Katarino and Mysilv have completed the double in the last five years.

Up at Haydock the **Greenalls Trial Handicap Chase** continues to blow hot and cold as far as the big one at Aintree is concerned.

Last season's winner, Young Kenny, was not even entered for the Grand National although he is already a leading fancy for the first one of the new Millennium after taking the Scottish version last April.

And second home Fiddling The Facts was backed down to favourite for Aintree only to fall at Becher's second time round when still travelling well.

Young Kenny won from 9lb out of the handicap, once again illustrating that in marathon slogs a low weight is a real bonus.

Only Party Politics (1993) has successfully carried more than 11st3lb in the last 15 years.

71

For die-hard jumps fans everywhere, March is the month to savour. The skirmishes of the previous four months have been little more than precursors to National Hunt's battle royal, the three-day Cheltenham Festival (Tues 14–Thurs 16).

Three days earlier, Sandown is the place to visit if you want to get some spare cash in the bank. The big race is the **Sunderlands Imperial Cup Handicap Hurdle** (Sat 11) which has a tasty carrot in the form of a £50,000 bonus courtesy of the sponsors.

That is the sum on offer for any horse that can win both the Imperial Cup and any race the following week at Cheltenham.

Just two horses — Olympian and Blowing Wind — have achieved the double, and both were trained by that man Martin Pipe. So the first rule here is to pay close attention to any of the Wellington Wizard's runners.

His Dr Jazz was sent off the 2-1 favourite last season but could only manage a close third to Irish raider Regency Rake.

With just two previous outings last season under his belt, the Rake conformed to the lightly-raced profile of the majority of Imperial Cup winners. You're best off going for something with less than four previous outings.

Last year's winner also weighed in when it came to how much he had to shoulder — only Blowing Wind has humped more than 11st to victory in the last decade.

Regency Rake was a little on the old side though — he was only the third horse in the last 12 years not to be aged five or six.

CHELTENHAM FESTIVAL

If you can't get excited about the heady three days in the middle of March that are jump racing's very own Olympics, you might want to check your own pulse.

Championship races and fiendishly competitive handicaps blend together to give the ultimate test of hurdler, chaser . . . and punter.

Beware! Enormous fields of horses boasting top-class form can leave the head spinning. Cheltenham can all too easily turn into a financial quagmire for even the most studious punter.

But follow my race-by-race analysis and hopefully you'll stay afloat . . . and relieve the ghastly bookies of a few quid rather than contributing to their next trips to Barbados.

First, a few general pointers.

Trainers. Martin Pipe had a relatively disappointing 1999 Festival with just two winners . . . but ignore him at your peril.

The previous two years the champion trainer saddled a modern-day record four winners. Pipe now needs just one more success to equal the legendary Vincent O'Brien's tally of 25 Festival victories. The other handlers with outstanding records are Nicky Henderson (20 career wins) and David Nicholson (17).

Jockeys. It's 'Richard Dunwoody first, the rest nowhere' when it comes to current riders' records at Cheltenham. Woody has 18 career winners at the Festival, stretching back to a double on Von Trappe and West Tip as a 21-year-old in 1985. He has only drawn a blank three times since.

Next best is Irishman Charlie Swan, whose career Festival tally stands at 13. However, Pipe-backed Tony McCoy threatens to overtake them both soon.

Though the Ulsterman only got off the mark at the 1996 meeting, he has already notched an incredible 11 successes.

Form. While the results of some Festival races will leave you wondering if the form book is written in Sanskrit, winning form is crucial. Indeed, you could do worse than eliminate all Cheltenham runners that hadn't scored on their previous run.

In 1998, 13 of the 20 winners at the meeting had won their last start, while last season 11 of the 20 fell into that bracket.

The Irish. Five winners probably didn't do Ireland's powerful squad full justice in 1999. Three years earlier the Irish carried off a record-equalling seven races at the meeting.

And you can bet your last punt that the Shamrock raiders won't be returning empty-handed this season for the first time since 1989 — if only because of Istabraq in the Champion Hurdle (although it's worth pointing out that the last time the Irish completed the big-race double by winning the Tote Gold Cup two days later was in 1950).

The average number of Irish-trained Festival winners since 1977 is 3.6.

Favourites. Since the war 258 jollies have won the 964 Festival races, a measly strike rate of just under 26%. Even without anal-

MARCH TRAINER FORM			
Trainer	Wins	Runs	%
M Pipe	87	534	16
Mrs M Reveley	56	289	19
P Nicholls	38	197	19
N Twiston-Davies	38	313	12
D Nicholson	37	295	13
N Henderson	36	213	17
P Hobbs	36	235	15
K Bailey	34	181	19
O Sherwood	33	149	22
Miss H Knight	33	215	15

ysing the SP records, the favourites' success rate is a lot lower than the one-in-three which is the rule of thumb for racing generally.

You only have to remind yourself of the ultra-competitive nature of the races, especially in the last 20 years (in the 1960s sometimes only four or five used to pitch up for the Gold Cup), to see why favourites have such a poor record.

Age: Stick with youth. The percentage of winners above the age of nine is very small. Rule out 10-year-olds and upwards and those without a recent win under their belt and you will quickly whittle down several of the fields to a manageable size.

Now on to the action.

Tuesday 14th

Citroen Supreme Novices Hurdle

Last year I warned of the rotten record Irish-trained favourites had in the curtain raiser, and Cardinal Hill's departure two out 12 months ago (he would almost certainly have only managed second to Hors La Loi III had he stood up) continued the run. Just three favourites have obliged in the last 21 years.

French import Hors La Loi III became the first non-five or six year-old to win in the last decade (and the first four-year-old to oblige since 1973).

But in common with all but two of the last ten winners, he had already won a hurdle and finished first or second on his last outing.

History also suggests the winner is highly likely to have had no more than five runs beforehand, of which just one or two will have been since January. He will also have shown winning form in a race of at least 12 runners.

Coincidentally — and it is surely nothing more — the last three winners have been the second-favourite, although don't let this stat deceive you into thinking the Festival opener is an easy race to solve.

It's usually a nightmare.

Finally, although the Supreme Novices is classified as a championship event, in reality few winners prove to be top class and it is similar to the Triumph in that the race can leave its mark on a horse.

But I have a sneaking suspicion Hors La Loi III will buck that trend.

Guinness Arkle Chase

Fortunately the two-mile championship event for novice chasers is a much more punter-friendly event — or at least it was until Flagship Uberalles sprang an 11-1 shock last year. The Flagship was the longest priced winner since Waterloo Boy in 1989 but, as the second five-year-old to win this in the last two years, he had a crucial 8lb weight allowance (as did runner-up Tresor De Mai).

However, a new weight-for-age scale will put a stop to the advantage enjoyed by precocious young steeplechasers — particularly those bred in France. Under the new scale, which takes effect from October, the allowance is only 4lb.

So don't necessarily expect the five-year-old trend to continue. In fact, before arch trend-buster Martin Pipe started the fashion of importing youngsters from France, the Arkle had been the preserve of six and seven-year-olds.

Make sure your selection was a winner last time out — that would have eliminated six of the 14-strong field last season.

Also don't be totally put off if your fancy hasn't had a foot-perfect jumping career to date. Four of the last 10 winners had failed to get round in one of their previous outings.

But chasing experience counts. Only Nakir (1994) had fewer than three previous sighters over fences.

Smurfit Champion Hurdle

A trend prevalent in the 1980s is re-establishing itself — namely, that the same old horses came back for second or even third wins.

And the beast who is single-handedly responsible for that is Istabraq, a genuine champion among Champion Hurdlers. Surely only injury can prevent Aidan O'Brien's brilliant gelding being Braq in business for a third time.

However, there is one horse who already has serious pretensions to the hurdling crown and that is Hors La Loi III.

This French-bred, now back with his original trainer Francois Doumen, won last season's Supreme Novices Hurdle in a time almost two seconds faster than Istabraq took to demolish his Champion Hurdle rivals for the second year running.

If everything goes to plan, Hors La Loi III will certainly go to Cheltenham as one of the more fancied runners, which history suggests he will need to be — the last double-figure price winner was 50-1 shocker Beech Road in 1989.

However, his age is against him — he will be seeking to become the first five-year-old to win since the legendary See You Then in 1985.

The optimum age is clearly six or seven.

Only three winners have come from outside this range since 1982. Vast hurdling experience is not necessary, as classy ex-Flat performers Alderbrook and Royal Gait, both of whom were novices, have shown.

But recent winning form over timber is crucial. Of the last 10 winners, only Granville Again secured the crown without a hurdle victory to his name that season.

William Hill National Hunt Chase

Betty's Boy's 25-1 shocker underlined what a miserable punting race this is, with little rhyme or reason to a bookie-friendly run of results.

Just one favourite has obliged in the last 20 years, and other recent winning SPs of 20-1 and 16-1 suggest this race is best given the big swerve.

If you must have a bet, pick out a light-weight — in the last two decades only Unguided Missile and Antonin have successfully humped round over 11st.

Fulke Walwyn Kim Muir Challenge Cup

The amateurs' big race on the opening day is another best confined to the 'too difficult' file. Avoid the favourites was the best advice the Sun guide could produce over the last two years, which would at least have steered you clear of 6-1 jolly Linden's Lotto who could only manage seventh last season.

It probably wouldn't have helped you, however, to select 20-1 scorer Celtic Giant, although he was a lightweight who again excelled in this notoriously tricky event for punters.

Stakis Casino Hcap Hurdle

Heavily-backed favourite Galant Moss attempted to give the dependable Pipe-McCoy combination another knockout blow following Unsinkable Boxer's demolition job in this event 12 months previously.

Unfortunately for the thousands of punters who climbed aboard the bandwagon, Galant Moss could only finish third behind 12-1 shot Generosa.

The winner fitted the trends by being a six-year-old running from within the handicap.

Although this staying event usually attracts a monster-sized field, you can normally whittle it down by eliminating any runner over eight or out of the handicap.

Applying those criteria would have chucked out half the 24-strong field last year in one fell swoop.

Royal & SunAlliance Novices Hurdle

If you thought the first day's final three races were nigh-on impossible to solve, help is at hand with day two's opening race, highlighted here 12 months ago as the **BEST** Festival event for backers.

And nothing has changed after heavily-punted Barton maintained his unbeaten record in great style . . . and maintained the outstanding record of favourites in this race. Six of the last 10 have done the business.

When the jolly doesn't oblige, it's almost always the second, third or fourth-favourite who does, so strap on your betting boots and wade in after the money.

Five and six-year-olds are the favoured age group — all bar two winners since 1985 have hailed from that age bracket.

Queen Mother Champion Chase

Here's another race that has been generally punter friendly down the years.

Last season's event looked a wide open affair beforehand with the tragic death of One Man leaving a gaping hole in the two-mile chasing ranks.

Even so, it was 7-2 second favourite Call Equiname who landed the spoils, with the second and third places falling to market-leader Edredon Bleu and third-favourite Direct Route respectively.

The market is certainly the best guide to this race — although there are some other useful pointers.

Make sure your pick has top-class winning 2m chase form to his name. Invariably recent champion chasers have been multiple scorers in the build-up to the big race.

But don't be put off by a horse with a blemish on their jumping record. Four of the last 10 winners had failed to complete in at least one prep run.

Champions also have a habit of doubling up.

So, if Paul Nicholls manages to get the rather fragile-legged Call Equiname back to Cheltenham fit and firing, he must enter the reckoning, even though at 10 he will be on the old side (of the last 10 winners only Martha's Son has been that old).

The optimum age is eight — five of the last 10 winners have come from this category.

Coral Cup Hcap Hurdle

Just seven runnings of this 2m5f race give us little history to work on. But one thing is clear — horses need to be laid out for this 30-

CALL COLLECT . . . Queen Mother Champion chaser Call Equiname in winning action

runner cavalry charge. Last year's hero Khayrawani had had just three outings since finishing runner-up in this event 12 months previously.

He was burdened with 11st3lb, and only Time For A Run has carried more. The other five winners have come from the foot of the handicap, so that is probably the best place to start your search for the winner.

This is also traditionally an event the Irish dominate. They have won it three times and in 1999 were responsible for the first **FIVE** home.

Royal & SunAlliance Chase
In this space last year I confidently predicted the eclipse of Florida Pearl in the Gold Cup, reasoning that SunAlliance winners have a dreadful record in chasing's Blue Riband and that the Irish challenger looked suspect on the stamina front as well.

You don't need to be Nostradamus to predict that Looks Like Trouble, the 1999 SunAlliance winner, will also fall short of Gold Cup standard.

In showing much improved form for his victory, Looks Like Trouble would never have won had favourite Nick Dundee not fallen so disastrously three out.

Three jollies have obliged in the last 10 renewals, and during that same period Looks Like Trouble (16-1) has been the longest-priced winner, so the market is, in the main, a reliable guide.

Ascot's Reynoldstown Chase is often a useful pointer — last season's winner Lord Of The River went on to finish runner-up in the SunAlliance.

National Hunt Chase
Another race confined to amateurs and also, at four miles, the longest at the Festival.

Add in the fact that it is restricted to horses without a win over hurdles or fences on May 1 of the previous year and you have a slippery combination which hardly inspires confidence when it comes to having a bet.

So, not surprisingly, wise backers sit this one out. If you do insist on getting involved, make sure you side with one of the better-known pilots. With a huge gulf between the decent riders and the also-rans, jockey bookings are usually one of the best guides.

Mildmay Of Flete Hcap Chase
Majadou's popular 16-length success gave master trainer Martin Pipe his second success here in the last three runnings. The winner was again making full use of the 8lb weight allowance five-year-old chasers received from the elders, a loophole that has now been tightened.

He was the first favourite to oblige since 1985 and with the recent role of honour reading like a horror story for punters (66-1, 33-1 and 20-1 included), let's hope last year's result has turned the tide.

Majadou was the second novice in the last five years to win, but they are the exceptions that prove the rule — this race has been a successful hunting ground for seasoned handicappers.

Majadou also became the fourth horse in the last 10 years to hump round exactly

11st. Five of the other six winners carried less, so top-weights are best avoided.

Champion Bumper NH Flat Race

Monsignor's 50-1 upset kept this prize this side of the Irish Sea for just the second time since it was inaugurated in 1992.

In all honesty, the only pointer to the winner's chance lay in his trainer's name — Mark Pitman. This young handler had already become a leading exponent in the bumper sphere by last year's Festival, even though it was only his first full season training. He now has his formidable mother as part of his team and should really start going places in the next few years. Keep an eye on him.

Back to the bumper and this race is often the scene of a monster gamble which goes astray.

Last year Monsignor foiled a massive plunge on runner-up Golden Alpha while Tiananmen Square and Joe Mac have been other talking horses which have expensively failed to justify the hype.

Willie Mullins (three out of the last four winners) is the trainer to note.

Thursday 16th

Elite Racing Triumph Hurdle

Two years ago Sun Guide readers were told: "the market has been no sort of guide to the destination of this race."

Last year I added: "Keep your wallet closed, the stats paint a glum picture when it comes to the Triumph."

Murphy's Law immediately swung into operation and Katarino became only the **SECOND** winning favourite since 1974 and just the sixth since 1965 when the race was first run at Cheltenham (for you historians, the others were Mysilv (1994), Attivo (1974), Moonlight Bay (1973), Boxer (1971) and Coral Diver (1969)).

More normally, with a maximum field of unexposed youngsters tearing off at a suicidal pace, the form book goes out of the window.

As far as the market leader winning again this time around, I don't expect lightning to strike twice!

But, with the benefit of hindsight, Katarino's subsequent exploits in the Punchestown mud (his fifth hurdle win on the trot) suggest Nicky Henderson's gelding is just a little bit special.

Because it is invariably run at a breakneck pace, stamina is always the trump card

for any Triumph candidate. Also make sure your selection has already tasted success over hurdles (preferably in the hurly-burly of a large field).

You have to go back to 1990 and Rare Holiday to find the last maiden to land this race.

The winner usually had some decent Flat form to his name before turning his attention to the winter game. But he won't have been over-busy in the build-up to the Triumph — five previous runs is the maximum.

This is often a race in which the Irish field a formidable presence. But be wary if the ground is riding on the fast side — most of their raiders' winning form will be on soft ground.

Bonusprint Stayers' Hurdle

For the third time in the same number of years, this event was won by a handicapper (this time Anzum), suggesting a non-vintage renewal.

And with winning SPs of 40-1, 16-1 and 20-1 (twice) in the last eight years, it has hardly been punter-friendly either.

What clues we can glean are these:

The majority of winners had decent form in top-class staying races (although not necessarily recent) and are aged between six and eight.

Notwithstanding the fact the Irish haven't won this since 1995, the Shamrock army has a very decent record (Aidan O'Brien's Le Coudray was just pipped last season, but last year's Sun Guide readers would have been alerted to the fact he couldn't win because he was only five).

The previous year's Royal & SunAlliance Novices Hurdle often throws up a leading contender while, surprise, surprise, Martin Pipe is the trainer with the best record (even though his Deano's Beeno was an expensive flop last year).

Tote Cheltenham Gold Cup Chase

While this is the undisputed Blue Riband of steeplechasing, it doesn't necessarily take a champion to win it, just a horse that is suited by the unusual demands that Cheltenham provides and who acts on the prevailing ground.

The roll of honour is littered with horses who were nothing more than decent handicappers. Into that category you can certainly put recent winners Cool Dawn, Mr Mulligan, Cool Ground, Garrison Savannah and Norton's Coin.

The first thing to bear in mind when examining the field for the first Gold Cup of the new Millennium is that you are pretty safe eliminating previous winners.

L'Escargot in the early 1970s was the last horse to win back-to-back Gold. And no horse has ever regained his Gold Cup crown after losing it. It seems the great race, a gruelling test of 21 fences which places unique demands on its contestants, also tends to bottom them.

So history is very much against See More Business, set alight by first-time blinkers last year, or for that matter Cool Dawn (1998 winner) or Imperial Call (1996).

Age is also the key. Eight to 10-year-olds have been dominant in recent years. Since 1982, the only horse younger than this to triumph was seven-year-old Imperial Call.

You can forget the veterans — the last horse older than 10 to triumph was What A Myth in 1969, though 12-year-old Tied Cottage was disqualified in 1980.

Novices don't win either, so you should concentrate on second or third-season chasers with top class form.

And those who will get the trip.

One factor all the winners have in common is they had all proved beforehand they stayed the Gold Cup distance or further.

Experience of Cheltenham's unique course is also vital.

Of last year's field, Double Thriller, who raced too keenly for his own good, could improve to become a leading candidate for this season's race — providing his first fence spill in the National has not left too much of a mental or physical scar and he learns how to settle a bit better.

Christie's Foxhunter Challenge Cup

This is the third of the three amateurs-only races at the Festival and was won last season by highly-rated Castle Mane who could well develop into a leading Gold Cup candidate this season.

The seven-year-old displayed winning form over three miles on his previous outing — a feature common to nine of the previous 10 winners.

West Country point-to-point maestro Richard Barber, the major backer of Paul Nicholls, has won this race four times in the last eight years, so if he has a runner, pay it due respect.

Grand Annual Hcap Chase

Former smart hurdler Space Trucker became the second favourite on the trot to land this, but was a rare success for the Irish here. It demonstrated that this race is becoming a pretty punter-friendly affair, with only Uncle Ernie (20-1) and Snitton Lane (33-1) providing much joy for the layers since 1990.

The other eight winners have started at 15-2 or less.

Space Trucker ran off 123 last year which is slightly lower than the usual 130-plus rated animals that have such an excellent record in this event.

Pay close attention to novices fielded by either Martin Pipe or David Nicholson.

Cathcart Challenge Cup Chase

This is invariably one of the weakest races of the Festival, restricted to first or second-season chasers which as a result almost always throws up a winner aged seven or eight.

Last year's hero, Stormyfairweather, fitted the bill on the age score, and was well supported at 9-1 because he also had solid form over two-and-a-half miles which is another strong trend.

Make sure you have Stormyfairweather and third home Edelweiss Du Moulin on your short list for the Murphy's at Cheltenham in November — the Cathcart is the key when it comes to analysing that race.

Vincent O'Brien County Hcap Hurdle

The curtain falls on the Festival in descending gloom with the traditionally tricky 'getting-out stakes' which last year saw a major plunge on Decoupage foiled by 10-1 shot Sir Talbot.

Which is as the script suggests — only one favourite has obliged in the last decade although rank outsiders rarely go in.

Sir Talbot's featherweight 10st was also in keeping with the stats.

They strongly suggest you want to side with an animal in the bottom half of the handicap.

As a five-year-old, he also came from the favoured five-to-six age bracket.

If that doesn't help you find the winner, don't panic . . . there are only 363 days until battle recommences!

Anyone with any stamina left after the rigours of Cheltenham must be on steroids, but the masochists head for Uttoxeter (Sat 18) for the 4m2f **Marstons Pedigree Midlands National**.

Progressive Young Kenny landed a gamble in this event last year, beating subsequent Grand National third Call It A Day.

Kenny should be on everyone's short list for Aintree 2000.

The start of the turf Flat season tends to overshadow the jumping game until the Grand National meeting takes centre stage.

Every year we point out the perils of relying on Cheltenham form at Aintree.

Last season, there was a three-week break between the two festivals, enough for the likes of Flagship Uberalles, Hors La Loi III, Barton, Khayrawani and Istabraq to score at both venues.

The gap is three weeks again this season so it's reasonable to expect the really good horses to complete the notable double.

However the point still remains valid — treat form from Cheltenham's undulating track with caution when analysing races on Aintree's flat, tight circuit — particularly where a horse had a hard race at Cheltenham.

The traditional highlight of the opening day of the Aintree meeting is the **Martell Cup Chase** (Thurs 6), billed as a valuable consolation event for horses beaten in the Gold Cup.

However the race has suffered in recent years through Friday's 2m4f Mumm Melling Chase which more often than not results in the Martell Cup attracting a small field.

Last year was a classic case with just five facing the starter. And the point of taking Cheltenham form too literally was immediately underlined with Gold Cup runner-up Go Ballistic and Mildmay of Flete winner Majadou finishing second last and last respectively!

Considering there are rarely more than 10 runners, the Martell Cup is a dire race for favourite-backers. Victory for unfancied 11-1 shot Macgeorge extended a miserable run for the market leaders which stretches back to 1992 when the last one, Kings Fountain, obliged.

Friday's **John Hughes Handicap Chase**, run over the unique National fences, is never short of numbers (mainly because it is limited to horses rated 145 or below) and last year Listen Timmy saw off 19 rivals for the valuable first prize.

The winner's 14-1 starting price was back to the norm following a win for 7-2 favourite Cyfor Malta 12 months earlier.

This is not a great race for well-fancied runners, so approach it with caution. That said, 9-2 favourite Gris D'Estruval was travelling as well as anything two out when breaking down fatally.

An hour earlier the **Mumm Melling Chase** often falls to the Queen Mother winner. But again, taking Cheltenham form too literally proved expensive with Direct Route, third home in the Queen Mother, turning round form with Call Equiname.

Notwithstanding that reverse, it normally pays to stick with the Queen Mother winner — four of the previous nine runnings have gone that way.

Friday's supporting card includes the 3m1f **Mumm Mildmay Novice Chase** which is usually an informative event.

The 1999 running confirmed that view with 100-30 favourite Spendid winning in a fast time. Spendid had previously been badly hampered when pulled up in the SunAlliance Chase at Cheltenham and he looks destined for top honours this season.

Saturday is, of course, National day and the big race tends to overshadow everything else.

But a decent supporting card includes the 2m4f **Martell Aintree Hurdle** which usually sees Champion Hurdle runners renew rivalry. Istabraq confirmed — if confirmation was needed — that he is the best hurdler around by some margin with a very cheeky win in this event last season.

Stick to the fancied runners here — shocks are as rare as defeats for Istabraq.

Martell Grand National

If there's one race in the calendar that still manages to capture the public's imagination then it's the National.

Of course we won't have the Des and Jenny show to keep us amused in the build-up, with Mrs P deciding she's had enough of training, while old smoothie Des has defected to ITV for the sort of transfer fee more normally associated with premiership footballers.

But what we still have is undeniably the greatest racing spectacle the world can offer — all the thrills and spills of more than 30 runners tackling four-and-a-half miles and 30 beautifully prepared spruce fences as they hurtle towards a place in racing history.

That's all very well, I can here you say, but what about finding the winner?

Well, contrary to popular belief, the National is **NOT** a lottery. In fact it is one of the best races of the year in which to have a bet. And here's why.

The recent modifications to the fences,

the drainage system and the entry requirements mean that the outcome is relatively easy to predict.

From a punting point of view, the National has become very much like any other long-distance chase — but at four-and-a-half miles a bit longer — and in most of those you can chuck out over half the field using various simple rules.

Start by eliminating any non-stayers. Among recent winners, only Rough Quest (1996) did not have previous winning form over at least three-and-a-quarter miles.

Don't be taken in by that ridiculous theory that two-and-a-half milers can somehow throttle back and win over a two-mile longer trip — history paints a very different picture. Out-and-out stayers win this race, full stop.

Then stick to the class animals. The winner normally comes from within the handicap proper or is an improving horse just a pound or two wrong.

Of course, last year's hero, Irish raider Bobbyjo, was a stone out of the handicap but that really was an exception.

With hindsight he was let in very lightly by the English handicapper, considering he had won the previous season's Irish Grand National, and he duly slammed a weak-looking field with his task made all the easier by the failure of some of the more fancied runners.

But weight does stop National contenders. Horses right at the top of the handicap have to be exceptional. The last one to carry more than 11st to victory was Corbiere in 1983.

You can now whittle down the field even further.

Go for experience. Don't be tempted by novices or those in their first season outside of novice company.

Your fancy needs to be at least eight and have a rock-solid jumping record. Of recent winners, only Rough Quest had fallen in the same season.

Recent winning form is not essential. But the last 10 winners finished in the first two at some point in the season leading up to their successful National bid.

The Hennessy, Welsh National and Gold Cup are often key races, as increasingly is Uttoxeter's Midlands National.

Call It A Day, subsequently third at Aintree, finished second to Young Kenny in that last-named event last season. Young Kenny skipped Aintree to put on an exhibition round in the Scottish National.

He is being aimed at the big one this season and, if any horse had 'future Grand National winner' written all over him, it is Young Kenny.

Ayr's **Stakis Casinos Scottish National** (Sat 15) is once again just a week after Aintree and that proximity inevitably causes it to suffer in terms of quality.

Last season Young Kenny was the first winning favourite since Red Rum in 1974. He demonstrated yet again that you need a fresh horse for this event, having not run since winning at Uttoxeter four weeks earlier.

Five of the last 10 Scottish National winners had already been successful in decent handicaps at around four miles, more proof that in marathon chases staying really is the name of the game.

The 2m **Scottish Champion Hurdle** on the same card is a limited handicap that usually attracts a small but select field.

Shocks are very rare as the longest winning SP of 11-2 in the last 10 years demonstrates.

Sandown's **Whitbread Gold Cup** (Sat 29) has long been the last hurrah for the jumps and is now officially recognised as such by marking the end of the campaign (May's action, including Haydock's **Swinton Hurdle** (Sat 6) is now part of the summer jumping season).

Sandown specialist Eulogy sprang something of a shock when winning the 1999 Whitbread, with National winner Bobbyjo predictably flopping after his Aintree exertions (Mr Frisk (1990) remains the only horse to have completed the National-Whitbread double).

Eulogy also continued a good run for lightweights.

Only Life Of A Lord has successfully humped more then 11st round, while six winners in the last decade have come from out of the handicap.

It's also worth noting that no favourite has won since Docklands Express in 1991.

So there you have it.

Wrap up warm and enjoy another jumps season. It promises to be a good one.

Best of luck.

APRIL TRAINER FORM

Trainer	Wins	Runs	%
M Pipe	80	402	20
P Nicholls	40	161	25
Mrs M Reveley	37	208	18
D Nicholson	35	214	16
N Twiston-Davies	35	256	14
P Hobbs	33	201	16
K Bailey	33	217	15
M Hammond	26	183	14
G Richards	24	143	17
N Henderson	23	175	13

BIG-RACE DATES '99-'00

OCTOBER

2 Sat	Chepstow	........Free Hcap Hurdle (2m 110yds)
21 Thu	Wincanton	........Desert Orchid South Western Pattern Chase (2m 5f)
30 Sat	Wetherby	..........Charlie Hall Chase (3m 1f)
	Wetherby	..........Tote West Yorkshire Hurdle (3m 1f)
	Wetherby	..........Wensleydale Hurdle (2m)

NOVEMBER

2 Tue	Exeter	..............William Hill Haldon Gold Cup Chase (2m 1f 110yds)
6 Sat	Wincanton	........Tanglefoot Elite Hurdle (2m)
	Chepstow	........Tote Silver Trophy Hcap Hurdle (2m 4f 110yds)
	Chepstow	........Mermaid Quay Rising Star Novices' Chase (2m 3f 110yds)
10 Wed	Worcester	........Worcester Novices' Chase (2m 7f 110yds)
12 Fri	Cheltenham	......The Sporting Index Cross Country Chase (3m7f)
13 Sat	Cheltenham	......Murphy's Gold Cup Hcap Chase (2m 4f 110yds)
14 Sun	Cheltenham	......Mitsubishi Shogun November Novices' Chase (2m)
		........................Murphy's Draughtflow H'cap Hurdle (2m)
19 Fri	Ascot	................Coopers & Lybrand Ascot Hurdle (2m 4f)
20 Sat	Ascot	..............First National Bank Gold Cup Hcap Chase (2m 3f 110yds)
21 Sun	Aintree	..............Becher Chase (3m 3f)
	Huntingdon	......Peterborough Chase (2m 4f 110yds)
27 Sat	Newcastle	......Newcastle Building Society Fighting Fifth Hurdle (2m)
	Newbury	..........Hennessy Cognac Gold Cup Hcap Chase (3m 2f 110yds)
	Newbury	..........Equity Financial Gerry Feilden Hurdle (2m 110yds)

DECEMBER

3 Fri	Sandown	..........Bovis Crowngap Winter Novices' Hurdle (2m 6f)
4 Sat	Sandown	..........Mitsubishi Shogun Tingle Creek Trophy Chase (2m)
	Sandown	..........William Hill Hcap Hurdle (2m 110yds)
	Sandown	..........Extraman Henry VIII Novice Chase (2m)
	Chepstow	........Rehearsal Hcap Chase (3m)
11 Sat	Cheltenham	......Bonusprint Bula Hurdle (2m 1f)
	Cheltenham	......Tripleprint Gold Cup Hcap Chase (2m5f)
	Cheltenham	......Bristol Novices' Hurdle (3m 110yds)
18 Sat	Ascot	................Smurfit Long Walk Hurdle (3m 1f 110yds)
	Ascot	................Betterware Cup Hcap Chase (3m 110yds)
	Ascot	................Book of Music Novices' Chase (2m 3f 110yds)
	Ascot	................Mitie Group Kennel Gate Hurdle (2m 110yds)
27 Mon	Wetherby	..........Rowland Meyrick Hcap Chase (3m 110yds)
	Kempton	..........Pertemps City Network Feltham Novices' Chase (3m)
	Kempton	..........Pertemps King George VI Chase (3m)
28 Tue	Wetherby	..........Castleford Chase (2m)
	Chepstow	........Welsh National Hcap Chase (3m 5f 110yds)
	Kempton	..........Pertemps Christmas Hurdle (2m)

JANUARY

3 Mon	Cheltenham	......Unicorn Hcap Chase (2m5f)
8 Sat	Sandown	..........Sun 'King of the Punters' Tolworth Hurdle (2m 110yds)
	Sandown	..........Mildmay & Cazalet Hcap Chase (3m 5f 110yds)

13 Thu	Wetherby	....	Towton Novice Chase (3m 110yds)
15 Sat	Ascot	....	Victor Chandler Hcap Chase (2m)
	Newcastle	......	Northern Echo Dipper Novices' Chase (2m 4f)
	Warwick	....	Tote Warwick National Hcap Chase (3m 5f)
21 Fri	Ascot	....	P M L Lightning Novice Chase (2m)
22 Sat	Kempton	....	Tote Lanzarote Hcap Hurdle (2m)
	Haydock	....	Peter Marsh Hcap Chase (3m)
	Haydock	....	Intercity Champion Hurdle Trial (2m)
	Haydock	....	Tote Premier Long Distance Hurdle (2m 7f 110yds)
29 Sat	Cheltenham	......	Marchpole Cleeve Hurdle (2m 5f 110yds)
	Cheltenham	......	Pillar Property Chase (3m 1f 110yds)
	Cheltenham	......	Wragge & Co Finesse Four-Year-Old Hurdle (2m 1f)
	Doncaster	....	River Don Novices' Hurdle (2m 4f)
	Doncaster	....	Stakis Westgate Casino Great Yorkshire Hcap Chase (3m)

FEBRUARY

5 Sat	Sandown	....	Agfa Diamond Hcap Chase (3m 110yds)
	Sandown	....	Tote Sandown Hcap Hurdle (2m 6f)
	Sandown	....	Scilly Isles Novices' Chase (2m 4f 110yds)
	Uttoxeter	....	Singer & Friedlander National Trial Hcap Chase (4m2f)
	Wetherby	....	Rossington Main Novice Hurdle (2m)
9 Wed	Chepstow	....	Persian War Premier Novices' Hurdle (2m 4f 110yds)
	Chepstow	....	John Hughes Grand National Trial (3m 2f 110yds)
12 Sat	Newbury	....	Mitsubishi Shogun Game Spirit Chase (2m 1f)
	Newbury	....	Tote Gold Trophy Hcap Hurdle (2m 110yds)
19 Sat	Ascot	....	Mitsubishi Shogun Ascot Chase (2m 3f 110yds)
	Ascot	....	Gerrard Group Reynoldstown Novices' Chase (3m 110yds)
	Newcastle	......	Tote Eider Hcap Chase (4m 1f)
	Warwick	....	Michael Page Group Kingmaker Novices' Chase (2m)
24 Thu	Wincanton	....	Axminster 100 Kingwell Hurdle (2m)
	Wincanton	....	Jim Ford Challenge Cup (3m 1f 110yds)
26 Sat	Kempton	....	Mitsubishi Shogun Pendil Novices' Chase (2m 4f 110yds)
	Kempton	....	Racing Post Hcap Chase (3m)
	Kempton	....	Money Store Rendlesham Hcap Hurdle (3m 110yds)
	Kempton	....	Weekender Dovecote Novices' Hurdle (2m)
	Kempton	....	Voice Newspaper Adonis Juvenile Novices' Hurdle (2m)
	Haydock	....	Greenalls Grand National Trial Hcap Chase (3m 4f 110yds)

MARCH

1 Wed	Chepstow	....	Prestige Novice Hurdle (3m)
4 Sat	Doncaster	....	Grimthorpe Hcap Chase (3m2f)
	Doncaster	....	Mitsubishi Shogun Trophy Hcap Chase (2m 3f 110yds)
11 Sat	Sandown	....	Sunderlands Imperial Cup Hcap Hurdle (2m 110yds)
14 Tue	Cheltenham	......	Guinness Arkle Challenge Trophy Novices' Chase (2m)
	Cheltenham	......	Smurfit Champion Hurdle Challenge Trophy (2m 110yrds)
	Cheltenham	......	Citroen Supreme Novices' Hurdle (2m 110yrds)
15 Wed	Cheltenham	......	Royal SunAlliance Novices' Chase (3m 1f)
	Cheltenham	......	Queen Mother Champion Chase (2m)
	Cheltenham	......	Royal & SunAlliance Novices' Hurdle (2m 5f)
	Cheltenham	......	Coral Cup Hcap Hurdle (2m5f)
	Cheltenham	......	Weatherbys Champion Bumper (2m 110yds)
16 Thu	Cheltenham	......	Elite Racing Club Triumph Hurdle (Novices') (2m 1f)
	Cheltenham	......	Bonusprint Stayers Hurdle (3m 110yds)
	Cheltenham	......	Tote Cheltenham Gold Cup Chase (3m 2f)
	Cheltenham	......	Vincent O'Brien County Hcap Hurdle (2m 1f)

| 18 Sat | Uttoxeter .... | Marstons Pedigree Midlands National Hcap Chase (4m 2f) |
| 25 Sat | Newbury .... | Hoechst Roussel Vet Panacur EBF Mares' NH Final (2m 5f) |

APRIL

5 Wed	Ascot	Grosvenor Casinos Long Distance Hurdle (3m)
6 Thu	Aintree..............	Glenlivet Anniversary Novices' Hurdle (2m 2f 100yds)
	Aintree..............	Sandeman Maghull Novices' Chase (2m)
	Aintree..............	Martell Cup Chase (3m 1f)
	Aintree..............	Barton Ans Guestier Top Novices' Hurdle (2m 110yds)
7 Fri	Aintree..............	Mumm Mildmay Novices' Chase (3m 1f)
	Aintree..............	Belle Epoque Sefton Novices' Hurdle (3m 110yds)
	Aintree..............	Mumm Melling Chase (2m 4f)
	Aintree..............	Martell Mersey Novices' Hurdle (2m 4f)
8 Sat	Aintree..............	Martell Aintree Hurdle (2m 4f)
	Aintree..............	Martell Grand National Chase (4m 4f)
	Aintree..............	Martell Red Rum Hcap Chase (2m)
	Aintree..............	Martell Champion Standard Bumper (2m 110yds)
15 Sat	Ayr	Stakis Casinos Scottish National Hcap Chase (4m 1f)
	Ayr	Samsung Electronics Scottish Champion Hcap Hurdle (2m)
	Ayr	Edinburgh Woollen Mill Champion Novices' Chase (2m 4f)
20 Thu	Cheltehham	Silver Trophy Chase (2m 5f)
29 Sat	Sandown	Whitbread Gold Cup Hcap Chase (3m 5f 110yds)

MAY

| 6 Sat | Haydock .... | Crowther Homes Swinton Hcap Hurdle (2m) |

JUNE

| 3 Sat | Stratford .... | Horse And Hound Cup Hunters' Chase (3m 4f) |

BIG IRISH DATES

DECEMBER
26 Sun	Leopardstown ..	Denny Gold Medal Chase
27 Mon	Leopardstown ..	Paddy Power Hcap Chase
28 Tue	Leopardstown ..	Ericsson Chase

JANUARY
8 Sat	Leopardstown ..	Ladbroke Hcap Hurdle
23 Sun	Leopardstown ..	A.I.G Europe Champion Hurdle
27 Thu	Gowran Park	Cuisine de France Thyestes Chase

FEBRUARY
| 6 Sun | Leopardstown .. | Hennessy Cognac Gold Cup |

APRIL
| 24 Mon | Fairyhouse........ | Jameson Irish Grand National |
| 25 Tue | Fairyhouse........ | Power Gold Cup |

MAY
2 Tue	Punchestown ..	BMW Hcap Chase
3 Wed	Punchestown ..	Heineken Gold Cup
4 Thu	Punchestown ..	IAWS Champion 4 Year Old Hurdle
4 Thu	Punchestown ..	Ballymore Properties Champion Stayers Hurdle
4 Thu	Punchestown ..	Triple Print Novice Chase

AUGUST
| 2 Wed | Galway.............. | Compaq Galway Plate Hcap Chase |
| 2 Wed | Galway.............. | Guinness Galway Hcap Hurdle |

Super SunForm

1 Wincanton, 2m 5f, £32,000, good, Oct 25 1998.
Vixen Desert Orchid S.W. Pattern Chase (Ltd Hcap)
1. **Super Tactics** (10-3) 5-2 fav although running from 2lb out of the handicap was always close up, and, taking it up at halfway, was clear approaching the third last.
2. **Bertone** (10-2) 4-1 held every chance until being put in his place by the winner.
3. **Gales Cavalier** (10-3) 4-1 weakened from halfway.
4. **Senor El Betrutti** (10-9) 9-1 made some progress at halfway before fading.
12l, 6l, 12l. (R Alner) 7 ran.

2 Ascot, 2m, £25,000, good to soft, Oct 31 1998.
United House Construction Hcap Chase
1. **Dontleavethenest** (10-5) 4-1 fav was held up early doors before making progress to lead two fences out and keeping on for a decisive victory.
2. **Chief's Song** (11-1) 8-1 having been prominent, lost his position four fences out before rallying to good effect.
3. **Mandys Mantino** (11-9) 12-1 made a decent enough seasonal debut, always in touch before running on at the one pace.
4. **Dr Bones** (10-2) 14-1 in front from the third, was headed two out.
3l, 4l, ¹/₂l. (R Curtis) 11 ran.

3 Wetherby, 3m 1f, £20,000, good, Oct 31 1998.
Tote West Yorkshire Hurdle (Grade 2)
1. **Marello** (11-2) 8-13 fav made it 11 wins from 13 outings, leading three out for a facile success.
2. **Nigel's Lad** (11-7) 11-2 fit from the Flat, was the early leader but proved no match for the winner once headed and was eased on the run to the line.
3. **Kerawi** (11-7) 13-2 looked in need of the run and, having disputed the lead until three out, faded.
11l, 4l, 1¹/₂l. (Mrs M Reveley) 6 ran.

4 Wetherby, 3m 1f, £30,000, Oct 31 1998.
Charlie Hall Chase (Grade 2)
1. **Strath Royal** (11-3) 14-1 was allowed to dictate the pace and kept up the gallop in great style all the way to the line.
2. **Boss Doyle** (11-3) 2-1 was upsides the winner when clobbering the fourth last which put paid to his chance.
3. **Simply Dashing** (11-3) 9-4 was always prominent and looked a danger three out only to find himself outpaced.

4. **Escartefigue** (11-11) 7-4 fav was under pressure from four out and was beaten soon after.
2l, 4l, 13l. (O Brennan) 5 ran.

5 Exeter, 2m 1f, £30,000, soft, Nov 3 1998.
William Hill Haldon Gold Cup Chase (Ltd Hcap)
1. **Lake Kariba** (10-6) 9-2 was never far away, and taking it up at the eighth fence, galloped home for a convincing success.
2. **Direct Route** (10-11) 5-2 looked a real danger until tiring over the last two fences.
3. **Or Royal** (11-10) 6-1 was never in with a shout and could only plug on at his own pace.
dis, 8l. (P Nicholls) 7 ran.

6 Chepstow, 2m 3f 110yds, £20,000, good to soft, Nov 7 1998.
Mermaid Quay Rising Stars Novices' Chase (Grade 2)
1. **Irbee** (11-4) 11-8 fav was really impressive, jumping well and leading five fences from home. He ran out a very comfortable winner.
2. **Calon Lan** (11-0) 12-1 led to halfway from where the winner asserted.
3. **Moor Lane** (11-0) 7-2 was prominent until weakening under pressure in the closing stages.
10l, 9l. (P Nicholls) 6 ran.

7 Chepstow, 2¹/₂m 110yds, £30,000, good to soft, Nov 7 1998.
Tote Silver Trophy Hcap Hurdle
1. **Mister Morose** (10-5) 10-1 landed a bit of a gamble having been off the course for the best part of two years. Leading four out, he was soon clear and won as he liked.
2. **L'Opera** (10-4) 8-1 appeared to be struggling three out but did pick up although it was all in vain.
3. **Buckhouse Boy** (11-2) 16-1 dropped six furlongs from home before rallying.
4. **Brave Tornado** (10-1) 15-2 ran in snatches before keeping on.
5. **Shooting Light** (11-3) 4-1 jt fav was always prominent until weakening in the closing stages.
13l, 2¹/₂l, 1l, 4l. (N Twiston-Davies) 10 ran.

8 Wincanton, 3m 1f 110yds, £25,000, good, Nov 7 1998.
Badger Beer Hcap Chase
1. **Teeton Mill** (11-4) 4-1 made an eyecatching debut in handicap company, leading on the bit three fences out and soon clear.
2. **Menesonic** (10-3) 3-1 fav stayed on from two out but never looked like troubling the winner.

83

3. **Jultara** (9-11) 10-1 faded, having been prominent for much of the way.
8l, 6l. (Miss V Williams) 7 ran.

9 Wincanton, 2m, £20,000, good, Nov 7 1998.
Tanglefoot Elite Hurdle (Ltd Hcap) (Grade 2)
1. **Grey Shot** (10-3) 10-11 fav rapped the first but was clear after the second and never looked in danger.
2. **Bellator** (10-10) 11-4 fit from the Flat, was always fighting a losing battle.
3. **Dreams End** (10-8) 9-1 was soon struggling.
10l, dis. (I Balding) 4 ran.

10 Cheltenham, 2¹/₄m 110yds, £75,000, good to soft, Nov 14 1998.
Murphy's Gold Cup Hcap Chase (Grade 3)
1. **Cyfor Malta** (11-3) 3-1 fav was 10lb higher than when winning the John Hughes in April but it made little difference. Left in the lead by the fall of Senor El Betrutti, he ran on well before idling up the hill.
2. **Simply Dashing** (11-12) 8-1 looked held until his stamina came into play. He almost gave the winner a real fright.
3. **Dr Leunt** (10-0) 7-1 made progress from rear before running on one pace.
4. **Challenger Du Luc** (11-13) 11-1 was 11lb higher than when winning this event two years ago and, although making progress from the rear, could never land a serious blow.
5. **Mandys Mantino** (10-8) 7-1 was also never able to put in a serious challenge.
1l, 7l, 17l, ³/₄l. (M Pipe) 12 ran.

11 Cheltenham, 2m 5f, £25,000, good, Nov 15 1998.
Stakis Casinos Intermediate Hcap Hurdle
1. **Lady Rebecca** (10-13) 5-2 fav was most impressive in her first handicap, never far away, and leading four out for an easy success.
2. **Dromhale Lady** (9-11) 25-1 did little wrong from just out of the handicap but found the winner in a different league.
3. **Melody Maid** (11-0) 11-1 held every chance two out.
4. **The Butterwick Kid** (10-1) 16-1 behind early, made progress from halfway before keeping on.
7l, 1¹/₄l, 10l. (Miss V Williams) 13 ran.

12 Cheltenham, 2m, £20,000, good, Nov 15 1998.
Greyhounds As Pets November Novices' Chase (Grade 2)
1. **Mister Morose** (11-0) 5-2 fav making his debut over fences, hit the third last before flying up the hill.
2. **Dines** (11-4) 4-1 looked set to score with his head in front at the last but was then outpaced by the winner.
3. **Desert Mountain** (11-0) 11-4 was always in the front rank before fading.
2¹/₂l, 3l. (N Twiston-Davies) 5 ran.

13 Cheltenham, 2m 110yds, £40,000, good, Nov 15 1998.
Murphy's Draughtflow Hcap Hurdle
1. **Grey Shot** (11-5) 11-4 fav would have been running off a 6lb higher mark if this had not been an early-closing race and he made full use of the lenient treatment, leading for much of the trip and running on well to shake off the persistent runner-up.
2. **Tyrolean Dream** (10-0) 16-1 was always in the front rank and made the winner pull out all the stops.
3. **Fatehalkhair** (10-0) 33-1 was behind early, before making progress from halfway and keeping on over a trip short of his best.
4. **Decoupage** (10-5) 7-1 improved from the rear before running on at one pace.
5. **Polar Prospect** (10-5) 16-1 was hampered early and was never nearer.
2l, 3l, ³/₄l, 7l. (I Balding) 16 ran.

14 Haydock, 3m, £40,000, good to soft, Nov 18 1998.
Edward Hanmer Memorial Chase (Ltd Hcap)
1. **Suny Bay** (11-10) 2-1 fav won this race for the second consecutive year, and was impressive to boot, disputing the lead all the way before scooting clear after the last.
2. **Escartefigue** (11-6) 3-1 stayed on willingly under a forceful ride.
3. **Strath Royal** (10-5) 8-1 looked the first beaten but then found fresh reserves and was galloping on well at the finish.
4. **See More Business** (11-12) 4-1 looked fairly well tuned up for his seasonal debut. Upsides at the third last, he made a bad mistake and that put paid to his chance.
5l, 1¹/₄l, nk. (S Sherwood) 6 ran.

15 Ascot, 2¹/₄m, £25,000, good to soft, Nov 20 1998.
Pricewaterhousecoopers Ascot Hurdle (Grade 2)
1. **Juyush** (11-0) 10-1 fav from the Flat, showed a good turn of foot to lead late on.
2. **Turnpole** (11-0) 9-1 tracked the leaders before taking it up two out, only to be made to look rather one-paced by the winner.
3. **Castle Sweep** (11-0) 7-1 made an encouraging return, having missed the whole of the previous season. Leading briefly entering the straight, he was then undone by a lack of fitness.
4. **Kerawi** (11-0) 11-4 fav was a disappointment, weakening from four out.
6l, ¹/₂l, 5l. (J Dunlop) 7 ran.

16 Aintree, 3m 3f, £40,000, good to soft, Nov 21 1998.
Tote Becher Chase (Hcap)
1. **Earth Summit** (12-0) 6-1 won for the first time on his seasonal debut, leading from halfway, and having been left clear, had little more than a schooling round for the last mile.
2. **Samlee** (10-6) 2-1 fav ran very disappointingly, never travelling at any stage.
3. **Back Bar** (10-0) 50-1 was 19lb wrong and completed the course in his own time.
16l, dis. (N Twiston-Davies) 8 ran.

17 Ascot, 2m 3f 110yds, £45,000, good, Nov 21 1998.

First National Bank Gold Cup Hcap Chase

1. **Red Marauder** (10-11) 5-1 maintained an unbeaten record over fences with an eyecatching victory, tracking the leaders until taking it up smoothly at the last.
2. **Chief's Song** (11-9) 9-1 didn't seem to be going well until improving from the rear in the last half mile. However, he could not match the winner's finishing burst.
3. **Northern Starlight** (11-10) 20-1 is only small so had no easy task under his big weight. Making most, he only weakened once headed at the last
4. **Ashwell Boy** (11-5) 12-1 was never placed to challenge despite vigorous assistance from the saddle.
11l, 3l, 11l. (N Mason) 11 ran.

18 Huntingdon, 2¹/₂m 110yds, £29,000, good, Nov 21 1998.

Independent Insurance Peterborough Chase (Grade 2)

1. **Edredon Bleu** (11-1) 5-1 benefited from a tongue-strap to make all for a fluent success over his ideal trip.
2. **Bertone** (11-1) 13-2 ran to form, making a couple of errors which told in the end.
3. **Or Royal** (11-5) 5-4 fav was the pick on the best of his form but showed he is becoming rather untrustworthy.
14l, 12l. (Miss H Knight) 6 ran.

19 Worcester, 2m 7f 110yds, £20,000, heavy, Nov 24 1998.

Tote Placepot Birthday Worcester Novices' Chase (Grade 2)

1. **Ocean Hawk** (11-1) 10-3 was helped considerably by the fall of Lord Of The River who had beaten him at Exeter. Not a natural jumper, his stamina enabled him to win this.
2. **Tiraldo** (10-13) 7-2 was left in the lead two out but could not maintain the gallop on the run to the line.
3. **Farfadet V** (10-13) 4-1 was struggling from halfway.
F. **Lord Of The River** (11-5) 5-2 fav was travelling as well as anything when getting the final open ditch all wrong.
4l, dis. (N Twiston-Davies) 7 ran.

20 Newbury, 2m 110yds, £30,000, good to soft, Nov 28 1998.

Equity Financial Gerry Feilden Hcap Hurdle (Grade 2)

1. **Wahiba Sands** (11-0) 6-1 set off in front and despite making mistakes was never headed.
2. **Decoupage** (10-7) 7-1 gave an excellent account of himself, always prominent but just unable to overhaul the winner.
3. **Zafarabad** (11-10) 3-1 fav stayed on from the rear.
4. **Lady Rebecca** (11-0) 9-2 was running over a distance short of her best and it was little surprise she was made to look rather one-paced.
5l, nk, 2¹/₂l. (M Pipe) 10 ran.

21 Newbury, 3m 110yds, £20,000, good to soft, Nov 28 1998.

Solaglas Long Distance Hurdle (Grade 2)

1. **Princeful** (11-7) 6-1 tracked the leaders before being hard ridden to lead close home.
2. **Shooting Light** (11-0) 11-1 forced the issue from four out but was eventually outstayed by the winner.
3. **The Proms** (11-4) 7-2 was short of pace down the back straight before staying on.
4. **Pharanear** (11-0) 10-1 was in need of his first run since injuring a leg in the Gold Card Final in 1997.
5. **Marello** (11-2) 5-6 fav ran a stinker, never travelling well. Her trainer blamed the soft ground.
2¹/₂l, 12l, 1³/₄l, 22l. (Mrs J Pitman) 6 ran.

22 Newbury, 3¹/₄m 110yds, £70,000, good to soft, Nov 28 1998.

Hennessy Cognac Gold Cup Hcap Chase (Grade 3)

1. **Teeton Mill** (10-5) 5-1 showed what a blot on the handicap he was, turning what had looked beforehand to be a competitive race into a procession. Always travelling ominously well, he took it up three out for a runaway success.
2. **Eudipe** (10-13) 14-1 ran up to his best form, always close up and leading from halfway until collared by the winner.
3. **Fiddling The Facts** (10-9) 9-1 faced a baptism of fire on her handicap debut but ran a cracker.
4. **Boss Doyle** (11-7) 8-1 was hard ridden from the 16th but could never land a blow.
5. **Him Of Praise** (10-2) 28-1 was never nearer.
P. **Seven Towers** (10-0) 3-1 fav was the subject of a massive gamble but ran no sort of race at all.
15l, 6l, 10l, 8l. (Miss V Williams) 16 ran.

23 Newcastle, 2m £35,000, good to soft, Nov 28 1998.

Newcastle Building Society 'Fighting Fifth' Hurdle (Grade 2)

1. **Dato Star** (11-8) 13-8 fav was never far away and, leading three from home, ran on readily.
2. **French Holly** (11-8) 10-3 ran encouragingly, staying on all the way home.
3. **Midnight Legend** (11-0) 16-1 was returning from a long lay-off and benefited from the run.
5l, 8l. (J Jefferson) 6 ran.

24 Fairyhouse, 2m, £30,000, good to soft, Nov 29 1998.

Avonmore Waterford Royal Bond Novice Hurdle (Grade 1)

1. **Alexander Banquet** (12-0) 4-1 chased the leaders before making headway to lead close home.
2. **Cardinal Hill** (11-9) 4-5 fav led three out before being hard ridden and headed close home.
3. **To Your Honour** (12-0) 5-1 held every chance from two out but could pull out no extra when required.
hd, 2¹/₂l. (W P Mullins) 8 ran.

25 Fairyhouse, 2¹/₂m, £40,000, good to soft, Nov 29 1998.

Chiquita Drinmore Novice Chase (Grade 1)

1. **Promalee** (11-10) 4-1 prominent throughout, led

approaching the last and then ran on strongly.

2. **Foxchapel King** (11-2) 7-2 led from four out until headed before the last.

3. **Inis Cara** (11-10) 6-1 made headway from three out before keeping on well enough.

4. **Feathered Leader** (11-5) 5-2 fav blundered at the sixth and could never land a serious blow thereafter.

3½l, 1l, sh hd. (Miss F M Crowley) 9 ran.

26 Fairyhouse, 2¹⁄₂m, £40,000, good to soft, Nov 29 1998.
Avonmore Waterford Hatton's Grace Hurdle (Grade 1)

1. **Istabraq** (12-0) 1-5 fav had little more than an exercise canter, leading three out for a facile win.

2. **Nomadic** (11-4) 11-2 could never trouble the winner.

3. **Master Beveled** (11-9) 8-1 was made to look rather one-paced.

¹⁄₂l, 6l. (A P O'Brien) 6 ran.

27 Chepstow, 3m, £30,000, good, Dec 5 1998.
Coral Rehearsal Chase (Ltd Hcap) (Grade 2)

1. **See More Business** (11-12) 10-11 fav was 15lb higher than when winning this race last year and appeared to be in trouble when clouting the first in the straight. But he picked up well to land the spoils driven out.

2. **Dom Samourai** (10-5) 5-1 was 5lb wrong at the weights but did little wrong, leading to halfway and rallying well.

3. **Escartefigue** (11-6) 13-8 seemed to have this in the bag entering the straight but found disappointingly little off the bridle, jumping badly right to boot.

1¹⁄₂l, 8l. (P Nicholls) 3 ran.

28 Sandown, 2m, £20,000, good, Dec 5 1998.
Extraman Henry VIII Novices' Chase (Grade 2)

1. **Dines** (11-4) 9-4 jt fav prefers going right-handed and showed it here, making all.

2. **Dawn Leader** (11-4) 10-3 chased the leader all the way, but to no avail.

3. **Billingsgate** (11-7) 6-1 was always prominent but could not quicken when popped the question.

1¹⁄₂l, 3l. (P Nicholls) 5 ran.

29 Sandown, 2m, £57,000, good, Dec 5 1998.
Mitsubishi Shogun Tingle Creek Trophy Chase

1. **Direct Route** (11-7) 7-1 jumped well in rear before making eye-catching headway to lead at the last.

2. **Edredon Bleu** (11-7) 9-4 fav set off in front and was only collared at the last.

3. **Mandys Mantino** (11-7) 14-1 took closer order at the Pond Fence but just couldn't quicken when asked thereafter.

4. **Hill Society** (11-7) 7-2 ran rather in snatches before plugging on at one pace.

5. **Lake Kariba** (11-7) 9-2 was never on terms after an early mistake.

2¹⁄₂l, 2l, ³⁄₄l, ¹⁄₂l. (J Howard Johnson) 10 ran.

30 Sandown, 2m 110yds, £50,000, good, Dec 5 1998.
William Hill Hcap Hurdle

1. **Polar Prospect** (10-0) 16-1 came good after some consistent efforts, improving from midfield to lead at the last.

2. **Serenus** (10-0) 11-1 was crusing entering the straight but then couldn't find the required extra up the hill.

3. **Out Ranking** (10-0) 14-1 was taking a huge step up in class but acqutted herself well, cutting out the donkey work up front before being collared at the last.

4. **Blowing Wind** (12-0) 11-8 fav was the subject of a monster gamble but failed to deliver under his big weight, making headway too late in the day.

2l, 3l, 6l. (P Hobbs) 13 ran.

31 Punchestown, 2¹⁄₂m, £45,000, heavy, Dec 6 1998.
John Durkan Memorial Punchestown Chase (Grade 1)

1. **Imperial Call** (12-0) 13-8 made virtually all the running before keeping on well.

2. **Dorans Pride** (12-0) evens fav was always prominent but could never find the extra gear required.

3. **Bob Treacy** (11-8) 25-1 disputed the lead briefly four out before a mistake at the last, and a violent swerve left soon afterwards, sealed his fate.

4. **Manhattan Castle** (11-8) 14-1 tracked the leaders before staying on from three out.

1¹⁄₂l, 2¹⁄₂l, 15l, 5¹⁄₂l. (R Hurley) 8 ran.

32 Cheltenham, 2m 5f, £75,000, good to soft, Dec 12 1998.
Tripleprint Gold Cup Hcap Chase (Grade 3)

1. **Northern Starlight** (10-1) 15-2 made virtually all before keeping on well under a typically robust Tony McCoy ride.

2. **Simply Dashing** (11-13) 11-2 tried in a visor, had to settle for second best again at Cheltenham, running on gamely after looking out of it turning for home.

3. **Mr Strong Gale** (10-3) 9-1 was tapped for toe turning in before staying on.

4. **Dr Leunt** (10-0) 10-1 plugged on at his own pace, having lost second place turning in.

5. **All The Aces** (10-0) 12-1 running from 8lb out of the handicap, stayed on well enough from off the pace.

³⁄₄l, 7l, 1³⁄₄l, ³⁄₄l. (M Pipe) 13 ran.

33 Cheltenham, 2m 1f, £35,000, good to soft, Dec 12 1998.
Bonusprint Bula Hurdle (Grade 2)

1. **Relkeel** (11-8) 8-1 was held up in rear but made progress throughout and, jumping the last better than the runner-up, led close home.

2. **Grey Shot** (11-0) 5-2 made most of the running but couldn't quicken up the hill after rapping the last flight.

3. **Midnight Legend** (11-0) 14-1 was never far away but was outclassed by the front two.

F. **Dato Star** (11-8) 11-8 fav stumbled and fell at the fifth.

¹⁄₂l, 9l. (D Nicholson) 5 ran.

34 Haydock, 3m, £40,000, soft, Dec 12 1998.
Tommy Whittle Chase (Grade 2)
1. **Suny Bay** (10-12) 4-11 fav was favoured by the race conditions but was rather disappointing. Although leading from halfway, he was never able to assert himself on the race.
2. **Earth Summit** (10-12) 5-1 running without blinkers for the first time in five years, turned in a game performance without quite being good enough to beat the below-par winner.
3. **The Grey Monk** (11-10) 11-1 was still a bit backward, leading to halfway before dropping away.
4. **Lord Gyllene** (10-12) 10-1 was having his first run in 20 months and gradually faded.
3½l, 30l, 17l. (S Sherwood) 5 ran.

35 Lingfield, 3m, £18,500, soft, Dec 12 1998.
Arena Leisure December Novices Chase (Grade 2)
1. **Executive King** (11-0) 11-2 maintained his unbeaten record for the season, making all. He was left clear by the runner-up's mistake three out.
2. **Lord Of The River** (11-4) 6-5 fav was losing the battle when blundering at the third last.
3. **See Enough** (11-0) 25-1 was having his first run for over a year and the writing was on the wall five fences from home.
4. **Ivy Boy** (11-4) 13-8 was never dangerous.
17l, 16l, 20l. (G Hubbard) 5 ran.

36 Ascot, 2m 3f 110yds, £19,000, good to soft, Dec 19 1998.
'Book Of Music' Novices' Chase (Grade 2)
1. **Kurakka** (11-3) 7-2 put up a bold front-running performance, winning with plenty in hand.
2. **Strong Paladin** (11-3) 16-1 had no chance with the winner but won the battle for second place with a gutsy display.
3. **Billingsgate** (11-10) 3-1 jt fav was made to look a bit one-paced by the winner.
13l, 2½l. (J Gifford) 7 ran.

37 Ascot, 3m 1f 110yds, £45,000, soft, Dec 19 1998.
Smurfit Long Walk Hurdle (Grade 1)
1. **Princeful** (11-7) 11-4 fav got the better of a titanic struggle with the runner-up under a masterful ride from Richard Dunwoody, leading in the shadow of the post.
2. **Deano's Beeno** (11-7) 7-2 set off in front and gave everything but was beaten by a better horse on the day.
3. **Ocean Hawk** (11-7) 9-1 lost his pitch after a bad error at the eighth before staying on.
4. **Paddy's Return** (11-7) 5-1 was never on terms with the leaders, struggling fully a mile from home.
5. **Castle Sweep** (11-7) 11-1 made some progress from the rear but the writing was on the wall half a mile out.
½l, 30l, 27l, 4l. (Mrs J Pitman) 11 ran.

38 Ascot, 3m 110yds, £40,000, good to soft, Dec 19 1998.
Betterware Cup (Hcap Chase)
1. **Torduff Express** (10-0) 9-2 relished this test, taking things up in Swinley Bottom before forging clear for a decisive success.
2. **Callisoe Bay** (10-10) 16-1 looked likely to drop away after pecking six out but struggled on well to claim the runner-up spot.
3. **King Lucifer** (10-5) 13-2 was always with the leaders but the petrol ran out going to the last.
4. **Dr Bones** (10-1) 6-1 was never on terms after an early mistake.
18l, 4l, 22l. (P Nicholls) 7 ran.

39 Kempton, 3m, £35,000, soft, Dec 26 1998.
Network Design International Feltham Novices' Chase (Grade 1)
1. **Lord Of The River** (11-7) 11-2 had had an extensive spell of schooling since his last run and it showed, jumping well from the front for a convincing win.
2. **Spendid** (11-7) 9-4 fav tended to get too close to many of the fences and that proved his undoing.
3. **King Of Sparta** (11-7) 12-1 got the third last all wrong but was already booked for third.
4. **Executive King** (11-7) 7-2 ran no sort of race, gradually fading.
1¼l, dis, dis. (O Sherwood) 7 ran.

40 Kempton, 3m, £100,000, heavy, Dec 26 1998.
Pertemps King George VI Chase (Grade 1)
1. **Teeton Mill** (11-10) 7-2 took the step up from handicap company in his stride, never far away, leading six out before cruising to victory.
2. **Escartefigue** (11-10) 6-1 ran his best race to date, always up with the leaders before staying on without ever seriously threatening the winner.
3. **Imperial Call** (11-10) 7-2 was bang in the firing line until weakening turning for home.
4. **Challenger Du Luc** (11-10) 12-1 was in one of his moods, completing in his own time.
P. **Simply Dashing** (11-10) 6-1 found the soft ground combined with his previous hard race at Cheltenham against him.
P. **See More Business** (11-10) 11-4 fav did not produce his running, his jumping going to pieces.
P. **Super Tactics** (11-10) 16-1 found the soft ground against him.
P. **Coome Hill** (11-10) 25-1 ran a stinker.
P. **Mulligan** (11-10) 25-1 showed very little.
6l, dis, 19l. (Miss V Williams) 9 ran.

41 Leopardstown, 2m, £20,000, soft, Dec 26 1998.
Denny Juvenile Hurdle (Grade 2)
1. **Knife Edge** (10-9) 9-4 produced a smart performance on only his second start over hurdles. Tracking the leaders, he held every chance at the last before running on well to lead in the shadow of the post.
2. **Golden Rule** (10-9) 7-4 fav was in front after the second last but could not withstand the winner's late burst.

3. **Persian Isle** (10-9) 25-1 was rather outclassed, needing to be ridden along from halfway.
4. **Simulacrum** (11-0) 3-1 led three out but was soon headed and returned lame.
¾l, 20l, 2⅔l. (M J O'Brien) 6 ran.

42 Leopardstown, 2m 1f, £40,000, soft, Dec 26 1998.
Denny Gold Medal Novice Chase (Grade 1)
1. **His Song** (11-4) 5-2 fav produced a very convincing performance, always going well and leading from two out before drawing clear.
2. **Native Estates** (11-6) 5-1 was having only his second run over fences, and although making headway from halfway, looked in need of a longer trip.
3. **Amberleigh House** (11-6) 25-1 had his limitations exposed, being made to look rather one-paced.
4. **Micko's Dream** (11-11) 6-1 led until headed two out.
8l, 10l, nk. (M Morris) 9 ran.

43 Wetherby, 3m 1f, £20,000, good to soft, Dec 26 1998.
Rowland Meyrick Hcap Chase
1. **Random Harvest** (9-11) 9-4 jumped for fun out in front for an easy success.
2. **The Last Fling** (10-0) 5-1 was never travelling particularly well and could never seriously threaten.
3. **River Lossie** (10-6) 9-4 needs to dominate from the front but was consistently outjumped by the winner.
P. **Strath Royal** (10-13) 2-1 fav never looked happy.
7l, dis. (Mrs M Reveley) 4 ran.

44 Leopardstown, 3m, £117,000, soft, Dec 27 1998.
Paddy Power Hcap Chase (Grade 2)
1. **Calling Wild** (11-3) 8-1 put up a dazzling display, foot-perfect apart from a slight error at the second last when he already had the race in firm keeping.
2. **Wylde Hide** (11-1) 25-1 put up his best performance for some time, going second two out and keeping on well without ever having a chance with the winner.
3. **Una's Choice** (10-3) 25-1 used his stamina to good effect, ridden along from six out but responding to pressure all the way.
4. **The Quads** (10-2) 10-1 started to get into things over the last two, also keeping on under pressure.
5. **Roundwood** (9-7) 33-1 chased the leaders before staying on at his own pace.
P. **Bob Treacy** (11-5) 13-2 fav looked well handicapped but was a major disappointment.
6l, 6l, 2l, 2l. (P Nicholls) 26 ran.

45 Chepstow, 2m 110yds, £25,000, soft, Dec 28 1998.
Finale Junior Hurdle Race (Grade 1)
1. **Hunt Hill** (11-0) 5-1 put his stamina to good use, stalking the runner-up all the way until taking it up two out.
2. **Miss Orphan** (10-9) 8-15 fav set off in front but set too strong a pace and the writing was on the wall four out.

3. **Legend Of Love** (11-0) 11-1 was outclassed but almost snatched second as the favourite faded.
17l, ⅓l. (J J O'Neill) 5 ran.

46 Chepstow, 3m 5f 110yds, £50,000, soft, Dec 28 1998.
Coral Welsh National (Hcap Chase) (Grade 3)
1. **Kendal Cavalier** (10-0) 14-1 seemed to have been freshened up by a recent change of stables. Running from 13lb out of the handicap, he looked to have the race in the bag jumping the last but needed to fight hard to repel the runner-up.
2. **Fiddling The Facts** (10-6) 11-2 made a couple of errors on the way round which may have cost her the race as she was staying on again having led between the third and second last.
3. **Forest Ivory** (10-0) 14-1 was tucked away in midfield until staying on under a vigorous ride.
4. **Eudipe** (10-12) 11-2 was found out by this marathon trip in very testing ground.
5. **Sail By The Stars** (10-0) 16-1 weakened from five out.
P. **Earth Summit** (11-10) 9-2 fav weakened from four out and looked in need of his old blinkers.
¾l, 6l, 12l, 4l. (N Hawke) 14 ran.

47 Kempton, 2m, £40,000, soft, Dec 28 1998.
Pertemps Christmas Hurdle (Grade 1)
1. **French Holly** (11-7) 5-2 stamped himself as England's top hurdler with a thoroughly professional display. Tracking the leader, he took it up at halfway and was clear from two out.
2. **Master Beveled** (11-7) 15-2 had no chance with the winner, unable to quicken at the business end.
3. **Dato Star** (11-7) evens fav finished slightly lame which possibly accounted for his below-par effort.
4. **Kerawi** (11-7) 11-2 chased the leaders to halfway before weakening.
9l, 8l, 18l. (F Murphy) 5 ran.

48 Leopardstown, 3m, £75,000, soft, Dec 28 1998.
Ericsson Chase (Grade 2)
1. **Dorans Pride** (12-0) 4-1 was in front when making a blunder six out but soon recovered and the departure of Florida Pearl left him with a simple task.
2. **Boss Doyle** (12-0) 9-1 was blinkered for the first time and would have only been a poor third but for Florida Pearl's exit.
3. **Buck Rogers** (12-0) 50-1 was totally out of his depth, soon tailed off before being left a distant third two out.
F. **Florida Pearl** (12-0) 11-10 fav was settling down for a head-to-head battle with Dorans Pride when getting the third last all wrong.
F. **Suny Bay** (12-0) 2-1 ran a stinker, already well beaten when falling two out.
dis, dis. (M Hourigan) 6 ran.

49 Wetherby, 2m, £30,000, soft, Dec 28 1998.
Castleford Chase (Ltd Hcap) (Grade 2)
1. **Cumbrian Challenge** (10-3) 16-1 showed improved form with a tongue-strap and dropping

back in trip. Always travelling well, he progressed to challenge at the last before leading close home.

2. **Direct Route** (11-10) 9-4 also travelled well until taking it up two out but could not answer the winner's late burst.

3. **Flying Instructor** (10-9) 11-4 held every chance four out but just failed to quicken on ground that was unsuitably soft for him.

4. **Lake Kariba** (11-8) 2-1 fav had an off day, never looking happy.

1¹/₄l, 3¹/₄l, 17l. (T Easterby) 5 ran.

50 Leopardstown, 2m, £20,000, heavy, Dec 29 1998.
A.I.B. Agri-Business December Festival Hurdle (Grade 2)

1. **Istabraq** (12-0) 1-10 fav had another breeze round, never off the bridle for a ludicrously easy success.

2. **Shantarini** (11-2) 10-1 challenged up the straight but could make no impression.

3. **Gazalani** (12-0) 20-1 led until headed after two out, then running on at the one pace.

8l, 15l. (A P O'Brien) 3 ran.

51 Cheltenham, 2m 5f, £25,000, good to soft, Jan 1 1999.
Unicoin Hcap Chase

1. **Eirespray** (10-7) 11-2 having raced in midfield, he made progress before effectively being handed the race by the runner-up's blunder three out.

2. **Mr Strong Gale** (10-7) 11-2 would almost certainly have won had he not tried to take the third last fence with him. Leading from halfway, in the end he was only just caught.

3. **Jathib** (10-0) 11-1 was left in the lead from three out but could not maintain his challenge.

4. **Fine Thyne** (10-9) 10-1 was in touch until a bad mistake at the 12th sealed his fate.

hd, ¹/₂l, 11l. (Mrs S Smith) 10 ran.

52 Newbury, 2m 5f, £25,000, soft, Jan 2 1999.
Challow Hurdle (Grade 1)

1. **King's Road** (11-7) 11-10 fav showed a really good fighting attitude, leading until collared at the fourth last but then rallying in game fashion to take it up again close home.

2. **Rio's King** (11-7) 7-2 might have won this had he not hung badly left over the last two hurdles when seemingly in control.

3. **Storm Of Gold** (11-7) 10-1 was beaten turning for home.

2l, 18l. (N Twiston-Davies) 5 ran.

53 Leopardstown, 2m, £75,000, heavy, Jan 9 1999.
The 13th Ladbroke (Hcap Hurdle) (Grade 1)

1. **Archive Footage** (11-8) 25-1 was never travelling particularly smoothly but responded to his rider's urgings throughout to take it up at the last and in the end could afford the luxury of being eased.

2. **Daraheen Chief** (10-9) 40-1 had previously won only a Listowel maiden so this was a fine effort, and he might have finished even closer but for a blunder at the last.

3. **Its Time For A Win** (10-0) 25-1 also came into

this a novice and so was far from disgraced, making his effort three out before plugging on.

4. **Palette** (10-12) 16-1 kept on under pressure from two out.

5. **Polar Prospect** (11-12) 25-1 did best of the British raiders although unable to quicken in the closing stages.

9l, 4l, hd, 4l. (D Weld) 25 ran.

54 Sandown, 2m 110yds, £25,000, soft, Jan 9 1999.
Sun 'King Of The Punters' Tolworth Hurdle (Grade 1)

1. **Behrajan** (10-9) 9-2 won with any amount in hand, happy to cut out the donkey-work and easily fending off the well-regarded runner up.

2. **Hidebound** (11-7) 2-5 fav disputed the lead from the off but found disappointingly little when asked for his effort from two out.

3. **Great Crusader** (11-7) 50-1 was held up and made steady headway before plugging on at the one pace.

4. **Jungli** (11-7) 7-1 weakened in the closing stages, having been prominent to halfway.

16l, 1¹/₄l, 5l. (H Daly) 6 ran.

55 Sandown, 3m 5f 110yds, £30,000, soft, Jan 9 1999.
Anthony Mildmay, Peter Cazalet Hcap Chase

1. **Eudipe** (12-0) 6-1 was given a masterful ride by Tony McCoy who was hard at work fully a mile from home but never gave in. The persistence paid off when a mistake by the runner-up at the last handed him the race.

2. **Glitter Isle** (10-9) 6-1 should have won this, leading after halfway, but throwing it away with a poor jump at the last.

3. **Callisoe Bay** (11-0) 14-1 ran a cracker, leading to halfway and rallying well thereafter.

4. **Call It A Day** (11-12) 7-2 fav was a big disappointment, never at the races.

1l, 1¹/₄l, dis. (M Pipe) 9 ran.

56 Wetherby, 3m 1f, £20,000, heavy, Jan 14 1999.
Towton Novices' Chase (Grade 2)

1. **Kadou Nonantais** (11-13) 7-4 fav made all, jumping well aside from one mistake at the 10th.

2. **Scotton Green** (11-9) 5-1 was hard at work some way from home but kept on responding without ever threatening the winner.

3. **Edmond** (11-9) 5-2 was let down by some sloppy jumping.

14l, dis. (O Sherwood) 5 ran.

57 Newcastle, 2¹/₂m, £20,000, heavy, Jan 16 1999.
Northern Echo Dipper Novices' Chase (Grade 2)

1. **Bobby Grant** (11-5) 9-2 made a whole series of mistakes but jockey Robbie Supple refused to give up and the pair recovered well enough to lead late on.

2. **Course Doctor** (11-5) 3-1 looked the winner two out but was outbattled in the dash to the line.

3. **No Retreat** (11-12) 10-11 fav tried to make all but

was found out by the testing conditions and could offer little response once headed two out.
4. **Carley Lad** (11-5) 11-2 was never fluent and was behind from halfway.
$^{1}/_{2}$l, 9l, dis. (C Grant) 5 ran.

58 Haydock, 2m 7f 110yds, £20,000, soft, Jan 23 1999.
Tote Premier Long Distance Hurdle (Grade 2)
1. **Deano's Beeno** (11-3) 4-11 fav showed his class, making all to thrash the opposition out of sight.
2. **Moorish** (11-3) 4-1 is a useful tool on his day but was made to look very ordinary by the winner.
3. **Pharanear** (11-3) 25-1 was never near enough to threaten.
4. **Paddy's Return** (11-10) 6-1 was outpaced the whole way round.
22l, 9l, 2l. (M Pipe) 5 ran.

59 Haydock, 3m, £42,500, soft, Jan 23 1999.
Peter Marsh Chase (Ltd Hcap) (Grade 2)
1. **General Wolfe** (10-12) 4-1 had been off the track since winning this event 12 months previously. Leading from halfway, he was clear when getting the last wrong.
2. **Simply Dashing** (11-10) 10-1 was unable to land a blow at the winner but did outstay the third.
3. **Random Harvest** (10-4) 4-1 improved from the rear before staying on well enough.
4. **Macgeorge** (10-11) 11-2 failed to handle the big fences and weakened after a bad mistake at the penultimate fence.
4l, $^{1}/_{2}$l, 18l. (Miss V Williams) 10 ran.

60 Haydock, 2m, £25,000, soft, Jan 23 1999.
Intercity Champion Hurdle Trial (Grade 2)
1. **Master Beveled** (11-7) 12-1 gained compensation for a string of near-misses against the best hurdlers around, racing in midfield before progressing to lead close home.
2. **Wahiba Sands** (11-3) 11-4 fav attempted to make all at a breakneck pace so it was little surprise he could not sustain the gallop all the way to the line — although only the winner ever threatened him.
3. **Toto Toscato** (11-7) 7-2 couldn't muster any extra when the heat was turned up between the last two flights.
4. **Pridwell** (11-10) 6-1 was soon struggling, losing touch from the fifth flight.
1l, 18l, 12l. (P Evans) 6 ran.

61 Kempton, 2m, £30,000, soft, Jan 23 1999.
Victor Chandler Hcap Chase (Grade 2)
1. **Call Equiname** (11-3) 15-2 maintained his unbeaten record over fences with a gutsy display, battling it out with the runner-up from the last.
2. **Get Real** (10-2) 15-8 fav dominated from the front until caught close home.
3. **Celibate** (11-3) 7-1 chased the leader all the way but was tapped for toe in the end.
4. **Manhattan Castle** (10-7) 9-1 stayed on late in the day.
nk, 6l, $^{1}/_{2}$l. (P Nicholls) 7 ran.

62 Kempton, 2m, £30,000, soft, Jan 23 1999.
Tote Lanzarote Hcap Hurdle
1. **Tiutchev** (11-2) 15-8 fav had fallen here on Boxing Day but made up for that tumble in no uncertain style, leading two out for a very smooth success.
2. **Mister Rm** (10-0) 16-1 took the field along until put firmly in his place by the winner.
3. **Serenus** (11-0) 4-1 gave his all but couldn't quicken in the straight.
4. **Davoski** (10-5) 10-3 tracked the leaders until tiring.
6l, nk, 1$^{1}/_{4}$l. (D Nicholson) 8 ran.

63 Leopardstown, 2m 1f, £28,000, soft, Jan 24 1999.
Baileys Arkle Perpetual Challenge Cup Novice Chase (Grade 2)
1. **His Song** (12-0) 1-2 fav was always in the front rank and leading two out, ran on for a narrow success.
2. **Padre Mio** (11-7) 12-1 also ran up with the pace and made the winner pull out all the stops.
3. **Cockney Lad** (11-7) 9-2 chased the leaders before keeping on at the same pace.
4. **Advocat** (11-7) 8-1 held up, could make no impression from three out.
nk, 9l, 12l. (M Morris) 6 ran.

64 Leopardstown, 2m, £55,000, soft, Jan 24 1999.
A.I.G. Europe Champion Hurdle (Grade 1)
1. **Istabraq** (11-10) 8-15 fav was always travelling supremely well, and, having taken it up at the last, was eased to a cosy victory.
2. **French Holly** (11-10) 9-4 made most of the running but was made to look second class by the winner.
3. **Zafarabad** (11-6) 16-1 was always prominent but lacked a turn of foot in this company.
4. **Theatreworld** (11-10) 16-1 got outpaced in rear and was never a factor.
1l, 7l, 2l. (A P O'Brien) 6 ran.

65 Cheltenham, 3m 1f 110yds, £30,000, soft, Jan 30 1999.
Pillar Property Chase (Grade 2)
1. **Cyfor Malta** (11-6) 10-11 fav chasing the leaders, was sent on three out and stayed on up the hill.
2. **Go Ballistic** (11-10) 16-1 threw away his chance with a bad mistake just as the race was hotting up.
3. **See More Business** (11-12) 7-4 had no excuses, prominent at halfway but finding precious little thereafter.
4l, 6l. (M Pipe) 5 ran.

66 Cheltenham, 2m 5f 110yds, £42,000, soft, Jan 30 1999.
Marchpole Cleeve Hurdle (Grade 1)
1. **Lady Rebecca** (11-3) 6-4 fav was very impressive despite some sloppy jumping, leading three out and running on gamely.
2. **Silver Wedge** (11-8) 9-1 was left behind by the winner on the long run to the last flight.

3. **Commanche Court** (11-8) 11-4 lost ground from halfway and was no danger thereafter.
20l, 9l. (Miss V Williams) 7 ran.

67 Cheltenham, 2m 5f, £25,000, soft, Jan 30 1999.
Ladbroke Trophy Hcap Chase
1. **Dr Leunt** (10-3) 11-4 fav beat a poor turnout, making most and readily asserting from the turn for home.
2. **Storm Damage** (10-0) 13-2 ran well enough from 6lb out of the handicap, moving up into a prominent position on the second circuit only to fade in the latter stages.
3. **Even Flow** (10-3) 7-2 chased along from halfway, was never dangerous
22l, dis. (P Hobbs) 6 ran.

68 Doncaster, 3m, £30,000, good to soft, Jan 30 1999.
Stakis Casino Great Yorkshire Hcap Chase
1. **Major Bell** (10-0) 20-1 caused a shock with an ultra-game display, always prominent and answering his rider's every urging to lead close home.
2. **Mr Strong Gale** (11-4) 8-1 led from halfway only to be caught close home.
3. **Cab On Target** (10-3) 25-1 made steady headway but could only run on at the one pace.
4. **Blue Charm** (10-8) 25-1 was always chasing the leaders.
¹/₂l, 9l, 4l. (A Whillans) 19 ran.

69 Sandown, 2¹/₂m 110yds, £35,000, good to soft, Feb 6 1999.
Scilly Isles Novices' Chase (Grade 1)
1. **Hoh Express** (11-6) 11-4 fav made all and, despite a bad jump out to the left at the penultimate flight, needed only to be shaken up to score.
2. **No Retreat** (11-6) 3-1 chased the leader all the way but to no avail.
3. **Bank Avenue** (11-6) 10-1 faded quickly in the closing stages.
4. **King Of Sparta** (11-6) 4-1 was outpaced at the finish.
3¹/₂l, 22l, sh hd. (P R Webber) 9 ran.

70 Sandown, 3m 110yds, £30,000, good to soft, Feb 6 1999.
Agfa Diamond Chase (Ltd Hcap) (Grade 2)
1. **Clever Remark** (10-5) 5-1 held up off the pace, made significant progress to take it up at the last.
2. **Nahthen Lad** (11-12) 12-1 had the blinkers refitted and they seemed to do the trick. Leading from the 14th he was only collared at the second last.
3. **King Lucifer** (11-9) 7-2 was prominent until fading in the latter stages.
9l, 6l. (J Old) 6 ran.

71 Sandown, 2³/₄m, £45,000, good to soft, Feb 6 1999.
Tote Sandown Hcap Hurdle (Grade 3)
1. **Teaatral** (10-2) 8-1 turned in an impressive display, racing in midfield until making headway to lead two out.
2. **Just Nip** (10-0) 14-1 held every chance but could not match the winner's well-timed run.
3. **Melody Maid** (10-0) 15-2 was in the front rank for most of the way but faded late on.
4. **Globe Runner** (9-7) 16-1 was always chasing the leaders.
3¹/₂l, 7l, 5l. (C Egerton) 13 ran.

72 Uttoxeter, 3¹/₄m, £55,000, heavy, Feb 6 1999.
Singer & Friedlander National Trial (Hcap Chase)
1. **Him Of Praise** (10-2) 12-1 dropped himself out with a circuit to go but, with the leaders tiring badly, he plugged on to lead close home.
2. **Fiddling The Facts** (10-9) 11-4 fav finished really tired, having taken it up four out.
3. **Forest Ivory** (10-0) 5-1 looked a major threat five out but the petrol soon ran out.
2l, 25l. (O Sherwood) 9 ran.

73 Leopardstown, 2m 5f, £50,000, good to soft, Feb 7 1999.
Dr P.J. Moriarty Novice Chase (Grade 2)
1. **Nick Dundee** (12-0) 4-6 fav made all for a bloodless victory.
2. **Sarsfield The Man** (11-7) 16-1 was always in touch and went second four out but could then only keep on at the one pace.
3. **Inis Cara** (12-0) 12-1 made progress from five out without seriously threatening.
15l, 9l. (E O'Grady) 6 ran.

74 Leopardstown, 3m, £100,000, good to soft, Feb 7 1999.
Hennessy Cognac Gold Cup (Chase Grade 1)
1. **Florida Pearl** (12-0) 8-15 fav was always prominent and took it up two out without ever shaking off the runner-up
2. **Escartefigue** (12-0) 10-3 showed stamina is his forte by galloping on all the way to the line.
3. **Addington Boy** (12-0) 33-1 stayed on after a mistake five out.
4. **Papillon** (12-0) 25-1 led to halfway before fading.
2l, dis, 4¹/₂l. (W P Mullins) 7 ran.

75 Newbury, 2m 1f, £30,000, good, Feb 13 1999.
Mitsubishi Shogun Game Spirit Chase (Grade 2)
1. **Celibate** (11-3) 7-2 took up the running four out and got the better of a good tussle after the last.
2. **Mulligan** (11-3) 7-2 failed to take advantage of the winner drifting right-handed on the run in.
3. **Nearly An Eye** (11-3) 11-2 kept on at the same pace after a couple of sloppy jumps.
4. **Ask Tom** (11-10) 5-2 fav was making a very belated seasonal debut and appeared to blow up in the home straight
2¹/₂l, 9l, 5l. (C Mann) 6 ran.

76 Newbury, 2m 110yds, £100,000, good, Feb 13 1999.

Tote Gold Trophy Hcap Hurdle (Grade 3)

1. **Decoupage** (11-0) 6-1 put up a career-best effort, improving from midfield to lead at the last.
2. **City Hall** (11-10) 20-1 ran his heart out, leading at halfway only to be collared late in the day.
3. **Sadler's Realm** (10-4) 16-1 stayed on from the rear.
4. **Amitge** (10-10) 50-1 was rather one-paced at the finish.
5. **Effectual** (10-12) 20-1 held up in the rear early doors, he ran on to some effect.

3l, sh hd, 2¹/₂l, 8l. (C Egerton) 18 ran.

77 Ascot, 3m 110yds, £32,000, good to soft, Feb 20 1999.

Gerrard Group Reynoldstown Novices' Chase (Grade 2)

1. **Lord Of The River** (11-12) 7-4 fav made all and was left clear when main rival Marlborough departed at the last.
2. **Collier Bay** (11-5) 11-2 was always prominent but could not quicken as well as the winner or Marlborough.
3. **Andsuephi** (11-5) 4-1 was soon struggling when the race warmed up in the last half-mile.
F. **Marlborough** (11-5) 5-2 would probably have finished second but departed with a tired-looking fall at the last.

15l, 28l. (O Sherwood) 6 ran.

78 Ascot, 2¹/₂m, £30,000, good to soft, Feb 20 1999.

William Hill Hcap Hurdle

1. **Ismeno** (10-10) 8-1 made all just as he had at Towcester on his last run off a 9lb lower mark.
2. **Polar Prospect** (11-13) 20-1 chased the winner after the third last but could never reel him in.
3. **Bluedonix** (10-11) 15-2 improved from midfield only to be outpaced at the finish.
4. **Castle Owen** (10-8) 11-2 made some late headway.

6l, 7l, 1l. (D Elsworth) 12 ran.

79 Ascot, 2m 3f 110yds, £62,000, good to soft, Feb 20 1999.

Mitsubishi Shogun Ascot Chase (Grade 1)

1. **Teeton Mill** (11-7) 6-4 fav was dropping considerably in trip after missing the Pillar Chase with a muscle problem. Jumping well, he blazed a trail on the second circuit and soon had his rivals in trouble.
2. **Senor El Betrutti** (11-7) 25-1 led early before fading and then getting his second wind, staying on to snatch second on the run-in.
3. **Super Coin** (11-7) 9-2 made steady headway but was rather one-paced at the finish.
4. **Direct Route** (11-7) 5-2 improved from halfway but could make no real impression.

4l, 1³/₄l, 7l. (Miss V Williams) 7 ran.

80 Newcastle, 4m 1f, £38,000, good to soft, Feb 20 1999.

Tote Eider Chase (Hcap)

1. **Hollybank Buck** (10-11) 10-1 was given a patient ride, making stealthy headway to lead at the last to give the Irish their first success in this marathon.
2. **Full Of Oats** (9-11) 8-1 gave his all but his challenge just failed.
3. **Feels Like Gold** (10-0) 14-1 led at halfway before getting outpaced close home.
4. **The Last Fling** (11-3) 25-1 was always in touch but could never land a blow.

nk, 1³/₄l, 10l. (A J Martin) 15 ran.

81 Warwick, 2m, £20,000, good to soft, Feb 20 1999.

Michael Page International Kingmaker Novices Chase (Grade 2)

1. **Flagship Uberalles** (11-0) 9-4 put his superior jumping to good effect in a very tactical affair.
2. **Tresor De Mai** (10-10) 1-3 fav could never quite master his wily rival.

hd. (P Nicholls) 2 ran.

82 Wincanton, 3m 1f 110yds, £20,000, good to soft, Feb 25 1999.

Jim Ford Challenge Cup Chase

1. **Double Thriller** (11-5) 1-6 fav made all before quickening clear for a hugely impressive handicap debut.
2. **Wayward King** (11-7) 6-1 could never get to grips with the Gold Cup-bound winner
3. **Melling** (11-2) 100-1 was always struggling.

dis, 8l. (P Nicholls) 4 ran.

83 Wincanton, 2m, £32,500, good to soft, Feb 25 1999.

Axminster 100 Kingwell Hurdle (Grade 2)

1. **Grey Shot** (11-2) 4-6 fav is normally a front-runner but settled for second here until taking it up two out and then stayed on despite not hurdling fluently.
2. **Midnight Legend** (11-7) 5-1 ran on at the end without ever threatening.
3. **Upgrade** (11-2) 16-1 kept on to grab third.

2¹/₂l, 4l. (I Balding) 6 ran.

84 Haydock, 3¹/₂m 110yds, £85,000, soft, Feb 27 1999.

Greenalls Grand National Trial Chase (Hcap)

1. **Young Kenny** (10-0) 9-1 showed himself an improving stayer, tracking the leaders before taking it up four out and then galloping on strongly.
2. **Fiddling The Facts** (10-12) 6-1 co fav made most only to weaken in the closing stages.
3. **Him Of Praise** (10-7) 7-1 was always about the same position and could only finish at the one pace.
4. **Forest Ivory** (9-9) 12-1 improved from the rear to snatch fourth.
5. **Cavalero** (10-0) 33-1 weakened, having been close up at halfway.

13l, 12l, 1¹/₂l, nk. (P Beaumont) 13 ran.

85 Kempton, 2½m 110yds, £20,000, soft, Feb 27 1999.
Mitsubishi Shogun Pendil Trophy Novices' Chase (Grade 2)
1. **Makounji** (10-2) 4-11 fav received an overly-generous weight allowance once again and made the most of it, setting the pace and running out an easy winner.
2. **No Retreat** (11-10) 9-2 was always in the front rank but could never get to grips with the winner.
3. **King Of Sparta** (11-7) 8-1 dropped away very tamely.
27l, 29l. (N Henderson) 4 ran.

86 Kempton, 3m, £60,000, soft, Feb 27 1999.
Racing Post Chase (Hcap)
1. **Dr Leunt** (11-5) 3-1 fav made much of the running and got the better of the runner-up without too much bother despite a mistake two out.
2. **The Land Agent** (10-7) 9-2 was the only danger to the winner in the straight despite making a hash of the 12th fence.
3. **Even Flow** (10-8) 5-1 was the early leader but faded in the closing stages.
4. **Mr Strong Gale** (11-0) 7-2 was already beaten when blundering through the last.
3½l, 7l, 6l. (P Hobbs) 8 ran.

87 Kempton, 3m 110yds, £20,000, soft, Feb 27 1999.
Money Store Rendlesham Hurdle (Ltd Hcap) (Grade 2)
1. **Pharanear** (10-7) 11-2 was 7lb out of the handicap but bounced back to form in great style, always going well and leading from two out.
2. **Anzum** (10-7) 8-1 ran on at the one pace, having been under pressure from some way out.
3. **Ivor's Flutter** (10-7) 16-1 made some progress from the rear before plugging on.
4. **Pridwell** (11-7) 3-1 jt fav was never a threat after a mistake at the seventh.
8l, 1½l, 8l. (D Nicholson) 8 ran.

88 Sandown, 2m 110yds, £30,000, good to soft, Mar 13 1999.
Sunderlands Imperial Cup Hurdle (Showcase Hcap)
1. **Regency Rake** (10-7) 7-1 needed to be hard ridden to lead close home and only just held on with his rider losing an iron.
2. **Coulthard** (10-8) 7-1 moved to the front two out and proved a real fighter in the dash to the line.
3. **Dr Jazz** (11-0) 2-1 fav was only outbattled close home, having been in with every chance jumping the last.
4. **Effectual** (11-10) 8-1 was losing the battle when getting the last all wrong.
sh hd, 1¼l, 7l. (A L Moore) 9 ran.

89 Cheltenham, 2m 110yds, £80,000, good, Mar 16 1999.
Citroen Supreme Novices' Hurdle (Grade 1)
1. **Hors La Loi III** (11-0) 9-2 registered a time two seconds faster than the Champion Hurdle. Never far away, he led three out for a really convincing success.
2. **Joe Mac** (11-8) 6-1 did nothing wrong but just couldn't match the winner's blistering turn of foot.
3. **Arctic Fancy** (11-8) 66-1 was the surprise package of the race, running a cracker and only outpaced in the closing stages.
4. **Colonel Yeager** (11-8) 10-1 stayed on late from midfield.
5. **Wither Or Which** (11-8) 20-1 found the trip on the short side, failing to quicken.
6. **Ricardo** (11-8) 25-1 was just a bit out of his depth.
17l, 7l, nk, 9l, nk. (M Pipe) 20 ran.

90 Cheltenham, 2m, £100,000, good, Mar 16 1999.
Guinness Arkle Challenge Trophy Chase (Grade 1)
1. **Flagship Uballes** (11-0) 11-1 was suited by the strong early pace, always close up before taking over two out.
2. **Tresor De Mai** (11-0) 14-1 was 4lb better off with the winner on Warwick form and battled on well without ever threatening to overhaul the winner.
3. **Nipper Reed** (11-8) 10-1 ran well enough on ground which was probably a bit too lively for him, making most and only weakening once headed when pecking two out.
4. **Gris D'Estruval** (11-0) 5-1 led at halfway only to fade at the business end of things.
5. **His Song** (11-8) 4-1 fav was never a factor and finished lame.
6. **Cockney Lad** (11-8) 25-1 found the pace a bit hot.
2½l, 14l, 4l, 1l, 1¾l. (P Nicholls) 14 ran.

91 Cheltenham, 2m 110yds, £240,000, good, Mar 16 1999.
Smurfit Champion Hurdle Challenge Trophy (Grade 1)
1. **Istabraq** (12-0) 4-9 fav was installed as low as 6-4 to complete the hat-trick next March after crusing to an effortless win, leading two out and demonstrating he is in a class of his own.
2. **Theatreworld** (12-0) 16-1 finished second for the third consecutive year, making steady headway before staying on under pressure.
3. **French Holly** (12-0) 11-2 was always in the front rank and nosed ahead after the third last. However, when Istabraq swept past before the penultimate flight, it was all over.
4. **Mister Morose** (12-0) 100-1 improved from halfway and kept on well enough.
5. **Nomadic** (12-0) 50-1 chased leaders before finishing rather one-paced.
6. **Tiutchev** (12-0) 40-1 made limited headway approaching three out.
3½l, 2½l, 1l, 1¼l, 2l. (A P O'Brien) 14 ran.

92 Cheltenham, 3m 1f, £60,000, good, Mar 16 1999.
William Hill National Hunt Chase (Hcap)
1. **Betty's Boy** (10-2) 25-1 showed he goes well fresh with a game display, tracking the leaders until taking it up approaching the last.

2. **Island Chief** (10-1) 10-1 led from halfway but was tiring badly when he got the last all wrong.
3. **Nahthen Lad** (10-10) 25-1 kept on at his own pace.
4. **Macgeorge** (11-8) 16-1 having been tucked away in midfield, was unable to quicken in the closing stages.
5. **King Lucifer** (10-6) 16-1 was never better than mid-division.
5l, 2l, 2¹/₂l, 4l. (K Bailey) 18 ran.

93 Cheltenham, 3m 1f, £35,000, good, Mar 16 1999.
Fulke Walwyn Kim Muir Cup Hcap Chase (Amateur Riders)
1. **Celtic Giant** (10-0) 20-1 led from six out and was soon clear for a bloodless victory.
2. **Tell The Nipper** (10-3) 16-1 was far from foot-perfect but did keep on until the death.
3. **Orswell Lad** (10-6) 25-1 improved from the rear before staying on.
4. **Strong Tel** (10-10) 33-1 found his jumping letting him down when the heat was turned up.
5. **Noyan** (10-8) 33-1 was the early leader before weakening in the closing stages.
14l, 1³/₄l, nk, 1¹/₂l. (L Lungo) 22 ran.

94 Cheltenham, 3¹/₂m, £45,000, good, Mar 16 1999.
Stakis Casinos Final (Hcap Hurdle)
1. **Generosa** (10-1) 12-1 was on the bridle turning for home and quickly had the issue settled, leading at the last and staying on gamely.
2. **Melody Maid** (10-3) 12-1 kept on, having improved from midfield from halfway.
3. **Galant Moss** (10-7) 3-1 fav progressed to lead two out but could not sustain his challenge.
4. **Shannon Gale** (10-0) 7-1 was always close up.
5. **Nibalda** (10-0) 33-1 made progress from halfway but could never get nearer.
5l, 1¹/₄l, 1l, 12l. (J Hassett) 24 ran.

95 Cheltenham, 2m 5f, £80,000, good, Mar 17 1999.
Royal & SunAlliance Novices' Hurdle (Grade 1)
1. **Barton** (11-7) 2-1 fav annihilated the strongest field he had yet faced, leading two out and then cruising up the hill for a devastating success.
2. **Artadoin Lad** (11-7) 28-1 was hard ridden from two out but to no avail.
3. **Winston Run** (11-7) 100-1 improved from midfield before keeping on.
4. **King's Road** (11-7) 16-1 was always in touch but just couldn't quicken.
5. **Behrajan** (10-12) 6-1 was in front four from home but an untidy leap at the next sealed his fate.
6. **Arctic Camper** (11-7) 16-1 weakened from two out.
9l, ¹/₂l, 3¹/₂l, 4l, 1¹/₄l. (T Easterby) 18 ran.

96 Cheltenham, 2m, £170,000, good, Mar 17 1999.
Queen Mother Champion Chase (Grade 1)
1. **Call Equiname** (12-0) 7-2 has had his problems

but produced a gutsy display, jumping fluently and making relentless headway to lead close home.
2. **Edredon Bleu** (12-0) 3-1 fav would have preferred fast ground but lost little in defeat, making almost all until giving way after the last.
3. **Direct Route** (12-0) 11-2 ran one of his better races, making good progress from the rear before keeping on up the hill.
4. **Green Green Desert** (12-0) 40-1 was never far away but was just outclassed on the day.
5. **Celibate** (12-0) 11-1 was never placed to challenge.
1¹/₄l, 3¹/₂l, 3¹/₂l, 1¹/₂l. (P Nicholls) 13 ran.

97 Cheltenham, 2m 5f, £65,000, good, Mar 17 1999.
Coral Cup Hurdle (Showcase Hcap) (Grade 3)
1. **Khayrawani** (11-3) 16-1 had clearly been laid out for this as it was his first run for four months. Racing in midfield for most of the way, he made stealthy headway to take it up at the last.
2. **Miltonfield** (10-0) 33-1 threw down a determined late challenge which only just failed.
3. **Generosa** (10-3) 12-1 was attempting a quick double under a 7lb penalty and lost little in defeat, although it later transpired she had broken a blood vessel.
4. **Darapour** (10-0) 14-1 ran on at the one pace, having sneaked up from the rear.
5. **Fishin Joella** (9-12) 33-1 improved from midfield and only lost out on the run from the last.
hd, nk, 5l, sh hd. (C Roche) 30 ran.

98 Cheltenham, 3m 1f, £100,000, good, Mar 17 1999.
Royal & SunAlliance Chase (Grade 1)
1. **Looks Like Trouble** (11-4) 16-1 was not travelling as well as the favourite when left clear three out.
2. **Lord Of The River** (11-4) 11-2 set off in front but stopped almost dead turning in. It later transpired he had twisted a plate.
3. **Billingsgate** (11-4) 25-1 lost his place from the 11th and was soon tailed off
4. **Collier Bay** (11-4) 25-1 weakened from the 12th.
5. **King's Banker** (11-4) 12-1 always in rear, was never dangerous.
F. **Nick Dundee** (11-4) 5-4 fav seemed to have the race in the bag when taking a horrible tumble at the downhill fence.
dis, 3l, 1³/₄l, 7l. (N Chance) 14 ran.

99 Cheltenham, 4m, £32,500, good, Mar 17 1999.
National Hunt Chase Challenge Cup (Amateur Riders)
1. **Deejaydee** (12-0) 13-2 survived a couple of mistakes to lead close home.
2. **Riot Leader** (12-7) 10-1 led from halfway and might have prevailed had his jockey not dropped his whip at the penultimate fence.
3. **Spot Thedifference** (12-4) 13-2 travelled well but just couldn't quicken when required.
4. **Derrymore Mist** (12-7) 6-1 fav clobbered three out which put paid to his chance.

5. Act In Time (12-0) 10-1 was in the front rank until the third last.

nk, 6l, 7l, 10l. (M Hourigan) 21 ran.

100 Cheltenham, 2¹/₂m 110yds, £55,000, good, Mar 17 1999.

Mildmay Of Flete Challenge Cup Hcap Chase

1. Majadou (11-0) 7-4 fav proved the Pipe banker of the meeting, being three out for an easy win.

2. King Of Sparta (10-0) 33-1 having raced in midfield, was outpaced at halfway but then kept on.

3. Wayward King (11-1) 25-1 ran on, having been tucked away in midfield.

4. The Outback Way (10-12) 10-1 made steady headway from the rear but it was never enough.

5. Philip's Woody (11-1) 40-1 kept on at his own pace.

16l, nk, nk, ³/₄l. (M Pipe) 18 ran.

101 Cheltenham, 2m 110yds, £30,000, good, Mar 17 1999.

Weatherbys Champion Bumper (Standard Open NH Flat) (Grade 1)

1. Monsignor (11-6) 50-1 finished over 10 lengths behind the runner-up on identical terms at Newbury a month previously. But he came into his own up the Cheltenham hill to beat close home.

2. Golden Alpha (11-6) 7-2 was sent on at the top of the hill and soon had a big lead, only then for his stride to shorten dramatically.

3. Canasta (10-13) 25-1 a stablemate of the winner, kept on nicely in the closing stages.

4. Queens Harbour (11-6) 40-1 was patiently held up in rear before running on to good effect.

5. Ballet-K (11-1) 25-1 behind early, made late progress.

1¹/₂l, ³/₄l, 4l, 2l. (M Pitman) 25 ran.

102 Cheltenham, 2m 1f, £80,000, good, Mar 18 1999.

Elite Racing Club Triumph Hurdle (Grade 1)

1. Katarino (11-0) 11-4 fav put up a truly astonishing display considering he was never travelling particularly well. Jumping well, he was scrubbed along to lead at the last but then fairly sprinted away from his rivals.

2. Balla Sola (11-0) 16-1 was covered up before progressing to lead jumping the second last only to find the winner's late burst too hot to handle.

3. Afarad (11-0) 8-1 looked ready to pounce turning in but found the front two too good for him.

4. Dangerus Precedent (11-0) 9-1 continued his improvement, always in touch and holding every chance two out.

5. Ballysicyos (11-0) 16-1 was never far away but was a little outpaced near the finish.

6. Scarlet Pimpernel (11-0) 16-1 held every chance until two out.

8l, 1¹/₄l, 2l, 5l, ¹/₂l. (N Henderson) 23 ran.

103 Cheltenham, 3m 110yds, £100,000, good, Mar 18 1999.

Bonusprint Stayers' Hurdle (Grade 1)

1. Anzum (11-10) 40-1 was given a peach of a ride by Richard Johnson who refused to give up on this tricky ride. Although looking beaten for much of the race, the jockey's efforts were rewarded when his mount's late spurt seized the prize in the dying strides.

2. Le Coudray (11-10) 2-1 jt fav was having his first crack at this extended trip but saw it out well, only to be caught right in the shadow of the post.

3. Lady Rebecca (11-5) 3-1 travelled well and nosed ahead after the last, only to find nothing more up the hill.

4. Sallie's Girl (11-5) 25-1 took on the other front-runner, Deano's Beeno, from the start and paid the price.

5. Juyush (11-10) 33-1 held every chance two out before fading.

nk, 2¹/₂l, 5l, 6l. (D Nicholson) 12 ran.

104 Cheltenham, 3¹/₄m 110yds, £260,000, good, Mar 18 1999.

Tote Cheltenham Gold Cup Chase (Grade 1)

1. See More Business (12-0) 16-1 got away with a mistake at the 12th to take it up at the last and win all out.

2. Go Ballistic (12-0) 66-1 ran the race of his life, progressing to lead from four out he only gave way after the last.

3. Florida Pearl (12-0) 5-2 fav made progress from the rear but could only run on at the one pace as his stamina gave out.

4. Double Thriller (12-0) 9-1 led from the seventh until four out before being outclassed.

5. Addington Boy (12-0) 66-1 was never really put into the race.

6. Simply Dashing (12-0) 20-1 hit four out and weakened out of contention.

7. Escartefigue (12-0) 11-1 weakened when the heat was turned up four out.

8. Dorans Pride (12-0) 11-2 was prominent until fading under pressure over the last three fences.

9. Senor El Betrutti (12-0) 50-1 set the early pace before fading badly.

P. Unsinkable Boxer (12-0) 14-1 broke a blood vessel.

P. Suny Bay (12-0) 14-1 made mistakes and was never travelling.

P. Teeton Mill (12-0) 7-2 broke down before the 10th.

1l, 17l, 14l, 3¹/₂l, 12l, nk, 12l, 29l. (P Nicholls) 12 ran.

105 Cheltenham, 3¹/₄m 110yds, £30,000, good, Mar 18 1999.

Christie's Foxhunter Chase Challenge Cup

1. Castle Mane (12-0) 9-2 showed his class to maintain an unbeaten record, making much of the running and stamping his authority on proceedings in the closing stages.

2. Elegant Lord (12-0) 3-1 fav is getting a bit long in

the tooth and his lack of pace showed in the last half mile.

3. **Last Option** (12-0) 20-1 was tapped for toe running to the penultimate fence but then stayed on again.

4. **Irish Stout** (12-0) 12-1 quickly weakened after a blunder three out.

13l, 1¹/₄l, dis. (Mrs C Bailey) 24 ran.

106 Cheltenham, 2m 110yds, £50,000, good, Mar 18 1999.

Cheltenham Grand Annual Chase Challenge Cup (Hcap)

1. **Space Trucker** (10-1) 7-2 fav sensibly tracked the leaders who set a strong pace, and, sent about his business two out, nosed ahead after the last.

2. **Dines** (10-8) 6-1 was sent on from the fifth and saw off all except the winner on the run to the line.

3. **Hurricane Lamp** (10-7) 16-1 recovered from some early mistakes to take a hand from the last.

4. **Country Star** (9-11) 14-1 was the early leader but was a spent force jumping the last.

5. **Amberleigh House** (10-0) 14-1 was always about the same position.

1¹/₂l, 1l, 2l, 1l. (Mrs J Harrington) 15 ran.

107 Cheltenham, 2m 5f, £55,000, good, Mar 18 1999.

Cathcart Challenge Cup Chase (Grade 2)

1. **Stormyfairweather** (11-3) 9-1 was never far off the pace and, despite a blunder four out, took it up at the last before running on well.

2. **Niki Dee** (11-0) 14-1 stayed on from the mid-division suggesting he needs a longer trip.

3. **Edelweis Du Moulin** (11-3) 5-1 challenged from two out and kept on near the finish.

4. **Potentate** (11-3) 4-1 cut out most of the running only to finish a little one-paced.

5. **Dr Leunt** (11-7) 11-4 fav shared the lead with Potentate until gradually fading at the business end.

2l, hd, sh hd, 11l. (N Henderson) 10 ran.

108 Cheltenham, 2m 1f, £50,000, good, Mar 18 1999.

Vincent O'Brien County Hcap Hurdle (Grade 3)

1. **Sir Talbot** (10-0) 10-1 tracked leaders before taking it up two out for an impressive win.

2. **Decoupage** (10-13) 10-3 fav was 13lb higher than when winning the Tote Gold Trophy but ran a blinder, just getting caught a little flat-footed turning in.

3. **Toto Toscato** (11-5) 25-1 found his big weight anchoring him in the closing stages.

4. **Sadler's Realm** (9-9) 25-1 made some late headway but never really threatened.

5. **Executive Decision** (9-9) 33-1 faded having led at halfway.

6l, 10l, nk, 3l. (J Old) 28 ran.

109 Kelso, 4m, £25,000, good, Mar 26 1999.

Ashleybank Investments Scottish Borders Hcap Chase

1. **Prime Example** (10-5) 3-1 raced in midfield until

making headway to lead three out. He ran on well to the line.

2. **Gigi Beach** (10-2) 5-2 fav was always in the front rank and stayed on nicely enough.

3. **Mister Muddypaws** (9-9) 20-1 kept on, having chased the leaders the whole way round.

1¹/₄l, sh hd. (M Todhunter) 12 ran.

110 Ascot, 2m 3f 110yds, £20,000, good to firm, Mar 31 1999.

Daily Telegraph Novices' Hcap Chase

1. **Supreme Charm** (10-12) 11-4 fav was close up but had to be hard-driven to lead at the last when he was left clear by the fall of Laredo.

2. **Kurakka** (11-13) 4-1 made the running but was quickly outpaced turning for home. He would have had to settle for third had Laredo not departed at the last.

3. **Fils De Cresson** (10-3) 7-2 was never in with a shout.

F. **Laredo** (10-12) 7-2 was just in front when falling at the last, otherwise he might well have won.

19l, 11l. (K Bailey) 6 ran.

111 Fairyhouse, 3m 5f, £125,000, good to soft, Apr 5 1999.

Jameson Irish Grand National Hcap Chase (Grade 1)

1. **Glebe Lad** (10-0) 8-1 co fav led three out, and although strongly pressed and needing to be hard ridden thereonin, he stayed on strongly.

2. **Feathered Leader** (10-4) 12-1 was vigorously ridden to dispute the lead approaching the last, but could do no more.

3. **Manus The Man** (10-6) 8-1 co fav was held up off the pace before joining issue three out, although his challenge never really hit top gear.

4. **Risk Of Thunder** (10-0) 14-1 was always prominent and held every chance at the last.

3l, 3l, 3l. (M J O'Brien) 18 ran.

112 Fairyhouse, 2¹/₂m, £50,000, good to soft, Apr 6 1999.

Power Gold Cup Chase (Grade 1)

1. **Rince Ri** (11-7) 9-2 chased the leaders until taking it up at the last and then scooting clear.

2. **Promalee** (11-7) 6-1 led after halfway but could not maintain the gallop.

3. **Micko's Dream** (11-7) 4-1 jt fav could produce no extra having been in the firing line two out.

4. **Cockney Lad** (11-7) 10-1 made his effort from the 10th but never got on terms.

9l, 11l, 5¹/₂l. (T Walsh) 14 ran.

113 Fairyhouse, 2m, £75,000, good to soft, Apr 6 1999.

Powers Hcap Hurdle (Grade 2)

1. **She's Our Mare** (10-2) 12-1 was produced with perfect timing to lead at the last.

2. **Owen Bart** (9-8) 20-1 challenged two out but could not quite pull out enough under a forceful ride.

3. **Tidjani** (10-1) 10-1 stayed on from the last.

2¹/₂l, 2l. (A J Martin) 16 ran.

114 Fairyhouse, 2m, £50,000, good to soft, Apr 6 1999.

Goffs Land Rover Bumper

1. **Berkeley Run** (11-4) 5-1 was always prominent, and, leading two furlongs out, was then strongly pressed close home, eventually all out to hold on.
2. **Intacta Print** (11-5) 12-1 was ridden to challenge inside the final furlong and only just failed in a thrilling finish.
3. **Sweet Deal** (11-3) 14-1 ran on under pressure in the final quarter-mile.
4. **Boley Lad** (11-3) 9-2 jt fav chased the leaders all the way round.

sh hd, 3l, 4l. (S Treacy) 22 ran.

115 Ascot, 3m, £31,500, good to firm, Apr 7 1999.

Grosvenor Casinos Long Distance Hurdle (Grade 2)

1. **Galant Moss** (11-3) evens fav was held up until the last possible moment under an inspired Tony McCoy ride to take it up close home.
2. **Lord Jim** (11-10) 12-1 made most of the running but could not withstand the winner's late show.
3. **Paddy's Return** (11-10) 11-4 was always prominent.

2¹/₂l, sh hd. (M Pipe) 5 ran.

116 Aintree, 2m 110yds, £35,000, good, Apr 8 1999.

Barton And Guestier Top Novices' Hurdle (Grade 2)

1. **Joe Mac** (11-8) 6-4 fav was never out of third gear and won this in tremendous style, leading at the last before breezing in.
2. **Grecian Dart** (11-5) 13-2 was always in the front rank but was fighting a losing battle all the way up the home straight.
3. **Piped Aboard** (10-8) 11-1 stayed on at the finish, having never been far off the pace.

4l, 3¹/₂l. (C Roche) 9 ran.

117 Aintree, 3m 1f, £65,000, good, Apr 8 1999.

Martell Cup Chase (Grade 2)

1. **Macgeorge** (11-5) 11-1 was given a determined ride by Adrian Maguire, leading from halfway then responding gamely when headed before two out to take it up again.
2. **Escartefigue** (11-5) 9-4 had the blinkers left off and gave the impression he wasn't always putting it all in, ducking in behind the winner on more than one occasion.
3. **Dr Leunt** (11-5) 12-1 was the early leader before fading in the closing stages.
4. **Go Ballistic** (11-5) 3-1 never showed the same dash as he had at Cheltenham.
5. **Majadou** (10-10) 13-8 fav was let down by his jumping and his hard race at Cheltenham obviously took its toll.

1¹/₂l, 11l, 1¹/₂l, 2¹/₂l. (R Lee) 5 ran.

118 Aintree, 2m, £55,000, good, Apr 8 1999.

Sandeman Maghull Novices' Chase (Grade 1)

1. **Flagship Uberalles** (10-11) 5-2 jt fav was never

far away, and, leading three out, ran on to win this in great style.
2. **Grimes** (11-4) 6-1 made a highly promising debut over fences, always going well but lacking the finishing kick of the winner.
3. **Dawn Leader** (11-4) 5-2 jt fav led to halfway before fading. He needs a longer trip.
4. **Clifton Beat** (11-4) 11-1 faded quickly having chased the leaders to halfway.
5. **Tresor De Mai** (10-11) 10-3 weakened after a series of mistakes.

9l, hd, 5l, 15l. (P Nicholls) 7 ran.

119 Aintree, 2³/₄m, £20,000, good, Apr 8 1999.

Martell Fox Hunters' Chase

1. **Elegant Lord** (12-0) 7-4 fav set the pace and the result was never in doubt once he was given the office approaching the elbow on the run-in.
2. **Mely Moss** (12-0) 11-2 was covered up until produced to challenge two out, only for a lack of fitness to tell.
3. **Kibreet** (12-0) 20-1 was prominent to halfway, but could not find the extra required at the business end.

7l, 13l. (E Bolger) 23 ran.

120 Aintree, 2m 110yds, £40,000, good, Apr 8 1999.

Glenlivet Anniversary 4YO Novices Hurdle (Grade 2)

1. **Hors La Loi III** (11-4) 8-15 fav looks destined for top honours based on this display of quick and accurate jumping from the front.
2. **Afarad** (11-0) 6-1 was always going well but could never peg back the winner.
3. **Golden Rule** (11-0) 11-1 was close up before running on at the one pace.
4. **Simply Gifted** (11-0) 6-1 travelled supremely well but found little when popped the question.

3¹/₂l, 3l, 3¹/₂l. (M Pipe) 6 ran.

121 Aintree, 3m 110yds, £17,500, good, Apr 8 1999.

Barton & Guestier Hcap Hurdle

1. **Papo Kharisma** (10-0) 12-1 put a poor effort at Cheltenham behind him, making ruthless progress to lead at the last.
2. **Darapour** (10-0) 4-1 fav travelled well and had his head in front until the winner swooped.
3. **Nocksky** (10-0) 16-1 made most of the running but could not quicken when asked.
4. **Lady Cricket** (11-8) 5-1 was clumsy at several flights before keeping on.

1¹/₄l, 2¹/₂l, ¹/₂l. (P Hobbs) 14 ran.

122 Aintree, 2¹/₂m, £30,000, good, Apr 9 1999.

Martell Mersey Novices' Hurdle

1. **Barton** (11-9) 2-7 fav had a real struggle, leading at the last and staying on determinedly as the runner-up threatened.
2. **Auetaler** (11-1) 14-1 touched down in the lead at the second last but did not quite have the firepower to foil the winner.

97

3. **Prominent Profile** (11-1) 10-1 set a strong pace, and although soon clear, he did not hurdle with any fluency and faded once headed.
4. **Polar Flight** (11-1) 25-1 weakened from halfway.
2l, 20l, 28l. (T Easterby) 6 ran.

123
Aintree, 2¹/₂m, £85,000, good, Apr 9 1999.

Mumm Melling Chase (Grade 1)
1. **Direct Route** (11-10) 7-2 was happier on this flatter track and, although he had a struggle maintaining the lead he had taken at the last, he never really looked like being headed.
2. **Mulligan** (11-10) 10-1 sweated up badly beforehand but ran really well, leading for much of the trip and rallying really well once tackled after the last.
3. **Call Equiname** (11-10) 11-10 fav was always prominent but the odd jumping error told.
4. **Opera Hat** (11-5) 8-1 faded from a promising position.
nk, 2¹/₂l, 12l. (J Howard Johnson) 6 ran.

124
Aintree, 3m 1f, £45,000, good, Apr 9 1999.

Mumm Mildmay Novices' Chase (Grade 2)
1. **Spendid** (11-9) 10-3 fav was driven out all the way to the line, having taken it up three from home.
2. **Village King** (11-4) 11-2 stayed on after getting outpaced down the back straight.
3. **Makounji** (10-11) 7-2 cut out the donkey work up front until forfeiting the lead three out as her stamina began to give out.
8l, 1³/₄l. (D Nicholson) 7 ran.

125
Aintree, 2³/₄m, £35,000, good, Apr 9 1999.

John Hughes Trophy Chase
1. **Listen Timmy** (11-8) 14-1 tackled the big fences with real enthusiasm, always to the fore before taking it up four out and galloping on strongly.
2. **Linden's Lotto** (11-5) 15-2 set the pace from halfway and didn't give up when passed by the winner.
3. **Maitre De Musique** (10-3) 16-1 kept on without ever posing a real threat..
4. **The Outback Way** (11-7) 9-1 was in touch from halfway before plugging on.
3l, 3l, 1³/₄l. (S Brookshaw) 20 ran.

126
Aintree, 3m 110yds, £40,000, good to soft, Apr 9 1999.

Belle Epoque Sefton Novices' Hurdle (Grade 1)
1. **King's Road** (11-4) 3-1 jt fav made most of the running and, despite mistakes at the third last and final flight, stayed on nicely.
2. **Ballysicyos** (10-10) 7-1 pursued the winner all the way up the straight and only went down after a prolonged battle.
3. **Santabless** (11-4) 25-1 improved from the rear before staying on.
4. **Lord Noelie** (11-4) 10-1 ran on from the mid-division.
1³/₄l, 2l, 6l. (N Twiston-Davies) 15 ran.

127
Aintree, 2¹/₂m, £20,000, good to soft, Apr 9 1999.

Oddbins Hcap Hurdle
1. **Khayrawani** (11-7) 7-2 fav had his second hard race in the space of a month, making headway under pressure to lead at the last where he was left clear by the fatal fall of Budalus (who probably would have won).
2. **Outset** (10-5) 14-1 kept on under pressure from two out.
3. **Sadler's Realm** (9-11) 7-1 improved from rear although he couldn't land a telling blow.
4. **Serenus** (10-8) 14-1 ran on at the one pace.
1¹/₂l, 4l, 5l. (C Roche) 15 ran.

128
Aintree, 2m 110yds, £30,000, good, Apr 10 1999.

Cordon Bleu Hcap Hurdle
1. **Kinnescash** (10-0) 7-1 proved very game in front, leading from four out and running on really well.
2. **Fadalko** (10-4) 8-1 looked a danger for the final two furlongs but couldn't overhaul the winner.
3. **Wakeel** (10-1) 20-1 ran on well enough.
4. **Bellator** (11-10) 12-1 was rather outpaced down the home straight.
1l, 2l, 5l. (P Bowen) 12 ran.

129
Aintree, 2m, £45,000, good, Apr 10 1999.

Martell Red Rum Chase (Ltd Hcap) (Grade 2)
1. **Flying Instructor** (11-5) 11-2 was touched off in the mud in this race last year but made no mistake here, leading three out before staying on well.
2. **Green Green Desert** (12-0) 4-1 has been called a few names in the past but didn't duck the issue, even if the winner proved too strong.
3. **Celibate** (12-0) 3-1 fav was always in touch but lacked a decisive finishing kick.
4. **Arctic Kinsman** (11-0) 11-2 made most until weakening once headed at the third last.
3¹/₂l, 5l, 10l. (P R Webber) 7 ran.

130
Aintree, 2¹/₂m, £80,000, good, Apr 10 1999.

Martell Aintree Hurdle (Grade 1)
1. **Istabraq** (11-7) 1-2 fav made it 16 wins from 18 starts over timber, tracking the leaders until taking it up at the last for another very cosy victory.
2. **French Holly** (11-7) 11-2 jumped better than he has done in the past but is not in the winner's class. A chasing career beckons.
3. **Midnight Legend** (11-7) 33-1 ran up to his best form, prominent until dropping away at the finish
4. **Mister Morose** (11-7) 10-1 was always under pressure.
1l, 6l, 24l. (A P O'Brien) 7 ran.

131
Aintree, 4¹/₂m, £420,000, good, Apr 10 1999.

Martell Grand National Chase (Showcase Hcap) (Grade 3)
1. **Bobbyjo** (10-0) 10-1 was never far away before being produced with an immaculately-timed run to take things up after the last.
2. **Blue Charm** (10-0) 25-1 jumped for fun out in front from halfway but his stamina gave out after the last.
3. **Call It A Day** (10-2) 7-1 saw out the trip well,

98

improving from midfield to almost snatch second spot.

4. **Addington Boy** (10-7) 10-1 stalked round off the pace for most of the way, he improved to look a danger over the second last only for his stamina to give way.

5. **Feels Like Gold** (10-0) 50-1 ran brilliantly considering he was 30lb out of the handicap, in touch for much of the race and only dropping away late on.

6. **Brave Highlander** (10-1) 50-1 took it up two out but was very tired jumping the last and faded,

7. **Kendal Cavalier** (10-0) 28-1 stayed on having been badly hampered at Becher's second time round.

8. **Earth Summit** (11-0) 16-1 wants much slower ground than he got here.

F. **Fiddling The Facts** (10-3) 6-1 fav travelled smoothly until departing at Becher's second time round.

F. **Double Thriller** (10-8) 7-1 overjumped the first and crumpled on landing.

10l, nk, 7l, 5l, 14l, 18l, hd. (T Carberry) 32 ran.

132 Aintree, 2m 110yds, £17,500, good, Apr 10 1999.
Martell Champion Standard National Hunt Flat (Grade 2)

1. **King Of The Castle** (11-2) 7-2 was always travelling well and, leading two furlongs out, ran out a ready winner.

2. **Errand Boy** (11-8) 12-1 was always close up but could not match the winner's finishing kick.

3. **Always Wayward** (11-2) 50-1 kept on, having raced in mid-division for most of the trip.

4. **Festival Leader** (10-13) 66-1 was slowly away and never really landed a blow.

4l, ½l, 2½l. (Mrs J Pitman) 17 ran.

133 Ayr, 2½m, £25,000, good to soft, Apr 17 1999.
11th Edinburgh Woollen Mill Future Champion Novices' Chase

1. **Bouchasson** (11-3) 50-1 jumped right at most of his fences but took it up from four out for a runaway success.

2. **Scotia Nostra** (11-3) 12-1 was always in touch but finished very tired.

3. **Irbee** (11-10) 7-2 ran as though a busy season had got to him, fading badly in the closing stages.

18l, 1¼l. (P Hobbs) 6 ran.

134 Ayr, 2m, £25,000, good to soft, Apr 17 1999.
Samsung Scottish Champion Hurdle (Ltd Hcap)

1. **Fadalko** (10-4) 4-1 proved a real fighter, leading on the run-in and all out thereafter.

2. **Potentate** (11-7) 3-1 made most of the running but wasn't quite as tenacious as the winner.

3. **Crazy Horse** (10-4) 5-4 fav travelled well in touch but didn't have the stomach for a fight at the business end.

4. **Bellator** (11-2) 4-1 dropped away after tracking the leaders for most of the race.

¾l, 2¾l, 24l. (P Nicholls) 4 ran.

135 Ayr, 4m 1f, £70,000, good to soft, Apr 17 1999.
Stakis Scottish Grand National Hcap Chase

1. **Young Kenny** (11-10) 5-2 fav looked a serious Aintree candidate on this performance, jumping for fun, leading from halfway before being driven out for a smooth success.

2. **Hollybank Buck** (11-0) 15-2 ran a cracker, always in touch, but the winner was always doing too much.

3. **Full Of Oats** (9-11) 20-1 ran up to his best but lacks a bit of pace these days.

4. **Clever Remark** (10-6) 7-1 ran on at his own pace.

5. **Farfadet V** (10-4) 25-1 was always behind, although he did make some late headway.

9l, 6l, 10l, 18l. (P Beaumont) 15 ran.

136 Sandown, 2½m 110yds, £20,000, soft, Apr 24 1999.
Brewers Fayre Novices' Hcap Chase

1. **Dark Stranger** (10-6) 4-1 bounced back from a poor run at Ayr to deliver his challenge at the last.

2. **Fanfaron** (10-2) 10-3 made most of the running until collared by the winner at the last.

3. **Andsuephi** (11-4) 11-4 fav was chased along down the back straight and struggled thereafter.

2½l, 29l. (M Pipe) 5 ran.

137 Sandown, 3m 5f 110yds, £100,000, soft, Apr 24 1999.
43rd Whitbread Gold Cup Chase (Showcase Hcap) (Grade 3)

1. **Eulogy** (10-0) 14-1 showed improved form going right-handed, tracking the leaders before taking it up at the last.

2. **Betty's Boy** (10-0) 15-2 seemd to see out the trip, leading from halfway and keeping on once tackled from the 16th.

3. **Jathib** (10-0) 20-1 progressed to lead from the 16th but could not pull out any extra when required.

4. **Fine Thyne** (10-0) 20-1 made steady headway but could only finish at the one pace.

5. **Cariboo Gold** (10-0) 50-1 was never better than mid-division.

6. **Bobbyjo** (10-0) 100-30 fav looked chucked in at the weights, running off an 11lb lower mark than when winning the Grand National, but the Aintree race had obviously taken its toll and he could only plod round without ever threatening.

3½l, 1l, 1½l, 8l. (R Rowe) 19 ran.

138 Sandown, 2½m 110yds, £30,000, soft, Apr 24 1999.
Pizza Hut Silver Trophy Chase (Grade 2)

1. **Super Tactics** (11-4) 5-1 loves going right-handed and, leading two out, kept on well.

2. **Northern Starlight** (11-0) 7-2 got the better of a real battle with Mulligan for the lead but that probably sealed his fate.

3. **Mulligan** (11-0) 2-1 fav forfeited the lead with an

error at the sixth and was in trouble after the Pond Fence.
4l, 10l. (R Alner) 7 ran.

139 Punchestown, 2m, £53,000, soft, Apr 27 1999.
Country Pride Champion Novice Hurdle (Grade 1)
1. **Cardinal Hill** (11-13) 1-2 fav was always close up, and leading at the last, ran on for an easy success.
2. **Greenstead** (12-0) 20-1 led three out, but was headed approaching the last, could offer no more.
3. **Dance So Suite** (12-0) 14-1 was under pressure from two out.
4. **Fadoudal Du Cochet** (12-0) 16-1 led until ridden and headed three out.
1¹/₄l, 5l, 15l. (N Meade) 5 ran.

140 Punchestown, 2m, £55,000, soft, Apr 27 1999.
B.M.W. Chase (Grade 1)
1. **Celibate** (11-9) 7-1 was given an excellent ride by Richard Dunwoody, making all and repelling all comers.
2. **Space Trucker** (11-9) 8-1 was never far away but just could not get his head in front.
3. **Direct Route** (12-0) 5-4 fav was beaten when making a mistake at the last and a late rally was to little effect.
4. **Hill Society** (11-6) 8-1 wasn't helped by a mistake three out and ran on rather one-paced thereafter.
1l, 1l, ¹/₂l. (C Mann) 6 ran.

141 Punchestown, 2¹/₂m, £24,000, soft, Apr 27 1999.
Bradstock Insurance Novice Chase (Grade 3)
1. **Ferbet Junior** (12-0) 3-1 overcame a blunder at the third to make all, clear from three out.
2. **Manus The Man** (11-11) 2-1 fav made a series of mistakes including a bad one two out, just when he was making progress.
3. **Micko's Dream** (12-0) 5-2 also jumped indifferently which effectively sealed his fate.
12l, 5l. (Mrs J Harrington) 7 ran.

142 Punchestown, 2¹/₂m, £50,000, good to soft, Apr 28 1999.
Stanley Cooker Champion Novice Hurdle (Grade 1)
1. **Native Upmanship** (12-0) 8-1 challenged two out having been held up off the pace for the first part of the race. Leading before the last, he needed only to be pushed clear for a convincing victory.
2. **Wither Or Which** (12-0) 12-1 kept on well enough without ever threatening the winner.
3. **Colonel Yeager** (11-13) 5-2 challenged from two out but was soon under pressure.
4. **Prominent Profile** (12-0) 14-1 failed to quicken in the closing stages, having cut out much of the donkey work.
5¹/₄l, 2l, 3¹/₄l. (A L Moore) 11 ran.

143 Punchestown, 3m 1f, £120,000, good to soft, Apr 28 1999.
Punchestown Heineken Gold Cup (Chase Grade 1)
1. **Imperial Call** (11-9) 8-1 made all, benefiting from a loose horse which distracted the rest of the field.
2. **Florida Pearl** (12-0) 4-7 fav was always in touch but could make no impression in the closing stages.
3. **Dorans Pride** (12-0) 10-3 weakened after a mistake four from home.
4. **Opera Hat** (11-9) 33-1 was always behind.
14l, dis, dis. (R Hurley) 5 ran.

144 Punchestown, 2m, £25,000, good to soft, Apr 28 1999.
Paddy Power Bookmakers Champion I.N.H. Flat Race (Grade 1)
1. **Our Bid** (12-1) 25-1 tracked the leaders before sneaking through to challenge in the straight and got up in the dying strides.
2. **Crocadee** (12-1) 8-1 was always in the front rank, and, although leading from halfway, was just outbattled in the closing stages.
3. **Ingonish** (12-4) 12-1 held every chance entering the final furlong.
4. **Ballinclay King** (12-0) 11-4 fav was placed with every chance two furlongs out but could only plug on at the one pace.
5. **Billywill** (12-3) 6-1 challenged in the straight only to weaken in the final furlong.
1l, nk, 3¹/₂l, ¹/₂l. (K Prendergast) 19 ran.

145 Punchestown, 2m £70,000, good to soft, Apr 29 1999.
I.A.W.S. Champion Four Year Old Hurdle (Grade 1)
1. **Katarino** (11-0) 7-4 fav responded to a vigorous ride, leading two out and staying on in really game fashion.
2. **Golden Rule** (11-0) 11-1 challenged for the lead briefly approaching the last but quickly had to settle for second-best.
3. **Afarad** (11-0) 6-1 made progress from midfield three out but could only finish at the one pace.
4. **Miss Emer** (10-9) 20-1 was never nearer.
5. **Balla Sola** (11-0) 2-1 held every chance two out.
1¹/₂l, 3¹/₂l, 2¹/₂l, 2¹/₂l. (N Henderson) 9 ran.

146 Punchestown, 2m, £47,500, good to soft, Apr 29 1999.
Tripleprint Novice Chase (Grade 1)
1. **Sydney Twothousand** (11-5) 11-2 disputed the lead throughout before staying on strongly after asserting from the last.
2. **Society Brief** (11-5) 9-1 made smooth progress to join the leaders two out, but couldn't pass the winner.
3. **Promalee** (11-9) 5-4 fav held every chance when blundering through the last.
4. **Wynyard Knight** (11-5) 3-1 led at halfway only to fade before the last
3l, 2¹/₂l, 4l. (N Meade) 6 ran.

KAT SUIT . . . top juvenile hurdler Katarino on his way to another success

147
Punchestown, 3m, £50,000, good to soft, Apr 29 1999.

Ballymore Properties Champion Stayers Hurdle (Grade 1)

1. **Anzum** (12-0) 7-1 is a really game animal and did things the hard way here, making all and responding to his rider's every call.
2. **Khayrawani** (11-11) 16-1 could never quite land a blow when it mattered most but stayed on well enough.
3. **Mister Morose** (11-11) 12-1 was going nowhere two out and could only plug on at the one pace.
4. **Pharanear** (11-11) 16-1 could never muster a serious challenge.

2¹/₂l, 3¹/₂l, 2l. (D Nicholson) 6 ran.

148
Punchestown, 3m 1f, £30,000, good to soft, Apr 29 1999.

Castlemartin Stud Pat Taaffe Hcap Chase (Grade 2)

1. **Emerald Gale** (9-9) 9-1 was the outsider of the trainer's three runners. Making progress under pressure four out, he led two out and then stayed on strongly on the flat.
2. **Miss Diskin** (10-2) 9-1 made most of the running but could not match the winner's well-timed burst.
3. **Hardiman** (10-0) 5-1 co fav was held up before progressing smoothly to challenge at the last without quite having the reserves to see things through.
4. **The Quads** (10-3) 5-1 co fav held every chance at the last.
5. **Ryhane** (10-12) 5-1 co fav made smooth head-

way to join the leaders three out but could not sustain his challenge.

1l, 2l, sh hd, 7l. (A L Moore) 11 ran.

149
Punchestown, 2m, £110,000, good, Apr 30 1999.

Shell Champion Hurdle (Grade 1)

1. **Istabraq** (12-0) 1-4 fav again demonstrted that no other current hurdler is in his league, leading two out for another easy win.
2. **Decoupage** (11-9) 9-1 was made to look rather one-paced by the winner.
3. **Limestone Lad** (11-9) 11-1 set the pace until collared at the business end.
4. **Space Trucker** (11-9) 11-1 tracked the leaders until outpaced from two out.

3¹/₂l, 5l, 5¹/₂l. (A P O'Brien) 7 ran.

150
Haydock, 2m, £40,000, firm, May 1 1999.

Crowther Homes Swinton Hcap Hurdle (Grade 3)

1. **She's Our Mare** (10-0) 10-1 was brought with a well-timed run to lead at the last.
2. **Papua** (10-0) 33-1 ran a cracker from 6lb out of the handicap, leading after halfway until collared late on.
3. **Auetaler** (10-9) 5-1 fav handled the lively ground well, putting in a bold show until outpaced close home.
4. **Dictamn** (10-9) 16-1 kept on, having made progress from the rear from halfway.

1¹/₄l, 2l, nk. (A J Martin) 22 ran.

103

Around the tracks

Your complete A-to-Z guide to every National Hunt racecourse in the UK

AINTREE

★ = evening fixture

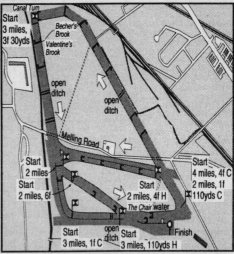

TicTac: The Grand National course is flat and 2m 2f round. The big race is run over two circuits, with 30 fences to be jumped before a 494yd run-in. The Mildmay course is 1m 4f round, with conventional birch fences.

How To Get There
Road: 5 miles N of Liverpool, on A59 Ormskirk Road. From North, M6-M58-A59.
Rail: Aintree Station adjoins course. Special trains run on National day.
Enquiries: Tel 0151 523 2600.
Top Trainers: M Pipe, D Nicholson, N Twiston-Davies. **Top Jockeys:** A P McCoy, A Dobbin, R Johnson.
Special Trainer Tip: Pipe's still 'the main man' but Tim Easterby is the new kid on the block.
Favourites: 1995-1999: Hurdles +£3.58, chases +£16.57. (Longest winning run 7, longest losing run 8). Best Bet: Favourites over the Mildmay fences can be followed with confidence.

(map labels) Canal Turn · Start 3 miles, 3f 30yds · Becher's Brook · Valentine's Brook · open ditch · open ditch · Melling Road · Start 2 miles · Start 2 miles, 6f · Start 4 miles, 4f C · 2 miles, 1f · 110yds C · Start 2 miles, 4f H · The Chair water · Start 3 miles, 1f C · open ditch · Start 3 miles, 110yds H · Finish

FIXTURES: Nov 21, Apr 6, 7, 8, May 19★

ASCOT

TicTac: Right-handed triangular track of 1m 6f. Ten stiff fences to a circuit, uphill finish and a 240yd run-in.
How To Get There
Road: From South and East, M3 at J3, take A332. From London and North, M4 at J6, A332. From West, M4 J10 to A329(M).
Rail: Frequent service from Waterloo to Ascot (46mins), then 7 minutes walk. Also from Guildford and Reading.
Enquiries: Tel 01344 622211.
Top Trainers: D Nicholson, M Pipe, K Bailey, N Twiston-Davies. **Top Jockeys:** A P McCoy, R Dunwoody, N Williamson, M A Fitzgerald.

(map labels) N · water · open ditch · Start 3 miles H · Start 3 miles 110 yds C · 3 miles 1f 110yds H · Finish · Start 2 miles, 3f 110 yds C · 2 miles, 4f H · Flat Course · Start 2 miles & 3 miles 5f C · 2 miles 110 yds H

Special Trainer Tip: Kim Bailey has left Lambourn but he'll still be a force here while Jim Old makes it pay with his chasers. **Favourites:** 1995-1999: Hurdles -£12.43, chases +£12.58. (Longest winning run 4, longest losing run 11). Best Bet: Long-distance hurdle jollies show a good profit.

FIXTURES: Oct 30, Nov 19, 20, Dec 18, Jan 15, 21, Feb 19, Apr 1, 5

AYR

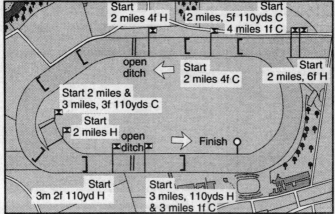

Start 2 miles 4f H
Start 2 miles, 5f 110yds C
4 miles 1f C
open ditch
Start 2 miles 4f C
Start 2 miles, 6f H
Start 2 miles & 3 miles, 3f 110yds C
Start 2 miles H
open ditch
Finish
Start 3m 2f 110yd H
Start 3 miles, 110yds H & 3 miles 1f C

TicTac: Left-handed flat track of 1m 4f with nine fences to a circuit and a 210yd run-in.

How To Get There

Road: NE of town centre between A70, A77 and A719.

Rail: From Euston and Glasgow Central to Ayr, then 1m bus or taxi ride.

Enquiries: Tel 01292 264179.

Top Trainers: Mrs M Reveley, L Lungo, P Monteith. **Top Jockeys:** A Dobbin, B Storey, R Supple, P Niven, S Taylor. **Special Trainer Tip:** Mary Reveley is still the punters' favourite around here but local boy Lennie Lungo is catching up fast.

Favourites: 1995-1999 Hurdles -£8.08, chases -£3.71. (Longest winning run 11, longest losing run 11). Best Bet: Treat hurdle favourites with caution.

FIXTURES: Nov 13, 14, Dec 6, 27, Jan 29, Feb 12, Mar 10, 11, Apr 14, 15

BANGOR

TicTac: Left-handed, tight track of 1m 4f with nine quite easy fences to a circuit, and a 1f run-in.

How To Get There

Road: 4 miles South East of Wrexham on A525, then B5069.

Rail: Euston Line to Wrexham General, taxi to Bangor Racecourse.

Enquiries: Tel 01978 780323.

Top Trainers: M Pipe, N Twiston-Davies, D Nicholson.

Top Jockeys: A P McCoy, C Llewellyn, S Wynne, R Johnson.

Special Trainer Tip: Philip Hobbs is making inroads and has a fine strike-rate.

Favourites: 1995-1999: Hurdles -£18.86, chases -£13.21. (Longest winning run 5, longest losing run 14). Best Bet: Poor all-round record here.

Start 2 miles 4f 110yds & 4 miles 1f C
Start 2 miles, 4f H
open ditch
Start 2 miles 1f 110yds & 3 miles 6f C
Start 2m 1f H
open ditch
water
Finish
Start 3 miles, 2f
Start 3 miles 110yds C 3 miles H

FIXTURES: Oct 9, 25, Nov 26, Dec 15, Feb 11, Mar 8, 25, Apr 15, May 5★, 20

CARLISLE

TicTac: Right-handed, undulating track of 1m 5f with nine fences and a punishing, uphill straight. The run-in is 300yd.

How To Get There
Road: Leave M6 at Junction 43 (from North) or 42 (from South). Track 1m South of Carlisle, between A6 and B5299.
Rail: Euston to Carlisle, then half a mile taxi ride.
Enquiries: Tel 01228 22504.
Top Trainers: Mrs M Reveley, L Lungo, Mrs S Smith.
Top Jockeys: A Dobbin, B Storey, P Niven, P Carberry, R Supple.
Special Trainer Tip: Mary Reveley

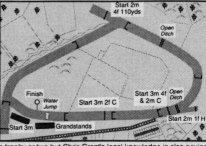

usually heads back to Saltburn with a trophy or two but Chris Grant's local knowledge is also paying dividends. **Favourites:** 1995-1999 Hurdles +£4.08, chases -£11.27. (Longest winning run 6, longest losing run 7). Best Bet: 3m hurdle jollies have a 60 per cent strike rate.

> **FIXTURES:** Oct 8, 23, Nov 8, 25, Dec 30, Jan 18, Feb 8, 21, Mar 9, 31, Apr 22, 24

CARTMEL

TicTac: Left-handed tight track of 1m 2f, with six fences to a circuit and a 4f run-in.
How To Get There
Road: 17 miles South West of Kendal, via A6, A590 and B5271.
Rail: Two miles from Cark and Cartmel Station (Carnforth-Barrow Line).
Enquiries: Tel 01539 536340.
Top Trainers: M Pipe, P Bowen, G M Moore. **Top Jockeys:** A P McCoy, A Dobbin, R Guest, R Johnson.
Special Trainer Tip: George Moore remains the man to follow.
Favourites: 1995-1999 Hurdles -£13.11, chases -£7.42. (Longest winning run 4, longest losing run 6). Best Bet: Hurdle jollies between 2m4f and 3m.

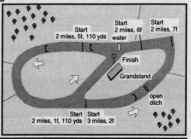

> **FIXTURES:** May 27, 29, 31

CATTERICK

TicTac: Left-handed, oval track of 1m 2f, with eight easy fences and a 240yd run-in.
How To Get There
Road: Adjacent to A1; Richmond 5m, Darlington 13m. **Rail:** Kings Cross to Darlington, then 16m bus from United Bus Station, or taxi. **Enquiries:** Tel 01748 811478.
Top Trainers: Mrs M Reveley, Mrs S Smith, T Easterby, M Hammond. **Top Jockeys:** P Niven, R Garritty, R Guest, A S Smith.
Special Trainer Tip: Another top track for Mary Reveley, who is miles clear of the rest.
Favourites: 1995-1999 Hurdles -£3.79, chases -£13.01. (Longest winning run 5, longest losing run 9). Best Bet: All hurdle jollies, bar those in 2m events, can be backed with confidence.

> **FIXTURES:** Nov 20, Dec 1, 15, 16, 31, Jan 5, 6, 22, Feb 4, 12, 29 Mar 8

CHELTENHAM

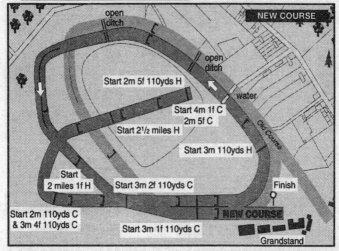

TicTac: Left-handed, 1m 4f round with nine fences to a circuit and a stiff climb to the winning post.

How To Get There

Road: 2m North of the town on A435.

Rail: Paddington Line to Cheltenham Spa; taxi or bus to course. **Enquiries:** Tel 01242 513014.

Top Trainers: M Pipe, D Nicholson, N Twiston-Davies, N Henderson. **Top Jockeys:** A P McCoy, R Dunwoody, N Williamson, M A Fitzgerald.

Special Trainer Tip: The big track brings out the big guns but watch out for Mark Pitman — he's already producing the goods and there's more to come.

Favourites: 1995-1999 Hurdles +£11.41, chases +£0.79. (Longest winning run 9, longest losing run 16). Best Bet: Hurdle jollies are the ones to focus on.

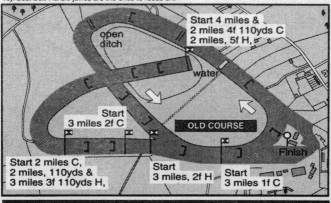

FIXTURES: Oct 26, 27, Nov 12, 13, 14, Dec 10, 11, 31
Jan 3, 29, Mar 14, 15, 16, Apr 19, 20, May 3★

CHEPSTOW

TicTac: Left-handed undulating course of 2m. There are 11 fences to a circuit and a 250yd run-in.

How To Get There

Road: Leave M4 at Junction 22, A466 to track.

Rail: Paddington to Chepstow, then one-and-a-half mile taxi or bus ride. Or via Bristol Parkway, then 15 min taxi ride.

Enquiries: Tel 01291 622260.

Start 3 miles C
3m 110yd H

Start
3 miles, 2f,
110yds

water

open ditch

open ditch

Finish

Start
2 miles 4f 110yd H
2 miles 3f 110yds C

Start
2 miles, 110 yds

Start
3 miles,
5f 110yds

Top Trainers: M Pipe, P Nicholls, P Hobbs, D Nicholson.

Top Jockeys: A P McCoy, R Johnson, R Dunwoody, C Llewellyn.

Special Trainer Tip: Martin Pipe has quality and quantity while Venetia Williams is the one to follow percentage-wise.

Favourites: 1995-1999 Hurdles -£48.77, chases -£8.84. (Longest winning run 3, longest losing run 31). Best Bet: 2m4f chase favourites show a good level-stake profit.

> **FIXTURES: Oct 2, 20, Nov 6, 24, Dec 4, 28, Feb 9, Mar 1, 11, 22, Apr 12, 24, May 10**

DONCASTER

TicTac: Left-handed mainly flat track of almost 2m, with 11 fences to a circuit and 240yd run-in.

How To Get There

Road: 1m SE of Doncaster, off A638 Bawtry Road. From South, M1-M18-A1M-A630. From North, leave M18 at J4, take A630 then A18.

Rail: 1hr 30 mins Kings Cross to Doncaster Central, then bus or taxi.

Enquiries: Tel 01302 320066.

Top Trainers: Mrs M Reveley, N Henderson, D Nicholson, T Easterby. **Top Jockeys:** P Carberry, M A Fitzgerald, R Garritty, P Niven. **Special Trainer Tip:** Nicky Henderson is the percentage man at the South Yorkshire track with Tim Easterby and Steve Gollings others to watch.

Favourites: 1995-1999 Hurdles -£30.79, Chases +£2.25. (Longest winning run 3, longest losing run 10). Best Bet: 3m chase favourites have a 60 percent strike rate.

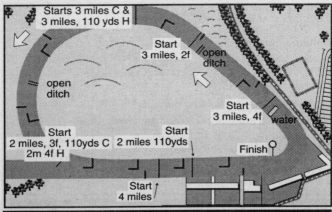

Starts 3 miles C &
3 miles, 110 yds H

Start
3 miles, 2f

open ditch

open ditch

Start
3 miles, 4f

water

Start
2 miles, 3f, 110yds C
2m 4f H

Start
2 miles 110yds

Finish

Start
4 miles

> **FIXTURES: Dec 10, 11, Jan 17, 28, 29, Feb 23, Mar 3, 4**

EXETER

TicTac: Right-handed undulating track of 2m, with 11 fences to a circuit and a 250yd run-in.

How To Get There

Road: At end of M5, take Plymouth road (A38) for 3 miles to Haldon.

Rail: Paddington Line to Exeter St Davids, then taxi.

Enquiries: Tel 01392 832599.

Top Trainers: M Pipe, P Hobbs, R Frost, Miss H Knight.

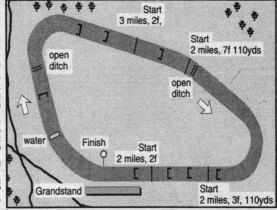

Top Jockeys: A P McCoy, R Dunwoody, J Frost. **Special Trainer Tip:** Oliver Sherwood and Rod Millman have fewer runners than the likes of Martin Pipe but decent strike-rates.

Favourites: 1995-1999 Hurdles -£12.69, Chases -£9.63. (Longest winning run 5, longest losing run 10). Best Bet: 2m hurdle jollies.

FIXTURES: Oct 6, 19, Nov 2, 19, Dec 3, 16, Jan 2, Mar 7, 21, Apr 4, 18, May 3, 9, 17

FAKENHAM

TicTac: Left-handed, undulating, tight track of 1m, with six fences to a circuit and a 250yd run-in.

How To Get There

Road: 21 miles East of Kings Lynn, on A419 and A148. Track 26 miles West of Norwich.

Rail: Liverpool Street to Norwich, then 25 miles by taxi.

Enquiries: Tel 01328 862388.

Top Trainers: Mrs D Haine, O Brennan, J Jenkins, S Gollings.

Top Jockeys: Mickey Brennan, R Johnson, A P McCoy.

Special Trainer Tip: Fewer stats than most tracks to go on here but Owen Brennan has a fair record and Pam Sly's runners must be respected.

Favourites: 1995-1999 Hurdles: +£4.41, Chases -£10.77. (Longest winning run 6, longest losing run 9). Best Bet: Nothing worth mentioning.

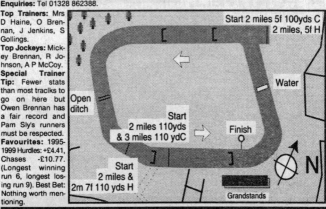

FIXTURES: Oct 22, Dec 6, Jan 10, Feb 18, Mar 17, Apr 24, May 10★

FOLKESTONE

TicTac: Right-handed track of 1m 3f, with seven fences to a circuit and a 1f run-in.
How To Get There
Road: A20, then M20, leaving at Junction 11. Track 7m outside Folkestone.
Enquiries: Tel 01444 441111.
Top Trainers: J Gifford, N Henderson, M Pipe. **Top Jockeys:** N Williamson, M A Fitzgerald, A P McCoy, R Dunwoody. **Special Trainer Tip:** Venetia Williams has a 50 per cent strike-rate from her few runners and must be followed.
Favourites: 1995-1999 Hurdles -£38.90, chases +£28.86. (Longest winning run 6, longest losing run 12). Best Bet: Market leaders over the bigger obstacles as the healthy profits show.

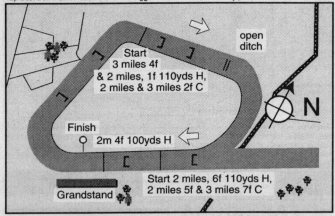

FIXTURES: Nov 18, 29, Dec 11, 17, Jan 3, 14, 18, 28, Feb 4, 15, 22, Mar 17, 20 May 5, 17★

FONTWELL

TicTac: Tight figure-of-eight chase course with seven fences to a circuit and a 230yd run-in. Hurdle course is a left-handed oval of about 1m.
How To Get There
Road: 6 miles East of Chichester, 4 miles West of Arundel, on A27.
Rail: From Victoria and London Bridge to Barnham, then taxi or free coach.
Enquiries: Tel 01444 441111.
Top Trainers: M Pipe, P Nicholls, J Gifford, R Buckler, P Hobbs. **Top Jockeys:** A P McCoy, P Hide, N Williamson, D Gallagher. **Special Trainer Tip:** The Pipe and Nicholls bandwagons continue to roll on but Bob Buckler takes on the big boys with some success.
Favourites: 1995-1999 Hurdles -£43.70, chases +£13.20. (Longest winning run 6, longest losing run 10). Best Bet: Long-distance chase favourites do well.

FIXTURES: Oct 5, 27, Nov 8, Dec 7, 31, Jan 10, 25, Feb 7, 21, Mar 6, 21, Apr 27, May 1, 29

HAYDOCK

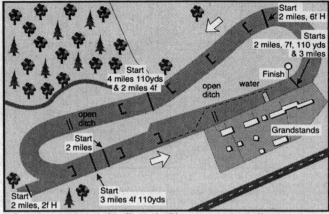

Start 2 miles, 6f H

Starts 2 miles, 7f, 110 yds & 3 miles

Start 4 miles 110yds & 2 miles 4f

Finish

open ditch

water

open ditch

Grandstands

Start 2 miles

Start 2 miles, 2f H

Start 3 miles 4f 110yds

TicTac: Left-handed, flat track of 1m 5f, with 10 stiff fences to a circuit and a 2f run-in.

How To Get There

Road: Leave M6 at Junction 23, track less than 1m away on A49 Wigan Road.

Rail: Euston to Wigan or Warrington, then two-and-a-half mile taxi ride.

Enquiries: Tel 01942 270879. **Top Trainers:** M Pipe, N Twiston-Davies, Mrs M Reveley.

Top Jockeys: L Wyer, R Dunwoody, C Maude, C Lewellyn, P Niven.

Special Trainer Tip: Martin Pipe gets the winners in the bag but Steven Brookshaw and Malcolm Jefferson make the game pay at the Lancashire track.

Favourites: 1995-1999 Hurdles -£20.18, chases +£1.47. (Longest winning run 8, longest losing run 7). Best Bet: 3-mile plus chase favourites can be followed with confidence.

FIXTURES: Nov 4, 13, 27, Dec 11, 29,
Jan 8, 22, Feb 12, 26, May 6 (mixed)

HEREFORD

TicTac: Right-handed, square track of 1m 4f, with nine fences to a circuit and a 300yd run-in.

How To Get There

Road: 28 miles North West of Gloucester, via A40 and A49. From North, M5-M50, A49.

Rail: Paddington Line to Hereford, then one mile taxi ride.

Enquiries: Tel 01432 273560.

Top Trainers: M Pipe, N Twiston-Davies, K Bailey, P Hobbs.

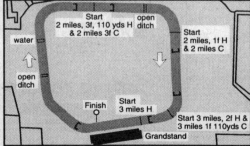

Start 2 miles, 3f, 110 yds H & 2 miles 3f C

open ditch

water

open ditch

Start 2 miles, 1f H & 2 miles C

Finish

Start 3 miles H

Start 3 miles, 2f H & 3 miles 1f 110yds C

Grandstand

Top Jockeys: A P McCoy, C Llewellyn, R Johnson, S Wynne. **Special Trainer Tip:** The main West Country stables have the edge in numbers while Jeff King and Henrietta Knight post excellent strike-rates. **Favourites:** 1995-1999 Hurdles +£2.17, chases -£8.64. (Longest winning run 7, longest losing run 10). Best Bet: Favourites do well when the ground is firm here.

FIXTURES: Oct 15, Nov 17, Dec 3, 14, 27, Jan 11
Feb 14, Mar 10, Apr 24, May 6, 16, 29

HEXHAM

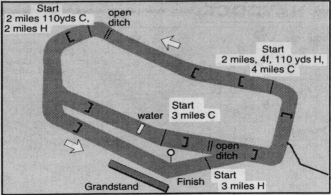

TicTac: Left-handed track of 1m 4f with 10 fences to a circuit and a 250yd run-in.

How To Get There

Road: 38 miles East of Carlisle, 20 miles West of Newcastle, both via A69. 1.5 miles South West of Hexham.

Rail: Kings Cross Line to Hexham, then short taxi ride.

Enquiries: Tel 01434 603738.

Top Trainers: L Lungo, G M Moore, Mrs S Smith, M Hammond.

Top Jockeys: B Storey, A Dobbin, R Garritty, R Supple, P Niven.

Special Trainer Tip: It's tight at the top between George Moore and Lennie Lungo while Malton-based John Quinn is a man on the up. **Favourites:** 1995-1999 Hurdles -£9.70, chases -£29.76. (Longest winning run 5, longest losing run 10). Best Bet: Little to recommend here.

> **FIXTURES: Oct 1, 9, Nov 5, 24, Dec 8, Mar 16, Apr 1, 17, May 13, 20★, 27, 30★**

HUNTINGDON

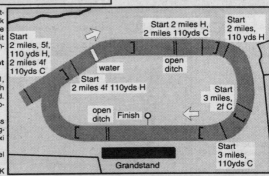

TicTac: Right-handed flat track of 1m 4f with nine fences to a circuit and a 200yd run-in.

How To Get There

Road: Just off A1, 21 miles North East of Bedford. Excellent approach roads.

Rail: Kings Cross Line to Huntingdon; 2 miles taxi ride.

Enquiries: Tel 01480 453373.

Top Trainers: K Bailey, Mrs M Reveley, G Hubbard, N Henderson.

Top Jockeys: R Dunwoody, M A Fitzgerald, J A McCarthy, A Thornton.

Special Trainer Tip: Josh Gifford used to be top man around here but has slipped a little and Kim Bailey leads the pack nowadays. Charlie Egerton places his runners well.

Favourites: 1995-1999 Hurdles +£16.19, chases -£10.49. (Longest winning run 6, longest losing run 10). Best Bet: Both hurdle and chase novices favourites show a good profit.

> **FIXTURES: Oct 8, Nov 9, 20, Dec 9, 27, Jan 19, 27, Feb 10, 24, Mar 4, 15, Apr 24, May 2★, 17★, 29**

KELSO

TicTac: Left-handed chase course of 1m 3f, with nine fences to a circuit and a testing 2f run-in. Separate hurdles course.

How To Get There
Road: 23 miles South of Berwick-upon-Tweed, via A 698. Track just outside town. **Rail:** Difficult, nearest station Berwick-upon-Tweed. **Enquiries:** Tel 01668 281611.

Top Trainers: Mrs M Reveley, M Hammond, P Monteith.
Top Jockeys: P Niven, A Dobbin, B Storey, R Garrity.
Special Trainer Tip: Mary Reveley dominates from nearby Cleveland while Anne Swinbank and Sue Smith make it a great track for the ladies.
Favourites: 1995-1999 Hurdles: +£4.05, Chases +£1.17. (Longest winning run 7, longest losing run 7). Best Bet: Hurdle jollies over the minimum trip are worth a second look.

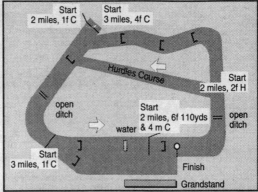

Start 2 miles, 1f C
Start 3 miles, 4f C
Hurdles Course
Start 2 miles, 2f H
open ditch
open ditch
open ditch
Start 2 miles, 6f 110yds & 4m C
water
Start 3 miles, 1f C
Finish
Grandstand

FIXTURES: Oct 16, 30, Nov 10, 29, Dec 20, Jan 21, Feb 3, Mar 3, 24, Apr 3, May 3★, 24

KEMPTON

TicTac: Right-handed, flat track of 1m 5f, with 10 fences to a circuit and a 175yd run-in.
How To Get There
Road: 15m SW of London, via A316 to start of M3, then A308 Kingston Road, From W leave M3 at J1, take A308 for half a mile.
Rail: Waterloo to Kempton Park station which adjoins the course.
Enquiries: Tel 01932 782292.

Top Trainers: D Nicholson, N Henderson, R Alner, N Twiston-Davies.
Top Jockeys: M A Fitzgerald, R Dunwoody, A Thornton, A Maguire.
Special Trainer Tip: David Nicholson heads the list for winners and his strike-rate is excellent. Paul Webber has a good record with his chasers.
Favourites: 1995-1999 Hurdles -£5.59, Chases +£6.54. (Longest winning run 4, longest losing run 9).
Best Bet: Favourites in handicap chases show decent returns to level stakes.

Thames Valley Line
Start 2 miles 4f 110yd C
2 miles 5f H
open ditch
open ditch
Lake
Start 3m 110yd H & 3miles C
water
Finish
Paddock
Start 2 miles, 3 miles 5f
Grandstand

FIXTURES: Nov 3, 17, Dec 27, 28, Jan 22, Feb 1, 25, 26

LEICESTER

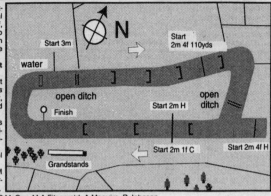

TicTac: Right-handed, oval track of 1m 6f, with 10 fences to a circuit and an uphill finish. The run-in is 250yd.

How To Get There

Road: Track is at Oadby, two miles SE of Leicester, between A50 and A6.

Rail: St Pancras to Leicester Midland, then two-mile bus ride.

Enquiries: Tel 0116 2716515.

Top Trainers: M Pipe, N Henderson, D Nicholson.

Top Jockeys: A P McCoy, M A Fitzgerald, A Maguire, R Johnson.

Special Trainer Tip: Martin Pipe leads the pack and Nicky Henderson also does well here. Richard Lee has made it pay from his relatively few runners.

Favourites: 1995-1999 Hurdles: -£18.27, chases -£6.66. (Longest winning run 5, longest losing run 10). Best Bet: Keep well clear of the market leaders here.

> **FIXTURES:** Nov 15, Dec 2, 8, 28, Jan 5, 11, 25, Feb 2, 16, Mar 7

LINGFIELD

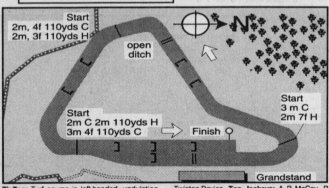

TicTac: Turf course is left-handed, undulating and just over 1m 4f round, with nine fences to a circuit and a 200yd run-in.

How To Get There

Road: From London, M25 to Junction 6, then A22 and B2029. **Rail:** Victoria or London Bridge to Lingfield Station, adjoining course. **Enquiries:** Tel 01342 834800.

Top Trainers: M Pipe, G L Moore, J Gifford, N Twiston-Davies. **Top Jockeys:** A P McCoy, R Dunwoody, M A Fitzgerald, P Hide.

Special Trainer Tip: Gary Moore has almost as many runners as Martin Pipe and plenty of winners.

Favourites: 1995-1999 Hurdles -£20.08, chases -£1.15. (Longest winning run 5, longest losing run 7). Best Bet: Novice hurdle market leaders have a 52 percent strike rate.

> **FIXTURES:** Dec 11

LUDLOW

TicTac: Right-handed, flat track of 1m 4f, with nine fences to a circuit and a 180yd run-in.

How To Get There

Road: 40 miles West of Birmingham (A49). **Rail:** Paddington or Euston to Ludlow, then 2 miles taxi ride. **Enquiries:** Tel 01981 250052.

Top Trainers: M Pipe, K Bailey, D Nicholson. **Top Jockeys:** R Johnson, A P McCoy, N Williamson, S Wynne.

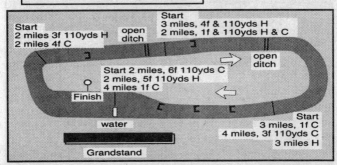

2m 5f 110yds H

Hurdle Course

N

2m 4f C

2m C

3m 2f 110yds H

3m C

Finish

open ditch

open ditch

Grandstand

2m H

Special Trainer Tip: It's 'tight at the top' here with Pipe, Bailey and Nicholson heading the line-up. Cumbria's Jonjo O'Neill has a tremendous strike-rate with his few runners. **Favourites:** 1995-1999 Hurdles -£11.59, chases -£8.01. (Longest winning run 5, longest losing run 7). Best Bet: Chase jollies up to 2m4f have proved profitable in recent seasons.

FIXTURES: Oct 7, 21, Nov 11, 22, Dec 9, 22, Jan 7, 20, Feb 9, 23, Mar 2, 22, Apr 5, 13, May 1

MARKET RASEN

Start
2 miles 3f 110yds H
2 miles 4f C

open ditch

Start
3 miles, 4f & 110yds H
2 miles, 1f & 110yds H & C

open ditch

Start 2 miles, 6f 110yds C
2 miles, 5f 110yds H
4 miles 1f C

Finish

water

Grandstand

Start
3 miles, 1f C
4 miles, 3f 110yds C
3 miles H

TicTac: Right-handed, sharp track of 1m 2f, with eight easy fences to a circuit and a 250yd run-in.

How To Get There Road: 16 miles North East of Lincoln (A46). **Rail:** Market Rasen station (Kings Cross-Cleethorpes line), then one-mile taxi ride. **Enquiries:** Tel 01673 843434.

Top Trainers: Mrs M Reveley, M Pipe, Mrs S Smith, M Chapman.

Top Jockeys: A P McCoy, N Williamson, R Johnson, P Niven.

Special Trainer Tip: Jimmy FitzGerald is not the force of old around here and Mary Reveley has taken over at the top. Toby Balding's strike-rate is second to none.

Favourites: 1995-1999 Hurdles -£64.03, chases -£1.29. (Longest winning run 6, longest losing run 13). Best Bet: Nothing can be recommended here.

FIXTURES: Oct 23, Nov 13, 23, Dec 2, 27, Feb 25, Mar 18, Apr 1, 24, 29 May 13★, 27★

MUSSELBURGH

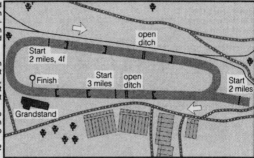

TicTac: Right-handed flat track of 1m 1f with eight fences to a circuit and a 150yd run-in (chases) and 250yd (hurdles).

How To Get There

Road: From South (A7, A68, A702); East (A1, A198); West (M8, A199). Course is at Musselburgh, 8m East of Edinburgh.

Rail: Kings Cross to Edinburgh, then 8 min Superior Sprinter to Musselburgh.

Enquiries: Tel 01292 264179.

Top Trainers: J Howard Johnson, M Hammond, P Monteith, F Murphy.

Top Jockeys: A Dobbin, P Carberry, B Storey, A S Smith.

Special Trainer Tip: Howard Johnson and Micky Hammond may be battling it out at the top but Ferdie Murphy is the man most feared by the bookies. **Favourites:** 1995-1999 Hurdles: -£9.90, Chases -£3.01. (Longest winning run 6, longest losing run 11). Best Bet: Chase favourites over 3m do well.

FIXTURES: Dec 14, 29, Jan 4, 14, Feb 1, 16, 26, Mar 6

NEWBURY

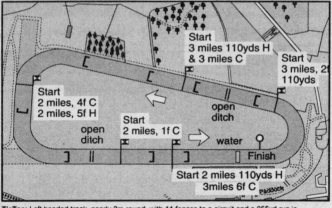

TicTac: Left-handed track, nearly 2m round, with 11 fences to a circuit and a 255yd run-in.

How To Get There

Road: From W, leave M4 at J13, take A34 into Newbury. From E, leave M4 at J12, take A4.

Rail: Paddington to Newbury racecourse station. (From London a special return ticket and course admission is available). **Enquiries:** Tel 01635 40015.

Top Trainers: M Pipe, D Nicholson, N Henderson, N Twiston-Davies.

Top Jockeys: R Dunwoody, M A Fitzgerald, A P McCoy.

Special Trainer Tip: All of the top yards do well here but the man to follow is James Fanshawe, whose strike-rate is almost 50 percent.

Favourites: 1995-1999: Hurdles +£8.70, chases -£4.93 (Longest winning run 6, longest losing run 9). Best bet: Stick to the hurdle favourites and you should not go too far wrong.

FIXTURES: Nov 9, 10, 26, 27, Feb 12, Mar 3, 4, 24, 25

NEWCASTLE

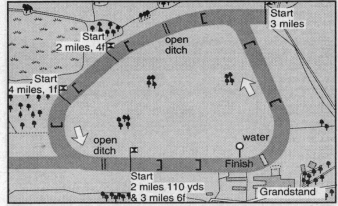

TicTac: Left-handed track of 1m 6f, with 11 fences to a circuit, a steady climb to the winning post and a run-in of 220yd.

How To Get There

Road: 5m North of Newcastle on A1. Track quarter of a mile from main road.

Rail: Kings Cross to Newcastle Central, then metro and special bus, or taxi (five miles).

Enquiries: Tel 0191 236 2020. **Top Trainers:** Mrs M Reveley, M W Easterby, M Hammond. **Top Jockeys:** P Niven, R Garrity, A Dobbin, B Storey.

Special Trainer Tip: Mary Reveley has almost twice as many runners here as anyone else and more than double the winners. Chris Thornton is the man to watch with his chasers.

Favourites: 1995-1999 Hurdles +£3.91, chases -£14.43. (Longest winning run 4, longest losing run 9). Best Bet: Jollies in handicap hurdles show a decent profit.

FIXTURES: Nov 12, 22, 27, Dec 13, 22
Jan 15, 19, Feb 2, 7, 19, 28, Mar 18, Apr 4, May 8★

NEWTON ABBOT

TicTac: Left-handed track of 1m 1f, with seven fences to a circuit and a short run-in.

How To Get There

Road: M5-A38-A380. **Rail:** Paddington Line to Newton Abbot, then one mile taxi or short walk. **Enquiries:** Tel 01626 775285.

Top Trainers: M Pipe, P Hobbs, P Nicholls, R Frost. **Top Jockeys:** A P McCoy, J Frost, R Dunwoody. **Special Trainer Tip:** It's a West Country bonanza with Pipe, Hobbs and Nicholls leading the charge.

Favourites: 1995-1999 Hurdles -£5.79, chases -£10.41. (Longest winning run 7, longest losing run 12). Best Bet: Novice hurdle favourites.

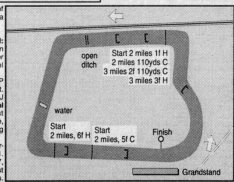

FIXTURES: Nov 3, 16, 30, Dec 27,
Mar 15, Apr 22, May 25, Jun 1

PERTH

TicTac: Right-handed, mainly flat track of 1m 2f with eight fences to a circuit.
How To Get There
Road: 3 miles North of Perth, off A93. **Rail:** To Perth station, then taxi.
Enquiries: Tel 01292 264179.
Top Trainers: M Hammond, Mrs M Reveley, J Goldie.
Top Jockeys: A Dobbin, P Niven, R Supple, R Garritty

Special Trainer Tip: Philip Hobbs generally farms races here and has an excellent strike rate.
Favourites: 1995-1999 Hurdles -£20.39, Chases -£15.15. (longest winning run 6, longest losing run 17). Best Bet: Nothing special to recommend.

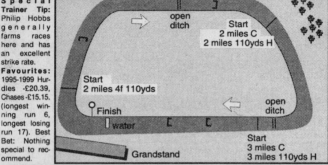

FIXTURES: Apr 26, 27, 28, May 17★, 18

PLUMPTON

TicTac: Left-handed, tight, undulating track of 1m 1f, with seven fences to a circuit and a 200yd run-in.
How To Get There
Road: Take A275 North of Lewes, then B2116. Or use M25-M23-A23.
Rail: From Victoria and London Bridge to Plumpton; short walk to the course.
Enquiries: Tel 01273 890383.
Top Trainers: M Pipe, J Jenkins, T McGovern, J Neville.
Top Jockeys: A P McCoy, M A Fitzgerald, M Bachelor, J R Kavanagh.
Special Trainer Tip: Henrietta Knight and Venetia Williams do very well on this tricky course.
Favourites: 1995-1999 Hurdles -£19.62, chases -£32.66. (Longest winning run 4, longest losing run 8). Best Bet: Steer clear of the market leaders.

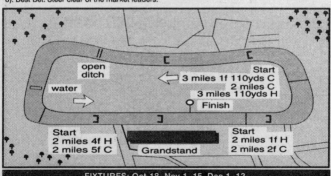

FIXTURES: Oct 18, Nov 1, 15, Dec 1, 13, Jan 2, 17, 31, Feb 14, 28, Mar 13, Apr 3, 22, 24

SANDOWN

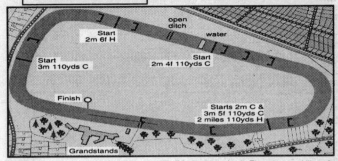

TicTac: Right-handed track of 1m 5f with 11 stiff fences to a circuit. There is an uphill run-in of 220yds.

How To Get There
Road: Course at Esher, off A3 London-Portsmouth road.
Rail: Waterloo to Esher, then short walk across the course.
Enquiries: Tel 01372 463072.
Top Trainers: D Nicholson, N Henderson, J Old, P Nicholls.
Top Jockeys: R Dunwoody, A P McCoy, M A Fitzgerald.
Special Trainer Tip: A real scrap at the top here but Jim Old and Paul Nicholls get the percentage call. Mark Pitman is on the up.
Favourites: 1995-1999 Hurdles -£14.68, chases -£25.61. (Longest winning run 5, longest losing run 10). Best Bet: Novice hurdle favourites show a profit backed blindly.

> **FIXTURES:** Nov 6, Dec 3, 4, Jan 8,
> Feb 5, 17, 18, Mar 10, 11, 28, Apr 29

SEDGEFIELD

TicTac: Left-handed, sharp, undulating track of 1m 2f, with eight fences to a circuit. There is a 220yd run-in for chases, 200yd for hurdles.

How To Get There
Road: Just off A1(M), via 689. **Rail:** Kings Cross Line to Darlington, then 8 miles taxi ride.
Enquiries: Tel 01642 557081. **Top Trainers:** Mrs M Reveley, B Ellison, J H Johnson, G M Moore.

Top Jockeys: P Niven, G Lee, R Supple, R Guest.
Special Trainer Tip: Mary Reveley's local gaff and the Cleveland trainer dominates events.
Favourites: 1995-1999 Hurdles: -£25.28, chases +£13.91. (Longest winning run 6, longest losing run 13). Best Bet: Market leaders over the bigger obstacles have kept punters in pocket recently.

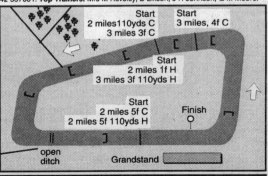

> **FIXTURES:** Oct 12, 28, Nov 9, 18, Dec 7, 27, Jan 12, 26,
> Feb 15, 22, Mar 7, 14, 21, Apr 7, 29, May 5★

SOUTHWELL

TicTac: The turf track is left-handed, 1m 1f round, with seven easy fences to a circuit.
How To Get There
Road: 5 miles West of Newark, via A617.
Rail: Kings Cross Line to Newark North Gate, then 4-mile taxi or connecting train to Rolleston Junction (adjoins course).
Enquiries: Tel 01636 814481.
Top Trainers: J O'Shea, M Pipe, P Bowen, B Llewellyn.
Top Jockeys: A P McCoy, R Johnson, Mickey Brennan, A Thornton.
Special Trainer Tip: John O'Shea takes advantage of the few meetings and is clear at the top of the table. **Favourites:** 1995-1999 Hurdles -£16.32, chases -£3.30. (Longest winning run 4, longest losing run 9). Best bet: Be wary of backing favourites over any distance.

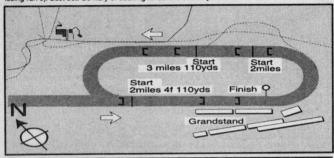

FIXTURES: Oct 4, Dec 30, Jan 26

STRATFORD

TicTac: Left-handed, flat track of 1m 2f, with eight easy fences to a circuit and a 200yd run-in.
How To Get There
Road: One mile outside Stratford, off A439.
Rail: Paddington Line to Stratford, then one mile walk or taxi.
Enquiries: Tel 01789 267949.
Top Trainers: M Pipe, D Nicholson, P Hobbs.
Top Jockeys: A P McCoy, R Johnson, M A Fitzgerald, R Dunwoody.

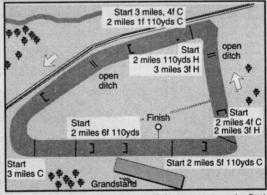

Special Trainer Tip: Martin Pipe has twice as many runners — and winners- — as anyone else. Frank Jordan has been known to produce a nice-price winner.
Favourites: 1995-1999 Hurdles -£10.63, chases -£18.83. (Longest winning run 7, longest losing run 13). Best Bet: A poor record suggests favourites are treated with caution here.

FIXTURES: Oct 16, 28, Dec 30,
Mar 13, Apr 15, May 12★, 19★, Jun 2★, 3

TAUNTON

TicTac: Right-handed track of 1m 2f with eight fences to a circuit and a 150yd run-in.

How To Get There

Road: Leave M5 at Junction 25; two miles south of Taunton off B3170.

Rail: Paddington Line to Taunton, then 3 miles taxi.

Enquiries: Tel 01823 337172.

Top Trainers: M Pipe, P Hobbs, R Hodges, P Nicholls.

Top Jockeys: A P McCoy, C Maude, T Dascombe.

Special Trainer Tip: All of the top West Country stables do well. Jim Old has by far the best strike rate from his few raiders so pay particular attention if he has a runner.

Favourites: 1995-1999 Hurdles +£10.99, chases - £10.55. (Longest winning run 4, longest losing run 8). Best Bet: Hurdle jollies over 3m have shown a profit of over £20 in the last five years.

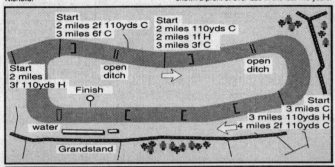

FIXTURES: Oct 14, Nov 11, 25, Dec 9, 29, Jan 6, 20, 31, Feb 17, Mar 2, 13, 30, Apr 6

TOWCESTER

TicTac: Right-handed testing track of 1m 6f, of which the last mile is uphill. There are 10 fences to a circuit and a 300yd run-in.

How To Get There Road: 9 miles South West of Northampton, via A43. **Rail:** Euston Line to either Milton Keynes (then taxi), or Northampton (then taxi or bus). Stations about nine miles from course.

Enquiries: Tel 01372 353414.

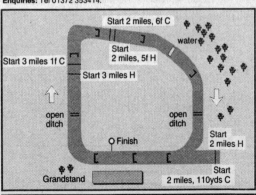

Top Trainers: D Nicholson, K Bailey, Miss V Williams.

Top Jockeys: R Johnson, A P McCoy, M A Fitzgerald, A Maguire.

Special Trainer Tip: This tough track is not for the faint-hearted and Robert Alner's runners are worth following.

Favourites: 1995-1999 Hurdles -£36.58, chases -£21.00. (Longest winning run 9, longest losing run 15). Best Bet: Favourites have the worse record here of any track!

FIXTURES: Oct 6, 29, Nov 4, 14, Dec 4, 16, Jan 7, Feb 3, Mar 9, 22, Apr 22, 24, May 1, 8, 15★, 26★

UTTOXETER

TicTac: Left-handed, undulating track of 1m 2f, with eight fences to a circuit and a short run-in.

How To Get There

Road: East of Stafford, via A518, or West of Derby via A516 and A50.

Rail: St Pancras Line to Derby, then to Uttoxeter station which adjoins the course.

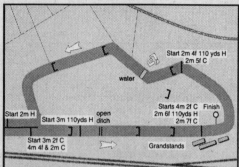

Enquiries: Tel 01889 562561.

Top Trainers: M Pipe, S Brookshaw, N Twiston-Davies, D Nicholson.

Top Jockeys: A P McCoy, R Johnson, N Williamson.

Special Trainer Tip: Steve Brookshaw and Tom George have been keeping punters happy of late.

Favourites: 1995-1999 Hurdles -£11.16, chases +£31.16. (Longest winning run 7, longest losing run 10). Best Bet: Leave out the handicap hurdle favourites and you will show a profit.

FIXTURES: Oct 2, Nov 5, 6, 13, 25, Dec 17, 18, Jan 2, Feb 5, Mar 18, 31, Apr 24, 25, May 6, 24★, 29

WARWICK

TicTac: Left-handed track of 1m 6f, with 10 fairly stiff fences and a 240yd run-in.

How To Get There

Road: 2m from Junc 15 of M40. Track off A46 Coventry-Stratford road, just south of Warwick.

Rail: Paddington to Leamington Spa, then three miles in a bus or taxi.

Enquiries: Tel 0192 6491553.

Top Trainers: M Pipe, D Nicholson, N Twiston-Davies.

Top Jockeys: R Johnson, A P McCoy, N Williamson, A Maguire.

Special Trainer Tip: Henry Daly has made his mark here since taking over from Tim Forster.

Favourites: 1995-1999 Hurdles +£13.58, chases -£26.23. (Longest winning run 4, longest losing run 9). Best Bet: Backing novice hurdle favourites produces healthy returns.

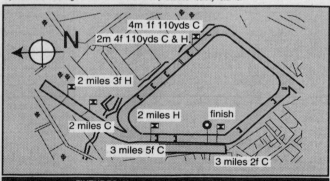

FIXTURES: Nov 2, 18, 27, Dec 18, Jan 8, 15, Feb 8, 19, Mar 4, May 13★

WETHERBY

TicTac: Left-handed, undulating track of 1m 4f with nine stiff fences to a circuit and a run-in of 200yd.

How To Get There
Road: 12 miles North East of Leeds, course right alongside the A1, on B1224.
Rail: Kings Cross Line to York or Leeds, then 13 miles taxi ride.
Enquiries: Tel 01937 582035.
Top Trainers: Mrs M Reveley, T Easterby, Mrs S Smith, D Nicholson.

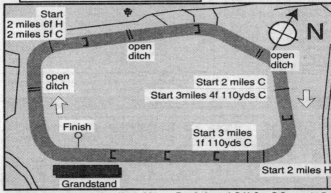

Start 2 miles 7¹/₂f H
open ditch
Start water
2 miles 4¹/₂f C
Start
2 miles 4f 110yds H
Starts 3 miles 1f H
3 miles 110yds C
Starts 2 miles H & C
3 miles 5f C
Finish
Grandstands

Top Jockeys: L Wyer, P Niven, A Dobbin, R Guest.
Special Trainer Tip: David Nicholson's southern raiders are always hot-to-trot at this Yorkshire venue. **Favourites:** 1995-1999 Hurdles -£9.74, chases -£9.52. (Longest winning run 7, longest losing run 13). **Best Bet:** Little to recommend here.

FIXTURES: Oct 13, 29, 30, Nov 16, 21, Dec 4, 27, 28, Jan 13, 24, Feb 5, Mar 1, Apr 24, May 10★, 29

WINCANTON

Start
2 miles 6f H
2 miles 5f C
open ditch
open ditch
open ditch
Start 2 miles C
Start 3 miles 4f 110yds C
Finish
Start 3 miles 1f 110yds C
Start 2 miles H
Grandstand

TicTac: Right-handed track of 1m 3f, with 9 fairly stiff fences and a 200yd run-in.

How To Get There
Road: Two miles north of Wincanton, just off A303.
Rail: Waterloo Line to Gillingham (Dorset), then seven miles taxi ride.
Enquiries: Tel 01963 32344.
Top Trainers: P Nicholls, M Pipe, R Alner.

Top Jockeys: A P McCoy, R Dunwoody, T J Murphy, A Thornton.
Special Trainer Tip: Oliver Sherwood and Nicky Henderson are also worth following while Paul Nicholls is tops for sheer numbers.
Favourites: 1995-1999 Hurdles -£11.32, chases -£33.57. (Longest winning run 5, longest losing run 14). **Best Bet:** Chase favourites here have a miserable record.

FIXTURES: Oct 7, 21, Nov 6, 21, Dec 2, 27, Jan 13, 27, Feb 10, 24, Mar 9, 23, Apr 24, May 12★

WOLVERHAMPTON

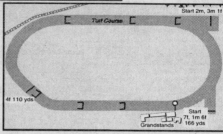

TicTac: Left-handed, flat, tight track of 1m 1f, with seven fences to a circuit and a 220yd run-in.

How To Get There
Road: M6-M54-A449. Track 1m NW of town. **Rail:** Euston to Wolverhampton, then 1.5m bus or taxi ride.

Enquiries: Tel 01902 421421.

Top Trainers: M Pipe, R O'Sullivan, J Jenkins, P Bowen.

Top Jockeys: A P McCoy, C Llewellyn, M A Fitzgerald, R Johnson.

Special Trainer Tip: Very little to go on at this rarely-used venue but Martin Pipe has had more than 50 per cent success. **Favourites:** 1995-1999 Hurdles -£0.93, chases -£0.61. (Longest winning run 2, longest losing run 3). Best Bet: Not enough statistics to go on.

FIXTURES: Jul 7, 17★

WORCESTER

TicTac: Left-handed, flat track of 1m 5f, with nine fences to a circuit and a 1f run-in.

How To Get There
Road: Leave M5 at Junction 7. Go through city and take A443.
Rail: Paddington Line to Worcester, then 15 minutes walk or short taxi ride.

Enquiries: Tel 01905 25364.

Top Trainers: M Pipe, D Nicholson, K Bailey, P Hobbs.

Top Jockeys: A P McCoy, R Dunwoody, C Llewellyn, R Johnson.

Special Trainer Tip: Paul Nicholls has a tremendous strike-rate while Charlie Mann is placing his horses well here. **Favourites:** 1995-1999 Hurdles -£3.75, chases -£3.15. (Longest winning run 5, longest losing run 10). Best Bet: Market leaders over the minimum trip show a healthy profit.

FIXTURES: Oct 9, 23, Nov 10, 29 May 13, 24

MULTIPLE BETS GUIDE

Bet	Selections	Doubles	Trebles	4-Folds	5-Folds	6-Folds	7-Folds	8-Folds	Total
TRIXIE	3	3	1	●	●	●	●	●	4
YANKEE	4	6	4	1	●	●	●	●	11
CANADIAN	5	10	10	5	1	●	●	●	26
HEINZ	6	15	20	15	6	1	●	●	57
SUPER HEINZ	7	21	35	35	21	7	1	●	120
GOLIATH	8	28	56	70	56	28	8	1	247

■**OTHER BETS: CROSS BET** (2 selections, 2 bets, one point win a, one point win b and vice-versa. **PATENT** (3 selections, 7 bets: Trixie plus three singles) **ROUND ROBIN** (3 selections, 10 bets: Trixie plus 3 cross bets) **LUCKY 15:** (4 selections, 15 bets: Yankee plus 4 singles) **FLAG** (4 selections, 23 bets: Yankee plus 6 cross bets)

FIXTURE CHECK '99-'00

OCTOBER

1	Friday	**Hexham**, *Lingfield*, *Newmarket*
2	Saturday	**Chepstow**, *Newmarket*, *Redcar*, **Sandown**, **Uttoxeter**, *★Wolverhampton*
4	Monday	*Brighton*, *Pontefract*, **Southwell**
5	Tuesday	*Catterick*, **Fontwell**, *Nottingham*
6	Wednesday	**Exeter**, **Towcester**, *York*
7	Thursday	**Ludlow**, **Wincanton**, *York*
8	Friday	**Carlisle**, **Huntingdon**, *Lingfield*
9	Saturday	*Ascot*, **Bangor**, **Hexham**, *York*
11	Monday	*Ayr*, *Leicester*, *Windsor*
12	Tuesday	*Ayr*, *Leicester*, **Sedgefield**
13	Wednesday	*Haydock*, **Wetherby**, *Wolverhampton*
14	Thursday	*Newmarket*, *Redcar*, **Taunton**
15	Friday	**Hereford**, *Newmarket*, *Redcar*
16	Saturday	*Catterick*, **Kelso**, **Kempton**, *Newmarket*, **Stratford**, *★Wolverhampton*
18	Monday	**Plumpton**, *Pontefract*, *Southwell*
19	Tuesday	**Exeter**, *Lingfield*, *Yarmouth*
20	Wednesday	**Chepstow**, *Newcastle*, *Nottingham*
21	Thursday	*Brighton*, **Ludlow**, *Nottingham*, **Wincanton**
22	Friday	*Doncaster*, **Fakenham**, *Newbury*
23	Saturday	**Carlisle**, *Doncaster*, **Market Rasen**, *Newbury*, **Worcester**
25	Monday	**Bangor**, *Leicester*, *Lingfield*
26	Tuesday	**Bath**, **Cheltenham**, *Redcar*
27	Wednesday	**Cheltenham**, **Fontwell**, *Yarmouth*
28	Thursday	**Sedgefield**, **Stratford**, *Windsor*
29	Friday	*Brighton*, *Newmarket*, **Towcester**, **Wetherby**
30	Saturday	*Ascot*, **Kelso**, *Newmarket*, **Wetherby**, *★Wolverhampton*

NOVEMBER

1	Monday	*Nottingham*, **Plumpton**, *Redcar*
2	Tuesday	*Catterick*, **Exeter**, **Warwick**
3	Wednesday	*Musselburgh*, **Kempton**, **Newton Abbot**
4	Thursday	**Haydock**, **Towcester**, *Windsor*
5	Friday	*Doncaster*, **Hexham**, **Uttoxeter**
6	Saturday	**Chepstow**, *Doncaster*, **Sandown**, **Uttoxeter**, **Wincanton**
8	Monday	**Carlisle**, **Fontwell**, *Lingfield*
9	Tuesday	**Huntingdon**, **Newbury**, **Sedgefield**
10	Wednesday	**Kelso**, **Newbury**, **Worcester**
11	Thursday	*Lingfield*, **Ludlow**, **Taunton**
12	Friday	**Cheltenham**, **Newcastle**, *Southwell*
13	Saturday	**Ayr**, **Cheltenham**, **Haydock**, **Market Rasen**, **Uttoxeter**, *★Wolverhampton*
14	Sunday	**Ayr**, **Cheltenham**, **Towcester**
15	Monday	*Leicester*, **Plumpton**, *Southwell*
16	Tuesday	*Lingfield*, **Newton Abbot**, **Wetherby**
17	Wednesday	**Hereford**, **Kempton**, *Wolverhampton*
18	Thursday	**Folkestone**, **Sedgefield**, **Warwick**
19	Friday	**Ascot**, **Exeter**, *Southwell*
20	Saturday	**Ascot**, *Catterick*, **Huntingdon**, *Wolverhampton*
21	Sunday	**Aintree**, **Wetherby**, **Wincanton**
22	Monday	**Ludlow**, **Newcastle**, *Southwell*
23	Tuesday	*Lingfield*, **Market Rasen**
24	Wednesday	**Chepstow**, **Hexham**, *Lingfield*

125

25	Thursday	**Carlisle, Taunton, Uttoxeter**
26	Friday	**Bangor,** *Lingfield,* **Newbury**
27	Saturday	**Haydock, Newbury, Newcastle, Warwick,** **Wolverhampton*
29	Monday	**Folkestone, Kelso, Worcester**
30	Tuesday	**Newton Abbot,** *Southwell*

DECEMBER

1	Wednesday	**Catterick, Plumpton,** *Wolverhampton*
2	Thursday	**Leicester, Market Rasen, Wincanton**
3	Friday	**Exeter, Hereford, Sandown**
4	Saturday	**Chepstow, Sandown, Towcester, Wetherby,** **Wolverhampton*
6	Monday	**Ayr, Fakenham,** *Lingfield*
7	Tuesday	**Fontwell, Sedgefield**
8	Wednesday	**Hexham, Leicester,** *Lingfield*
9	Thursday	**Huntingdon, Ludlow, Taunton**
10	Friday	**Cheltenham, Doncaster,** *Lingfield*
11	Saturday	**Cheltenham, Doncaster, Lingfield, Haydock,** **Wolverhampton*
13	Monday	**Newcastle, Plumpton,** *Southwell*
14	Tuesday	**Musselburgh, Hereford**
15	Wednesday	**Bangor, Catterick,** *Wolverhampton*
16	Thursday	**Catterick, Exeter, Towcester**
17	Friday	**Folkestone,** *Southwell,* **Uttoxeter**
18	Saturday	**Ascot,** *Lingfield,* **Uttoxeter, Warwick**
20	Monday	**Kelso,** *Wolverhampton*
21	Tuesday	**Folkestone,** *Southwell*
22	Wednesday	*Lingfield,* **Ludlow, Newcastle**
27	Monday	**Ayr, Hereford, Huntingdon, Kempton, Market Rasen,**
		Newton Abbot, Sedgefield, Wetherby, Wincanton, *Wolverhampton*
28	Tuesday	**Chepstow, Kempton, Leicester, Wetherby**
29	Wednesday	**Musselburgh, Haydock,** *Lingfield,* **Taunton**
30	Thursday	**Carlisle, Southwell, Stratford**
31	Friday	**Catterick, Cheltenham, Fontwell, Warwick**

JANUARY

2	Sunday	**Exeter,** *Lingfield,* **Plumpton, Uttoxeter**
3	Monday	**Ayr, Cheltenham, Folkestone,** *Southwell*
4	Tuesday	**Musselburgh,** *Wolverhampton*
5	Wednesday	**Catterick, Leicester,** *Lingfield*
6	Thursday	**Catterick, Taunton,** *Wolverhampton*
7	Friday	**Ludlow,** *Southwell,* **Towcester**
8	Saturday	**Haydock,** *Lingfield,* **Sandown, Warwick,** **Wolverhampton*
10	Monday	**Fakenham, Fontwell,** *Southwell*
11	Tuesday	**Hereford, Leicester,** *Wolverhampton*
12	Wednesday	**Kempton,** *Lingfield,* **Sedgefield**
13	Thursday	**Wetherby, Wincanton,** *Wolverhampton*
14	Friday	**Musselburgh, Folkestone,** *Southwell*
15	Saturday	**Ascot,** *Lingfield,* **Newcastle, Warwick**
17	Monday	**Doncaster, Plumpton,** *Southwell*
18	Tuesday	**Carlisle, Folkestone,** *Wolverhampton*
19	Wednesday	**Huntingdon,** *Lingfield,* **Newcastle**
20	Thursday	**Ludlow, Taunton,** *Wolverhampton*
21	Friday	**Ascot, Kelso,** *Southwell*
22	Saturday	**Catterick, Haydock, Kempton,** *Lingfield,* **Wolverhampton*
24	Monday	*Southwell,* **Wetherby**
25	Tuesday	**Fontwell, Leicester,** *Wolverhampton*
26	Wednesday	*Lingfield,* **Sedgefield, Southwell**
27	Thursday	**Huntingdon, Wincanton,** *Wolverhampton*
28	Friday	**Doncaster, Folkestone,** *Southwell*
29	Saturday	**Ayr, Cheltenham, Doncaster,** *Lingfield*
31	Monday	**Plumpton,** *Southwell,* **Taunton**

FEBRUARY

1	Tuesday	**Musselburgh, Kempton,** *Wolverhampton*
2	Wednesday	**Leicester,** *Lingfield,* **Newcastle**
3	Thursday	**Kelso, Towcester,** *Wolverhampton*
4	Friday	**Catterick, Folkestone,** *Southwell*
5	Saturday	*Lingfield,* **Sandown, Uttoxeter, Wetherby,** **Wolverhampton*
7	Monday	**Fontwell, Newcastle,** *Southwell*
8	Tuesday	**Carlisle, Warwick,** *Wolverhampton*
9	Wednesday	**Chepstow,** *Lingfield,* **Ludlow**
10	Thursday	**Huntingdon, Wincanton,** *Wolverhampton*
11	Friday	**Bangor, Newbury,** *Southwell*
12	Saturday	**Ayr, Catterick, Haydock,** *Lingfield,* **Newbury**
14	Monday	**Hereford, Plumpton,** *Southwell*
15	Tuesday	**Folkestone, Sedgefield,** *Wolverhampton*
16	Wednesday	**Musselburgh, Leicester,** *Lingfield*
17	Thursday	**Sandown, Taunton,** *Wolverhampton*
18	Friday	**Fakenham, Sandown,** *Southwell*
19	Saturday	**Ascot,** *Lingfield,* **Newcastle, Warwick,** **Wolverhampton*
21	Monday	**Carlisle, Fontwell,** *Southwell*
22	Tuesday	**Folkestone, Sedgefield,** *Wolverhampton*
23	Wednesday	**Doncaster,** *Lingfield,* **Ludlow**
24	Thursday	**Huntingdon, Wincanton,** *Wolverhampton*
25	Friday	**Kempton, Market Rasen,** *Southwell*
26	Saturday	**Musselburgh, Haydock, Kempton,** *Lingfield*
28	Monday	**Newcastle, Plumpton,** *Southwell*
29	Tuesday	**Catterick, Leicester,** *Wolverhampton*

MARCH

1	Wednesday	**Chepstow,** *Lingfield,* **Wetherby**
2	Thursday	**Ludlow, Taunton,** *Wolverhampton*
3	Friday	**Doncaster, Kelso, Newbury**
4	Saturday	**Doncaster, Huntingdon,** *Lingfield,* **Newbury, Warwick,** **Wolverhampton*
6	Monday	**Musselburgh, Fontwell,** *Southwell*
7	Tuesday	**Exeter, Leicester, Sedgefield**
8	Wednesday	**Bangor, Catterick,** *Lingfield*
9	Thursday	**Carlisle, Towcester, Wincanton**
10	Friday	**Ayr, Hereford, Sandown**
11	Saturday	**Ayr, Chepstow, Sandown,** *Wolverhampton*
13	Monday	**Plumpton, Stratford, Taunton**
14	Tuesday	**Cheltenham, Sedgefield,** *Southwell*
15	Wednesday	**Cheltenham, Huntingdon, Newton Abbot**
16	Thursday	**Cheltenham, Hexham,** *Wolverhampton*
17	Friday	**Fakenham, Folkestone,** *Southwell*
18	Saturday	**Lingfield, Market Rasen, Newcastle, Uttoxeter**
20	Monday	**Folkestone,** *Southwell*
21	Tuesday	**Exeter, Fontwell, Sedgefield**
22	Wednesday	**Chepstow, Ludlow, Towcester**
23	Thursday	*Doncaster,* **Wincanton,** *Wolverhampton*
24	Friday	*Doncaster,* **Kelso, Newbury**
25	Saturday	**Bangor,** *Doncaster,* **Kempton, Newbury,** **Wolverhampton*
27	Monday	*Southwell, Windsor*
28	Tuesday	*Newcastle,* **Sandown,** *Wolverhampton*
29	Wednesday	*Catterick, Lingfield, Nottingham*
30	Thursday	*Musselburgh, Leicester,* **Taunton**
31	Friday	**Carlisle,** *Southwell,* **Uttoxeter**

APRIL

1	Saturday	**Ascot, Haydock, Hexham, Market Rasen**
3	Monday	**Kelso, Plumpton,** *Warwick*
4	Tuesday	**Exeter, Newcastle,** *Nottingham*
5	Wednesday	**Ascot, Ludlow,** *Ripon*
6	Thursday	*Leicester,* **Aintree, Taunton**
7	Friday	*Lingfield,* **Aintree, Sedgefield**
8	Saturday	*Hamilton,* **Hereford, Aintree**
10	Monday	*Southwell, Windsor*
11	Tuesday	*Pontefract, Wolverhampton*
12	Wednesday	**Chepstow,** *Lingfield,* **Warwick**
13	Thursday	*Brighton, Musselburgh,* **Ludlow**
14	Friday	**Ayr,** *Newbury, Thirsk*
15	Saturday	**Ayr, Bangor,** *Newbury,* **Stratford,** *Thirsk,* ***Wolverhampton**
17	Monday	**Hexham,** *Pontefract, Windsor*
18	Tuesday	**Exeter, Folkestone, Newmarket**
19	Wednesday	*Beverley,* **Cheltenham,** *Newmarket*
20	Thursday	**Cheltenham,** *Newmarket, Ripon*
22	Saturday	**Carlisle,** *Haydock, Kempton,* **Newton Abbot,** *Plumpton,* **Towcester**
24	Monday	**Carlisle, Chepstow, Fakenham, Hereford, Huntingdon,** *Kempton,* **Market Rasen,** *Newcastle, Nottingham,* **Plumpton, Towcester,** **Uttoxeter,** *Warwick,* **Wetherby, Wincanton**
25	Tuesday	*Southwell,* **Uttoxeter, Wetherby**
26	Wednesday	*Catterick, Epsom,* **Perth**
27	Thursday	*Beverley,* **Fontwell, Perth**
28	Friday	**Perth,** *Sandown, Wolverhampton*
29	Saturday	*Leicester,* **Market Rasen,** *Ripon,* **Sandown, Sedgefield**

MAY

1	Monday	*Doncaster,* **Fontwell,** *Kempton,* **Ludlow,** *Newcastle,* **Towcester,** *Warwick*
2	Tuesday	*Bath,* ***Huntingdon,** *Nottingham,* ***Windsor**
3	Wednesday	*Ascot,* ***Cheltenham, Exeter,** ***Kelso,** *Pontefract*
4	Thursday	*Brighton, Redcar, Wolverhampton*
5	Friday	***Bangor,** *Musselburgh,* **Folkestone,** *Newmarket,* ***Sedgefield**
6	Saturday	**Haydock, Hereford,** *Newmarket, Thirsk,* **Uttoxeter**
7	Sunday	*Hamilton, Newmarket, Salisbury*
8	Monday	***Newcastle,** *Southwell,* **Towcester,** ***Windsor**
9	Tuesday	*Brighton, Chester,* **Exeter**
10	Wednesday	**Chepstow,** *Chester,* **Fakenham,** ***Wetherby**
11	Thursday	*Chester, Hamilton, Wolverhampton*
12	Friday	*Carlisle, Lingfield, Nottingham,* ***Stratford,** ***Wincanton**
13	Saturday	*Beverley,* **Hexham,** *Lingfield,* ***Market Rasen,** ***Warwick, Worcester**
15	Monday	*Redcar, Southwell,* ***Towcester,** ***Windsor**
16	Tuesday	**Hereford,** *York*
17	Wednesday	*Brighton,* **Exeter,** ***Folkestone,** ***Huntingdon,** ***Perth,** *York*
18	Thursday	**Perth,** *Salisbury, York*
19	Friday	***Hamilton,** ***Aintree,** *Newbury, Nottingham,* ***Stratford,** *Thirsk*
20	Saturday	**Bangor,** ***Hexham,** ***Lingfield,** *Newbury, Nottingham, Thirsk,* ***Wolverhampton**
22	Monday	*Bath,* ***Musselburgh,** *Southwell,* ***Windsor**
23	Tuesday	*Beverley, Goodwood*
24	Wednesday	***Brighton,** *Goodwood,* **Kelso,** ***Uttoxeter, Worcester**
25	Thursday	*Goodwood, Newcastle,* **Newton Abbot**
26	Friday	*Brighton, Haydock,* ***Pontefract,** *Southwell,* ***Towcester**
27	Saturday	**Cartmel,** *Doncaster, Haydock,* **Hexham,** *Kempton,* ***Lingfield,** ***Market Rasen,** ***Warwick**
29	Monday	**Cartmel,** *Chepstow,* **Fontwell, Hereford, Huntingdon,** *Leicester, Redcar, Sandown, Uttoxeter,* **Wetherby**
30	Tuesday	***Hexham,** *Leicester, Redcar,* ***Sandown**
31	Wednesday	**Cartmel,** ***Newbury,** ***Ripon,** *Southwell, Yarmouth*